The Aryan Debate

Oxford in India Readings

DEBATES IN INDIAN HISTORY AND SOCIETY

Series Editors: Sabyasachi Bhattacharya, B.D. Chattopadhyaya, Richard M. Eaton

BIDYUT CHAKRABARTY (EDITOR)	*Communal Identity in India* Its Construction and Articulation in the Twentieth Century
G. BALACHANDRAN (EDITOR)	*India and the World Economy 1850–1950*
DAVID N. LORENZEN (EDITOR)	*Religious Movements in South Asia 600–1800*
AMIYA P. SEN (EDITOR)	*Social and Religious Reform* The Hindus of British India
THOMAS R. TRAUTMANN (EDITOR)	*The Aryan Debate*
BHAIRABI PRASAD SAHU (EDITOR)	*Iron and Social Change in Early India*
SCOTT C. LEVI (EDITOR)	*India and Central Asia* Commerce and Culture, 1500–1800
BISWAMOY PATI (EDITOR)	*The 1857 Rebellion* (Forthcoming)

The Aryan Debate

Thomas R. Trautmann

OXFORD
UNIVERSITY PRESS

OXFORD
UNIVERSITY PRESS

YMCA Library Building, Jai Singh Road, New Delhi 110001

Oxford University Press is a department of the University of Oxford. It furthers the University's objective of excellence in research, scholarship, and education by publishing worldwide in

Oxford New York
Auckland Cape Town Dar es Salaam Hong Kong Karachi
Kuala Lumpur Madrid Melbourne Mexico City Nairobi
New Delhi Shanghai Taipei Toronto

With offices in
Argentina Austria Brazil Chile Czech Republic France Greece
Guatemala Hungary Italy Japan Poland Portugal Singapore
South Korea Switzerland Thailand Turkey Ukraine Vietnam

Published in India
by Oxford University Press, New Delhi

First published 2005
Oxford India Paperbacks 2007
Third impression 2009

ISBN-13: 978-0-19-569200-6
ISBN-10: 0-19-569200-4

Typeset in NalandaGaramond 10.5/12.5
By Le Studio Graphique, Gurgaon 122 001
Printed in India by De Unique, New Delhi 110 018
Published by Oxford University Press
YMCA Library Building, Jai Singh Road, New Delhi 110 001

Contents

PART THREE
THE VEDA AND THE INDUS CIVILIZATION

Archaeology

Horses

The Indus Script

Series Editors' Note

The Debates in Indian History and Society series focuses on the diversity of interpretations in historical discourse. The series addresses widely debated issues in South Asian history (including contemporary history) through edited volumes centring around sharply-focused themes or seminal writings which have generated arguments and counter-arguments resulting in worthwhile debates. In this context, the debates represent not simply differences in opinions but also offer important interpretative frameworks, which result in them acquiring a certain historiographic status. The approach encourages the interrogation of history, as distinct from presenting history as a collection of 'given' facts. The aim is to bring to readers significant writings, interpretations, and sources and to open to students bridge-heads into research.

SABYASACHI BHATTACHARYA
B.D. CHATTOPADHYAYA
RICHARD M. EATON

Preface

There is no mistaking the urgency and importance of the Aryan debate in India just now. When the series editors invited me to do a volume on the topic, I knew that it would be difficult and that I would need lots of help.

The editors themselves—Sabyasachi Bhattacharya, Brajadulal Chattopadhyaya, and Richard Eaton—gave abundant comments on the overall plan for the book and the draft of the introduction, and the comments were exceptionally acute. Dilip Menon gave vigorous and searching criticism of the penultimate version, when I badly needed one last outside reading of the text. To all of these I am greatly obliged. What merit the text may have is due to their invaluable help, while the remaining faults can doubtless be attributed to the fact that I did not always follow their advice. Arpita Das, with great intelligence and unfailing good cheer, guided me through the various stages of production, and after she departed from Oxford University Press, Parnal Chirmuley saw it to press. I am immensely grateful to them for their help.

I had previously taught a course with my colleague Carla Sinopoli on the history and archaeology of ancient India, a collaboration which gave me the advantage of access to her wide knowledge of the archaeological scholarship. While struggling with the problem of selecting writings to include in the book I had long discussions with Madhav Deshpande, David Lorenzen, and Romila Thapar, and benefited a great deal from their good advice. It was due to Madhav Deshpande that I decided to exclude articles that, however good in substance, were excessively polemical and personal in their attacks. I also decided, in the course of my discussions with these four, to exclude writings that are widely read and discussed but are not backed up by the special skills relevant to the Aryan debate, in philology, archaeology, or history. I also decided to choose writings that were neither too technical nor too long, and have abridged several of them to achieve both goals. The discussions with these four helped me clarify the criteria for inclusion and exclusion, and they suggested a number of individual papers. I am very much in their debt. Even with the exclusions I have mentioned, there still remained a very large universe of articles on the topic from which to choose. The selection I settled on is my own, and is governed by the three parts into which I analyse the Aryan debate: the founding discoveries, the Aryan/Dravidian distinction, and the question of the relation of the Veda to the Indus Civilization. Inevitably a great many very good and important contributions to the Aryan debate have been left out. Readers must keep it in mind that this is just a sampler, intended to convey an overview of the issues and provide some suggestions about how they should go about weighing the arguments advanced on each side.

Sarah Whitney Womack was a most efficient research assistant as I was choosing and assembling the parts of the book. Jeanette Diuble transcribed the Ellis selection. I thank them both for their good work.

The writing of this book (and a related work on the Dravidian proof of F.W. Ellis and his associates in early nineteenth century Madras) was made possible by sabbatical research leave from the University of Michigan and support from the American Council of Learned Societies, the National Endowment for the Humanities, and the Social Science Research Council. A grant from the American Institute of Indian Studies supported a trip to India for research that greatly helped the composition of this book. The College of Literature, Science, and the Arts of the University of Michigan was generous with research support. I am deeply indebted to these institutions, and the persons connected with them, for this aid.

Lastly, my special thanks go to Theodore and Thilaka Baskaran for arranging for me to air the ideas of this book before the Madras Book Club, and for many kindnesses over the course of a long friendship.

THOMAS R. TRAUTMANN

Introduction

What is the Aryan Debate?

The Aryan debate has been raging in books, newspapers, and public forums of India for the last decade or so. It concerns this question: did the Sanskrit-speaking Aryans enter India from the north-west in about 1500 BC, or were they indigenous to India and identical with the people of the Indus Civilization of 2600–1900 BC?

The first position, the *immigrant Aryan* position that the Aryans came to India from outside in about 1500 BC, I will call the *standard view* because it is the interpretation that has prevailed in school and university history textbooks and in academic journals and books. The second position, the *indigenous Aryan* position that the Aryans were the makers of the Indus Civilization, I will call the *alternative view*, because it is challenging the established, standard view.

While the standard or immigrant Aryan view has prevailed among scholars, the alternative or indigenous Aryan view is not a recent invention, and there have always been some scholars who supported it. For example, both are represented in the multi-volume series called *History and Culture of the Indian People*, that was published shortly after Independence. The series was intended to overcome the inadequacy of histories of India written under colonial rule, and to show the world how India's past might be described by Indians.[1] In

[1] *The Vedic Age* (*History and Culture of the Indian People*, vol. 1), eds R.C. Majumdar and A.D. Pusalker, p. 7. These are the words of K.M. Munshi, the president of the Bharatiya Vidya Bhavan, which sponsored the series.

the first volume, called *The Vedic Age*, the editor, the distinguished historian R.C. Majumdar, stated that while the coming of the Aryans to India at the end of the prehistoric period 'may be regarded as the beginning of history proper', this was not unanimously accepted, and some scholars regarded India as the original home of the Aryans, while others referred the Aryans to so many thousands of years ago that there could be no question of any historical period prior to the Aryans.[2] Accordingly, Majumdar included chapters expressing the standard view and others expressing the alternative view, respecting both sides to the Aryan debate and not imposing on it a premature conclusion.

Thus, even though it is only recently that the Aryan debate has become a large, noisy public debate, it has been with us for a long time at a lower level of intensity and public participation, and the issues remain unsettled. But times have changed, and today the civility with which these things used to be debated—the respect participants showed to the view of the opposing side, so noticeable in Majumdar's volume on the Vedic age—has gone out the window, unfortunately. Moreover, what used to be a debate among scholars has boiled up and spilled over into the public arena, and the sober works of academics are now swamped by the often overheated writings and websites of those who are not scholars trained in the history, linguistics, and archaeology of ancient India. Partisan politics have entered into the debate. What used to be a polite disagreement among scholars has become a strident public shouting match in which personal insults are all too freely thrown about. Scholarship, of course, always involves disagreement and debate, and indeed we must have disagreement and debate so that interpretations of history are rigorously tested, for without them there is no hope of progress in historical knowledge. But when the debate becomes too heated and polemical, such that writers attack one another with ferocity, as has been the case of the Aryan debate in recent years, it becomes more difficult to determine the truth of the matter, and easier to be thrown off the track of historical truth in favour of political or religious objectives.

[2] Ibid., p. 25.

Why is it that historical questions of times so far in the past have become so intensely interesting to the public, outside the circle of scholars? We may say, in a general way, that the history of the deep past often becomes the object of intense public debate because ancient history serves as a *charter* for society or for a particular vision of what society should be. When there are deep divisions within a society over its future direction, it sometimes leads to debates about the interpretation of the deep past, too. Such debates often have at their core a disagreement about the boundaries of society, about who is foreign and who is native, and such matters are apt to be highly sensitive and contentious.

How do we find the truth under such conditions? The search for truth in respect of times long past is difficult under the best conditions, because the evidence is incomplete and fragile. When we try to reconstruct the ways of life in Vedic times, for example, we are often baffled by the difficult, metaphysical, and allusive poetic style and the archaic language of the Rig Veda. The Veda was not composed to give us a lesson in history, and it is only with difficulty that we can derive the history of the Vedic age from it. Difficulties of this kind are the normal problems of history-writing, and they are generally greater the further back we go in time. We only establish the facts of the ancient past after the sources have been analysed with a great deal of careful, technical work requiring special skills of archaeology, of linguistics, and of the historical evaluation of documents. This delicate work is best conducted in silence, not in loud voices. The great Japanese historian of South India, Noboru Karashima, speaks of the 'whispering' of the inscriptions, by which he means the subtle facts that can only be found by paying close attention to the small details of a text.[3]

Our task would be much easier if the documents gave us a large body of hard facts on which all scholars agreed. Unfortunately the *facts* of ancient history are not hard facts, for a couple of reasons. One of them has to do with the many steps in the scholarly processing of such facts before they become recognized facts—there can be

[3] Noboru Karashima, 'Whispering of inscriptions', in Kenneth R. Hall, ed., *Structure and Society in Early South India: Essays in Honour of Noboru Karashima*, pp. 44–58 (New Delhi: Oxford University Press, 2001).

disagreement about every stage of such processing, and hence of the facts it establishes. A second is that facts only become significant facts for history in respect of some general view of things, some intellectual paradigm. There are no facts that exist truly independently of the interpretations that are made of them. Thus, there are always several grounds upon which the supposed facts can be challenged. The *interpretations* of facts, too, can always be challenged by an opposing interpretation because the record of the past available to us is always incomplete. We can only make statements about the past that are probable, to a greater or lesser degree, and can never attain certainty.

Under the best of circumstances, the community of scholars debates the questions of ancient history continuously, and in so doing subjects all interpretations to the criticism of those who have the special skills necessary to be well-informed judges of them. By the *community of scholars*, I mean those who have been trained in the special skills for the analysis of historical evidence, who make arguments supported by careful reference to that evidence, and whose writings are tested by other scholars through processes of review and criticism in scholarly seminars and publications. The community of scholars is not infallible, to be sure. It can be mistaken, and has in fact changed its collective mind on many occasions. The view that the planets revolve around the sun was established in opposition to the earth-centred view of the community of scholars, and became, in its turn, the prevailing view. Such 'paradigm shifts' in science are brought about by powerfully argued alternative interpretations, such as Kepler's sun-centred astronomy and Darwin's theory of natural selection in biology, and similar shifts of interpretation occur among historians.[4] Moreover, many good and useful histories are written by individuals who are not trained scholars and we do not want to exclude them from discussion. Nevertheless, the community of scholars who have the relevant expert knowledge, fallible though it is, remains the best resource we have for testing interpretations and establishing historical truth.

[4] The idea of reigning paradigms in science and the revolutions in scientific thought that result in paradigm shifts is that of Thomas Kuhn, *The Structure of Scientific Revolutions* (Chicago: University of Chicago Press, 1962).

The circumstances we find ourselves in today, however, are not the most favourable for reaching the truth of ancient history. In the last several years a number of popular books and websites on the Aryan debate have appeared, many of them—but not all—by authors who are not scholars qualified by their training in the skills of ancient history. Moreover, partisan politics and governments of the day have been making pronouncements about ancient history, and ordering changes in textbooks. The new writings have pressed various versions of the alternative view very strongly, arguing that the Aryans are indigenous to India and were the builders of the Indus Civilization. There has been a flood of new books purporting to prove that the idea of an Aryan invasion—meaning the idea of an Aryan immigration—is a myth.

Now, India is a free country, and everyone is entitled to publish any interpretation of history they wish. If one wants to say that the Taj Mahal was built by the Vedic rishis, or that the moon is made of green cheese, or that the earth is flat, one is entirely free to do so. But not all views of history are equal, or deserve to be taken seriously by scholars. Writers can only gain the respect of the community of scholars by demonstrating the skills necessary to study the sources and by the careful use of evidence and logic in constructing an argument that will be persuasive. These are the qualities needed for original work in history. A great many of the new writings on the Aryan debate do not qualify.

Nevertheless, while many of the books challenging the standard, immigrant Aryan view are written by persons ill qualified to pronounce on the topic, and are of no value to those who earnestly seek the truth of ancient history, there are others taking up the alternative, indigenous Aryan position who are very well qualified, and whose scholarly credentials entitle them to a respectful hearing. Moreover, the alternative view has been around, as a minority view within the community of scholars, for a long time. These are reasons why the alternative view merits serious consideration. But the principal reason is that the alternative view challenges the current consensus in the scholarly community, and seeks to overturn it. A challenge of this kind requires scholars to re-examine the basis of the standard view, to see if it remains sound, and to replace it if it does not.

History and Historiography

Before coming to the substance of the Aryan debate, we need to think through the issue of politics in history, and how it affects the search for truth.

The training of historians teaches them how to evaluate historical sources (generally texts), to draw historical facts from them, and make of the facts an interpretation of the past. The historical study of a document always involves careful attention to the questions of what group of people produced the text and for what purpose it was written. That is, historians always try to determine the *social–historical location* of the document. For example, when studying the Veda we need always to be aware that it was produced and perpetuated by a category of religious specialists and reflects the outlook and interests of that category, and not those of all segments of society in that time. In ancient India, as in other ancient civilizations, literacy is monopolized by a few, and we need to make special efforts to capture the thoughts and intentions of those who are *not* the producers of texts. This attention to the social location of texts as a means to evaluating them is a fundamental aspect of the historian's work.

Besides evaluating documents and writing histories, historians also evaluate the histories written by other historians. Thus historians study history—what *happened* in the past—and they also study historical *writing* about the past. Because the English word *history* denotes both what happened in the past and writings about the past, we sometimes use the word *historiography* to distinguish the latter from the former.

When historians study historiography, they employ the very same methods they use in the study of historical documents, namely, they begin by determining the social and historical location of the historical writings they are studying. Just as it helps us to evaluate what historical documents say, it helps us to understand how historical writings came about if we can identify the social and historical position from which they come. This may involve identifying the political, religious, and other tendencies of the historian whose writing we are studying, or such personal attributes as nationality and gender, or the more general features of the period in which the historian wrote. Such personal matters and group affiliations and historical conditions of the period may help us understand how interpretations of history have been shaped. However, they do NOT tell us whether they are true or false.

This is the most important thing to be kept in mind by everyone wishing to reach the truth of history. Because of its importance I repeat, for emphasis: *Identifying the social-historical location of a piece of history-writing does NOT tell us whether it is true or false.*

The reason this needs emphasis is that, as the Aryan debate has become more heated, unflattering labels such as 'Hindu nationalist' and 'Marxist fundamentalist', or 'pseudo-secularist' and 'so-called champions of Hindutva', are thrown about. These labels are often used as if they were proofs that the arguments of the writer's opponent are not true. And often enough they are flung back at the writer of them, and the argument turns into a futile shouting match.

We need to be clear about this problem. It is not wrong to identify the political movements associated with the Hindutva ideology as major advocates of the alternative view in the Aryan debate, and to identify some (though by no means all or even most) of the leaders of the standard view as secularists or Marxists. Most historians belong to neither the one nor the other of these two alternatives, and occupy a large middle ground between the positions, but it is perfectly acceptable and indeed useful to try to identify the intellectual, religious, or political sources of attraction for the different interpretations of history. It helps us to understand why the Aryan debate has become so heated. To take another example, it is perfectly acceptable to say that the work of a particular writer, a European or American let us say, is influenced by Christian religion or colonial ideology, if there is good evidence to say so, and indeed it may help us understand why such a writer is attracted to a particular interpretation of history.

But the truth of ancient history is indifferent to our wishes, our politics, our religion, in short, our own social and historical location. The idea of truth in history involves the idea that it exists independent of our will, and is therefore inherently difficult to know, because our interpretations are will-bound, and our facts are never independent of our theories. It is well to keep in mind how very difficult it is to attain historical truth, and to remember that it is what it is, whether it is useful to one kind of politics or another. For that reason, it is never legitimate historical practice to dismiss a view of history merely on account of its politics. This means that *after* we have completed the investigation of historiography, and have identified the social and historical location of a given interpretation of history, we *still* have to evaluate its truth or falsity. The two evaluations, of historiography and of history, have their own logic and should not be collapsed into each other. Very often in the heat of argument, this process gets cut short, and we assert that because a person has an evident political, religious, or other stake in an interpretation of history, that disproves the truth of the interpretation. When we think calmly, we recognize the error of that way of arguing.

Three Fundamental Discoveries

The Aryan debate itself has a history, and a beginning in time that we can identify. It arose from three fundamental discoveries about the ancient history of India. These discoveries have come about through philology (or linguistics) and archaeology, which have been the two main avenues by which we have acquired new knowledge about ancient India, adding greatly to what we may know of the ancient past from the king-lists and genealogies to be found in the Puranas, the Mahabharata and the Ramayana. The three discoveries and the dates at which they were first published—for they were made at widely distant times—are:

- the discovery of the Indo-European language family (1786);
- the discovery of the Dravidian language family (1816); and
- the discovery of the Indus Civilization (1924).

These discoveries are fundamental in the sense that the historical facts they uncovered have survived the critical scrutiny of the community of scholars worldwide and are therefore well-established truths of history today and as far as we can see into the future.

Of course, all historical interpretations are subject to criticism and change because all are based on probabilities and cannot be proven absolutely. But these three discoveries have been examined critically for a very long time and have passed the scrutiny of generations of scholars, which is good reason to believe they are true, subject to correction by some new, contrary bit of information that the future may hold and that is hidden from us now, or some new 'paradigm shift' caused by a powerfully persuasive demonstration of an alternative view. The three discoveries are subject to correction by new information that may come to light, but as far as we can see there is no reason to think that they will be shown to be false in the future. This being so, any argument advanced in the Aryan debate that rejects one of these discoveries would not be acceptable to the community of scholars worldwide. We could not entirely rule out the possibility that such an argument is true, but the probability against it being true would be very, very high. And since such an argument would attack fundamental beliefs of the community of scholars, to be successful it would have to contain a fully-worked out, convincing demonstration of the alternative way of explaining the data.

Let me now explain the nature of each of these three discoveries.

The Indo-European Language Family

The first published expression of what scholars today call the Indo-European language family was made in Calcutta in 1786, by Sir William Jones, in a lecture given before the Asiatic Society of which he was the president and founder. What he said was that six ancient languages—Sanskrit, Latin, Greek, Gothic (ancestor of the Germanic languages), Celtic (ancestor of Irish and Welsh), and Old Persian—are so similar that they must have been descended from a common original language, 'which, perhaps, no longer exists'. In saying this he posited a genealogical relationship among the six languages and, by implication, their modern descendants, which constitute six of the branches of the family tree of languages now called Indo-European. These are the six branches of the Indo-European language family:

1. Indo-Aryan languages of North India and Sri Lanka (from Sanskrit)
2. Iranian languages such as Farsi (from old Persian)

3. Romance languages including French, Spanish, and Italian (from Latin)
4. Greek or Hellenic languages (from ancient Greek)
5. Germanic languages such as English, Dutch, and German (from Gothic)
6. Celtic languages such as Irish and Welsh (from ancient Celtic)

There are other branches of the Indo-European family of languages which Jones failed to include in this statement, such as the Baltic and Slavonic languages including Russian and languages such as Armenian and Albanian but the list is correct as far as it goes. The ancestor of all these languages and branches is now called Proto-Indo-European. We have no writing in this language, and it is known wholly by inference from comparison of the daughter languages of the Indo-European family.

Jones interpreted the similarities to be seen in the grammar and vocabulary of the six ancient languages in terms of a common genealogy. In doing so, he regarded Sanskrit as a historical language like any other, as a language having come into existence at some point in the past and being subject to change over time. This was a departure from the doctrine of eternal Sanskrit commonly found among the pandits of the time. Moreover, he treated Sanskrit as a *sister* language to the other four ancient languages, not as the *mother* language from which all others have derived. This new way of looking at Sanskrit was quite revolutionary, for it proposed a new and unexpected linkage between the history of India and the histories of nations lying to the west of India. The discovery that languages of India, Iran, and Europe are related to one another, even though separated from one another by a large block of territory in which Arabic and Turkish are now the dominant languages, was unexpected and utterly new, departing from previous ideas that Indians, Iranians, and Europeans held about their own histories.

The study of comparative philology, or historical linguistics as it is called today, developed rapidly from the comparison of these languages, especially after the German scholar Franz Bopp published (in 1816) his sketch of the comparative grammar of Indo-European, and Jacob Grimm showed the law-like regularity of the sound shifts, which had overtaken languages of the Indo-European family as they drifted apart from one another. Jones' proposal has been abundantly justified by subsequent generations of linguists, and it is fundamental to historical linguistics today. It was bound to have profound effects on the way we understand India's ancient history. The most important effect was that India's most ancient history was now connected with that of Iran and Europe.

The Dravidian Language Family

The second discovery, that of the Dravidian language family, is usually credited to a missionary, Bishop Robert Caldwell, whose classic work, *A Comparative Grammar of the Dravidian or South-Indian Languages*, was published in 1856 and is still in print.

This, however, is mistaken. Fully forty years previous to Caldwell's book, in the very year in which Bopp was laying the foundations of the comparative study of Indo-European languages in Europe (1816), Francis Whyte Ellis, Collector of Madras, published an elegant proof of the Dravidian language family. He showed that Tamil, Telugu, and Kannada shared a common stock of roots and forms of grammar that were different from those of Sanskrit, a finding he extended also to Malayalam, Tulu, Kodagu, and 'Rajmahali' or Malto, a tribal language of the Gangetic basin, far to the north. The Dravidian proof was developed through the work of Ellis and of Indian scholars at the College of Fort St. George (where the South Indian languages were taught to arriving civil service recruits) such as Pattabhiraman Shastri, and of Shankariah or Shankara Shastri who was chief of staff to Ellis in the collectorate of Madras.

Here, too, the results were durable and productive, and remain accepted today by the great majority of linguists worldwide. Here again the effects on our understanding of Indian history were profound, and in some ways complementary to the discovery of Indo-European. These results tended to undermine the traditional view of eternal Sanskrit as the source of all other languages. The new discovery tended to show that Indian civilization is a *fusion* of cultures belonging to different linguistic groups.

These two discoveries, made two centuries ago, have stood the test of time and remain accepted by linguists today. They have proven to be permanent additions to knowledge, so far as we can see. The methods employed in the discoveries of Indo-European and Dravidian were so successful they were extended to other parts of the world, and helped to elucidate the histories of peoples without writing, in Africa and the Americas. The success of these methods means that to deny the truth of the Indo-European or the Dravidian discovery, one would be opposing the whole worldwide development of historical linguistics. Conversely, the success of that worldwide development is reason to believe the truth of the Indo-European and Dravidian findings, subject, of course, to future discoveries, or a persuasive demonstration of an alternative way of reading the evidence for these relationships.

The two discoveries, then, were the beginnings of a wider application of the new methods of language history. They announced unexpected truths that departed from previous beliefs and revolutionized knowledge both in Europe and in India. They began in India, under colonial rule, where European and Indian scholars were brought together, and in so doing both European and Indian forms of language analysis were joined in producing this new knowledge. I may mention two other discoveries coming from British India. Both Sir William Jones and another East India Company servant, William Marsden, contributed to the discovery that the Romani language of the Rom or Gypsies of Europe is Indo-Aryan and came from India long, long ago. And Marsden published the first proof of what is now called the Malayo-Polynesian language family, joining Madagascar, off the coast of Africa, with Indonesia and, in the far Pacific, Hawaii.

In all these cases, historical relations among languages showed the connection among peoples who had no distinct historical memory of their connection. I mention this because the absence of historical memory of a distant homeland by the Aryans of the Veda is often used as evidence for the belief that India is the homeland of the Aryas. Making this argument, however, ignores the very large number of cases around the world, such as that of the Rom or the speakers of Malayo-Polynesian languages, for whom historical linguistics has been able to reveal historical connections where memory cannot. This ability to reveal historical connections that were lost to collective memory was the source of the method's appeal and remains one of its very great strengths.

The discovery of the Indo-European and Dravidian language families was not a simple matter of observing similarities among the languages, because the languages of India have borrowed large numbers of words and grammatical features from one another over thousands of years of interaction, with the result that they resemble one another to a large degree, whether they are genealogically related or not. Thus the Dravidian languages have many, many loanwords from Sanskrit and Prakrit that make them resemble the Indo-Aryan languages in the north and in Sri Lanka. India, as the American linguist M.B. Emeneau says, is a linguistic area, the languages of which have many common features, which have come about over many thousands of years of co-residence in the subcontinent,[5] and this of course is also true of many other aspects of Indian culture. Indian civilization is a fusion of different linguistic and cultural components that have converged over time.

Philologists or linguists have developed analytical methods that are very technical and have a logic of their own. The fundamental step in this analysis is to separate later, borrowed words and grammatical features from the ancient core of the language. This core retains traces of its deep past, rather like the DNA of living cells. Thus, as we shall see, Ellis showed that certain common words for things in the languages of South India are traceable to roots in Dravidian languages but not to the roots of Sanskrit collected in texts of Indian linguistic science called *dhatu-patha*s or *dhatu-mala*s. Sanskrit and Prakrit loans in Telugu, for example, had already been identified in Indian grammars of Telugu, written in Sanskrit, which called such loans *tatsama*s and *tadbhava*s, and are distinguished from *deshya*s or 'country words'. In this and other matters, modern, scientific linguistics absorbed and benefited from the highly developed Indian tradition of linguistic analysis, from Panini in the North to Tolkappiyar in the South. One should note that the historical relationships which linguists discern apply to the ancient core of the

[5] M.B. Emeneau, 'India as a linguistic area', *Collected Papers*, article 11, pp. 172–86 (Annamalainagar: The Annamalai University, 1967). First published in *Language* 1956: 3–16.

language from which borrowings have been removed, an abstraction from the whole, living language. That process of abstraction allows us to see the traces of their own history within languages which are, through borrowing, growing ever more similar to their neighbours.

One can get a good sense of the logic of analysis in historical linguistics in this volume, from the Dravidian proof of Ellis, and the articles by Mehendale and Deshpande. Mehendale shows how the relations of Indo-Aryan and Iranian languages are inferred from the patterning of shared and non-shared features. Deshpande talks about retroflexion, the series of consonants (ṭ, ṭh, ḍ, ḍh, ṇ) which are found in Dravidian and Indo-Aryan languages, but not in other Indo-European languages, an example of a telling pattern showing Dravidian influence on Indo-Aryan (and not vice versa).

The Indus Civilization

The discoveries of Indo-European and Dravidian language families were momentous, and there was an Aryan debate of sorts even before it was further complicated by the equally momentous discovery of the Indus Civilization, by the archaeologists.

Archaeologists had examined sites of the Indus Civilization such as Harappa since the times of Alexander Cunningham, the first head of the Archaeological Survey of India (ASI), beginning in 1853, but without realizing the significance of the evidence. Cunningham's programme for the ASI was oriented toward ancient Buddhist sites that were mentioned in the itineraries of Chinese Buddhist pilgrims to India, and in his report on the Indus Civilization site of Harappa he speculated that it was one of the cities visited by the Chinese Buddhist pilgrim Hsüang Tsang in the seventh century. He had no idea of its very great antiquity, and that it belonged to the Bronze Age.[6]

During excavations in 1922–3, R.D. Banerji found inscribed seals in an unknown script at Mohenjo-daro in Sindh (present-day

[6] Alexander Cunningham, Archaeological Survey of India: Report for the years 1872–3 (1875), pp. 105–8. Reprinted in Gregory L. Possehl, ed., *Ancient Cities of the Indus*, pp. 102–4 (Durham, North Carolina: Carolina Academic Press, 1979).

Pakistan) beneath the level of Buddhist monuments, similar to ones known from Harappa and previously published by Cunningham. On the basis of Banerji's excavation at Mohenjo-daro, and Daya Ram Sahni's excavations at Harappa, Sir John Marshall, then Director-General of the ASI, published the find in the *Illustrated London News* in 1924, announcing the discovery of a new civilization and appealing for assistance in determining the age of the finds. Within two weeks of its publication, letters from specialists in Mesopotamian archaeology identified the seals as similar to ones recovered from Mesopotamian sites of the third millennium BC, among them the cities of Susa and Ur. The Indus Civilization had been discovered, and acquired a place in world history.

But what was its place in the history of India? The discovery of a Bronze Age civilization in India greatly complicated the picture of India's beginnings. There came about two quite different ways of thinking about the relation of the Indus Civilization to the rest of Indian history. One of them, which was Marshall's view, was that the newly-discovered civilization was a wholly new first chapter in the history of India, prior to the arrival of the Aryans and the Veda. The reason had to do with chronology. If the Indus Civilization belonged to the third millennium BC (and radiocarbon testing has since confirmed this finding, giving brackets of approximately 2600–1900 BC for the urban phase), it seemed to be earlier than the Veda. The language of the Veda, according to the philologists, is closely related to the language of the ancient Iranians, whose oldest text is the Avesta, dating to about 700 BC. The Avestan language and the language of the Veda are so similar that many words and grammatical forms are identical except for the sound changes that separate the two. The form of the Vedic language as it has come down to us cannot, therefore, be very much earlier than the Avesta, so that 1000 BC or perhaps 1200 BC seems an outer limit. The entry of the Aryans into India must have been prior to the composition of the Rig Veda, but it could not be much earlier than about 1500 BC.

If, as Marshall thought, the Indus Civilization *preceded* the Veda, it opens a problem of continuity between the Indus Civilization and the later history of India, that is, the question of what aspects of the culture of that civilization were passed on to later ages. Marshall thought such continuities existed. He believed, for example, that the worship of Shiva is indicated on a seal of the Indus Civilization, and that Shiva-worship was passed on and absorbed into the Vedic religion. This entailed a view that Hinduism is a fusion of Vedic and pre-Vedic practices and beliefs.

If the Sanskrit language was brought into India from without, and at a period after the Indus Civilization, what then was the language of the Indus Civilization's population? Here we can only speculate, on the basis of suggestive but inconclusive facts. The most probable candidate is a language of the Dravidian family. This is because there are Dravidian languages in the Gangetic valley (Malto) and the Indus valley (Brahui) that remain to this day, as well as traces of Dravidian languages in the earliest Vedic texts (loanwords and retroflexion), suggesting that Dravidian languages were once spoken throughout North India. Emeneau and Burrow have developed strong evidence for this position,[7] which is widely accepted by other scholars, but it is not a certain proof of the language of the Indus Civilization. Other languages would be possible. Munda, the third major language family of India is not a serious contender among scholars for the language of the Indus Civilization, but there are other languages in the valley of the Indus (Burushaski, for example, in the Gilgit region of Pakistan) which belong to no known language family and suggest the possibility that the language of the Indus Civilization may have belonged to a completely different family of which we know little or nothing. What is well-established is that Dravidian languages were current in North India prior to Sanskrit, and that tends to support the hypothesis that a Dravidian language was the language of the Indus Civilization.

The view that the Indus Civilization preceded the arrival, from without, of Sanskrit, which is the standard view in works of history, accepts the findings of the philologists and the Aryan/Dravidian difference. But even before the discovery of the Indus Civilization, there were some who rejected the Aryan/Dravidian difference, and who posited a greater antiquity for the Veda than allowed for by philologists. After the discovery of the Indus Civilization, the

[7] T. Burrow and M.B. Emeneau, *A Dravidian Etymological Dictionary* (Oxford: Clarendon Press, 1961), provides the linguistic foundation for this interpretation.

alternative view that the Indus Civilization *is* the Vedic civilization, the Aryans are indigenous to India, and the Indo-European languages radiated out from a homeland in India to their present locations, began to take shape. The problematic nature of the relation of the Indus Civilization to the rest of Indian history was dissolved in that interpretation. It was no longer a question of a few specific continuities—the continuities are massive.

These two broad positions are very different indeed, and both cannot be true. Why has the Aryan debate been so difficult to resolve? The underlying difficulty is that the Aryan debate entails two very different kinds of evidence. The Indus Civilization is represented by the *material remains*, which archaeologists study according to the methods of stratigraphy and so forth, and the Vedic civilization is represented largely by the *texts* of the Veda, studied by philologists in the context of historically-related languages such as Avestan, ancient Greek, Latin, and the like. Controversy continues over whether the content of the Veda refers to objects that archaeology identifies, and the great difference between linguistic and material evidence makes it difficult to resolve the matter.

The seals of the Indus Civilization, which are both material and linguistic objects, hold the greatest hope for resolving the Aryan debate. If it could be determined that the language of the seals is Dravidian, or Sanskrit or a close relative, or some third possibility, that would be a giant step toward the resolution of the debate, at least among scholars. Unfortunately, although there have been many attempts to decipher the seals under both the Dravidian and the Aryan hypotheses, and others, none of the proposed decipherments have attained general acceptance.

The Racialization of History

The new discoveries of philologists about the histories of languages were also discoveries about the history of peoples. But how should we understand the relation of languages and peoples?

These days we understand that the relation between languages and peoples is not a *necessary* relation but a *contingent* one. That is, we recognize that any child can be brought up to speak the language it is taught regardless of its race or national origin. But that understanding, which is common sense today, was not the one that was current at the time the discoveries of Indo-European and Dravidian were made. In those days it was thought that languages and races or nations—the words were used interchangeably then—were necessarily and permanently connected. Thus the Orientalist Max Müller said that the comparison of languages shows that the same blood flowed in the veins of the soldiers of Clive as flows in the veins of the 'dark Bengalese'. He was saying that language is a truer sign of race ('blood') than is complexion. In his later years, when it came to be generally understood that language and physical features are not necessarily connected, Max Müller repented having said this and argued that language and race are completely independent of one another. There are, he said, no dolichocephalic (long-headed) languages.[8]

In the first half of the nineteenth century, the classification of races by European scientists was governed by the historical genealogies of languages fashioned by comparative philology, and bodily signs such as complexion were subordinated to linguistic classifications. By mid-century it had become apparent that the presumed necessary connection of language and race was mistaken, and a new race science came into existence which challenged 'the tyranny of the Sanskritists', that is, the dominance of philological classifications of languages in the study of race. In this period, there was a growing interest in race history and the formation of a race science based on the study of the features of the human body. One of the most influential expressions of this impulse was a large, four-volume book by a French aristocrat, Arthur de Gobineau, called the *Essay on the Inequality of the Human Races* (1853–5).[9] In it he argued that the white race is responsible for all the ancient civilizations, and that the decline of civilizations is everywhere due to the intermixture

[8] F. Max Müller, *The Languages of the Seat of War in the East.* (London: William and Norgate, 1855); Thomas R. Trautmann, *Aryans and British India*, pp. 172–8; 194–8 (Berkeley and Los Angeles: University of California Press, 1997).

[9] Joseph Arthur, comte de Gobineau, *Essai sur l'inégalité des races humaines*, 4 vols (Paris: Firmin Didot Freres, 1853–5).

of the white race with other races. Of the speakers of Indo-European languages, only the Germanic race (from which the French aristocracy was supposed to have descended) remained pure. In so arguing, Gobineau invented the racial interpretation of world history—the view that race is the deep cause of the most fundamental changes in history, namely the formation and decline of civilizations.

This argument contributed directly to the politics of racial hatred of the Nazi Party of Germany, and its policy of ridding the German population of contamination by foreign racial elements, especially Jews, but also including Indo-European-speaking peoples the Nazis regarded as degenerated through mixture, such as Gypsies and Slavs. Thus the classifications of the linguists had to be overthrown by the idea of racial intermixture, in order to form the idea of a single remaining population of the pure white race. The defeat of Germany in World War II did not entirely destroy this noxious idea, and the politics of whiteness and racial hatred continues to be propagated by small, violent groups in Europe and the United States. Thus there has been, and is, an Aryan debate in the West, quite different in substance from the current Aryan debate in India, but like it in involving deep divisions about social boundaries, about the native and the foreign.

The growing influence of racial ideas in the West had its effects in India, too. Although the Sanskritists and philologists were seen as obstacles by the new proponents of race science and the racial interpretation of history, the Orientalists made their peace with the new ideas of race. Thus the linguistic difference between Indo-Aryan and Dravidian language groups was interpreted as a sign of an ancient clash between a light-skinned race bringing Sanskrit and civilization to an India inhabited by dark-skinned, savage speakers of Dravidian languages. The clash of these races resulted in the caste system, taken to be the formative, central institution of Indian civilization. This interpretation of history, which I call 'the racial theory of Indian civilization',[10] took form in the second half of the nineteenth century and has been widely influential. Indeed, for a long time it was the master narrative of the history of Indian civilization.

[10] Trautmann, *op. cit.*, Ch. 7.

As we will see later in this volume, the racial theory of Indian civilization depended upon a very small number of passages in the Rig Veda, which were interpreted to show the existence of a dark-skinned, broad-nosed enemy population to the Aryans. But the evidence is clearly *over*-interpreted, and the matter of broad noses rests on a single passage which is probably *mis*interpreted. These facts are very soft facts, because they rely on interpretations of difficult texts in poetic language, and they may not be facts at all. What is certain is that the Aryans of the Rig Veda had enemies who differed in language and religion, as the texts make abundantly clear. There *may* have been differences of complexion and other physical features, but we should be sceptical of evidence that we know to have been interpreted too enthusiastically up to now. And in any case it is obvious that language and religion were more salient signs of difference than complexion to the ancient Aryans.

The racial theory of Indian civilization was formed in a period after the ending of slavery in Europe and the United States, in the aftermath of which there grew up a racialized division of labour, combined with social segregation on the basis of race. The system of indentured labour, involving large numbers of Indian workers being shipped to distant colonies of the British Empire after the abolition of slavery to work for very low wages, contributed to the racialization and globalization of the division of labour. The origin of the caste system of India thousands of years ago was often explained by its supposed similarity to the system of segregation in the southern states of the United States of that period, and in South Africa, where Gandhi was soon to make his contribution to the dismantling of racial barriers. This kind of explanation of caste assumed that it was the result of unchanging features of human nature and of racial feeling that history was powerless to alter—ideas that now seem dated.

The discovery of the Indus Civilization in the 1920s showed that the racial theory of Indian civilization could not be true, in that a Bronze Age civilization pre-existed the coming of the Aryans to India (in the standard view). At the very least, it undermined the belief that the Aryans had brought civilization to a savage population of India, for it showed that civilization was very, very early in India, whatever the complexions and other body features of ancient Indians.

The Aryan Debate Today

With this history as background, let us now examine the Aryan debate as it stands now.

We begin with the three fundamental discoveries. Let us arrange the three terms as two pairs of terms. The Aryan debate concerns this question: what is the relation between the first of the discoveries, the Indo-European idea (more specifically the Aryans of the Veda) and the last discovery, that of the Indus Civilization? This indeed is the big question. But there is a middle term, the Dravidian concept, and the question of the relation of Aryans and Dravidians, which arose in the nineteenth century, preceded and still precedes the question of the relation of the Veda and the Indus Civilization. Therefore we group the readings which follow under three heads: (Part 1) The Three Fundamental Discoveries, (Part 2) Aryans and Dravidians, and (Part 3) The Veda and the Indus Civilization. The three discoveries and the two pairs of relations between them of course are not neatly separated in practice, but are intertwined, so that it is artificial to separate these questions from one another. However, it helps us analyse the Aryan debate if we can break it down into three steps in this way, so that we may be sure that all the relevant, well-established facts of ancient Indian history are taken into account.

The relation between Aryans and Dravidians is in the first instance a question of the relation of the two language families, Indo-Aryan (as a branch of the larger Indo-European family) and Dravidian. For its analysis, we depend heavily upon the philologists or linguists, who have the special skills needed. Historians have to be familiar with the debate among linguists about these two language groups. The case is entirely different when we turn to the second relation, between the Vedas and the Indus Civilization. To understand the historical import of the Vedas, which are texts, we must again rely on the special skills of the philologist, while for the analysis of the material remains of the Indus Civilization we must rely entirely on the skills of the archaeologist, at least until the Indus script is deciphered and its language is identified and read. Thus the evidence and the special skills needed to analyse this relation are of two different kinds. Because of this difference in the nature of the evidence, the evaluation of the relation between the Vedas and the Indus Civilization is especially difficult. Let us now examine each of these relations.

Aryans and Dravidians

The work of linguists has solidified our knowledge of the Indo-European and Dravidian language families subsequent to the publications of Jones and Ellis, and they remain as enduring contributions to knowledge. While some linguists are willing to speculate that Indo-European and Dravidian may be two branches of a single tree of languages—that is, they may be connected further back in the past by a common ancestor language—the difficulty is that the further back we go in time, the weaker and more ambiguous the evidence becomes. These more remote possible relationships are, therefore, not widely accepted by linguists. For our purposes, the solid result to grasp is that the Indo-Aryan and the Dravidian languages belong to two different historical families of languages, and the first is a part of the larger Indo-European family. Because this departs from the traditional conception of Sanskrit as eternal and the mother of all languages, there have been a number of scholars in India who have resisted this view, but most have supported and many have contributed greatly to this well-settled finding of the scientific study of language. Any argument which rejects that well-established fact must produce a convincing proof, or it will be regarded as non-scientific.

Which came first, Sanskrit or the Dravidian languages? Of course, every language has a past which extends back to the beginning of speech, so that in a sense all are equally old. But in India, the work of Emeneau, Burrow, and others has shown that the oldest Sanskrit text, the Rig Veda, incorporates loanwords from Dravidian languages, words that have become fully naturalized Sanskrit words, such as *daṇḍa* (staff), *piṇḍa* (ball or lump), and *mayūra* (peacock). Moreover, the retroflex consonants (*ṭ*, *ṭh*, *ḍ*, *ḍh*, *ṇ*, as in words like *daṇḍa* and *piṇḍa*) are found in all the Indian languages, including Indo-Aryan and Dravidian ones, but not in other Indo-European languages. This patterning of the evidence makes it virtually certain that Sanskrit acquired retroflexion from Dravidian (or Munda, the third Indian language family) and not vice versa. Deshpande gives further analysis of retroflexion in the Veda in the readings to follow. This evidence, together with the continuing existence of small pockets of Dravidian language in the valleys of the Ganga (Malto) and the Indus (Brahui), go to show that Dravidian languages were once distributed throughout North India. They were not driven out of North India and into South India by the speakers of Sanskrit, as is often said, but largely remained in place and, after a long period of bilingualism during which Sanskrit acquired features from Dravidian, early inhabitants of North India, over a course of generations, lost their Dravidian languages in favour of exclusive use of Sanskrit-derived languages.

Finally, the relation of Indo-Aryan to the other Indo-European languages, especially the Iranian languages to which it is most closely related, has been an object of much study, and we will see the logic of that kind of investigation in the article by Mehendale in this volume.

The Vedas and the Indus Civilization

We now come to the main question: the relation of the Vedas and the Indus Civilization.

What is the date of the Rig Veda? We have no very secure dates in Indian history prior to the time of the Buddha—which itself is not beyond dispute. In the nineteenth century, groping for an answer to the question, Friedrich Max Müller suggested we reckon back from the date of the Buddha, assuming that the emergence of Buddhism presupposes the full development of several successive strata of Vedic texts: the Samhitas or hymn collections, the Brahmanas or prose texts explaining their mythology and ritual application, and the Upanishads or prose philosophical works. Allowing several hundred years for the development of each layer, he came up with 1200 BC as an approximate date of the Rig Veda.

This approximation agrees with other facts the philologists have uncovered. In the first place, the language of the Veda is very close to that of the oldest Iranian religious text, the Avesta, which, in its present form, is datable to about 700 BC. Philologists would find it difficult to believe that the language of the Veda is very much older than the approximate date Max Müller arrived at, which would put it too far in time from the Avesta. Then, an archaeological excavation in what is now Turkey, at a site called Boghaz Keui, yielded a document, in cuneiform script, in which a king of the Mitanni people calls on his gods to guarantee his promises in a treaty with the king of the Hittites. The gods of the Mitanni are Vedic gods even though the body of the document is not in Sanskrit but in Akkadian. They are Indra, Varuna, Mitra, and the Nasatyas. Both in linguistic form and in religious conception, these gods appear to be closer to Sanskrit than to Iranian; indeed, they are virtually identical to Vedic forms. The Boghaz Keui treaty, which is datable to c.1380 BC by reliable king-lists of the region, provides plenty of puzzles for interpretation, but there is considerable agreement among linguists that the language of the Veda cannot be much earlier than this date.

Turning to the Indus Civilization, its Bronze Age dating, shown in Marshall's article in this volume, has since been confirmed by radiocarbon dating. This involves measuring the decay of forms of carbon from larger to smaller molecules, which proceeds at a steady, measurable pace, in samples of organic material from Indus sites. These datings show that the high period of the Indus Civilization, the 'urban phase', was from about 2600 BC to about 1900 BC. On the face of it, the findings of philology and of archaeology have served to reinforce Marshall's initial conception that the Indus Civilization came *before* the Veda. This is the standard view, that is being increasingly challenged by the alternative view, which argues that the Indus Civilization *is* the Vedic civilization.

Let us now examine the standard view and the alternative view as they stand today.

The Standard or Aryan Immigration View Examined

I have already given the reasons supporting the standard or Aryan immigration view, and need not repeat them. It is sufficient to say that it has developed under continual scholarly debate and scrutiny over the two centuries since Jones, with many refinements and some major changes. It is a well-tested interpretation, and that is why it has become the scholarly standard. We need at this point to examine the main changes in the standard view.

One of the recent changes concerns attacks upon the racial aspect—the racial theory of Indian civilization—of which I have already spoken. Since the 1950s, physical anthropology has been abandoning the idea of race, in favour of the idea of biological populations each having its own statistical range of variation of traits, which overlap with the ranges of other biological populations. It is now understood that there are no discrete races, clearly distinct from one another, and this explains the notorious fact that race science experts of the past could never agree on what the number of different races was. As the biological anthropologist Frank Livingston has said, 'There are no races, there are only clines,'[11] that is, continuous gradations of bodily traits such as complexion without sharp discontinuities that could be taken as the boundaries between races. While anthropologists are abandoning the idea of race, many historians have come to the conclusion that there is no certain racial aspect to the Aryan/Dravidian difference, and do not wish to import modern notions of race back in time to the Vedic period.

A second notable change is a tendency among adherents of the standard view to abandon the idea of *invasion*, in the sense of a rapid military penetration, in favour of a slower, more gradual migration of Aryans into India, accompanied by warfare, to be sure, but spread over a long period of time. This change is welcome. The idea of the Aryan invasion from a Central Asian homeland was long linked to the idea of pastoral nomadism, of which Central Asia supplied the purest examples, such as the Huns or Hunas and the Mongols, with their expansionist, predatory warfare against agrarian societies. However, the Aryans of the Rig Veda were not pure nomads of this pattern. They did have cattle, goats, and other animals, but they also practised agriculture, which is not possible for a fully nomadic way of life and therefore the Aryans must have been sedentary. Thus they were pastoral, but they were not nomadic. They had wheeled vehicles; fixed, year-round settlements; and a complex, ranked social system, all of them absent from the classic pastoral nomads of Central Asia. In part, the invasion thesis reflects an older

[11] Frank B. Livingstone, 'On the non-existence of human races', *Current Anthropology*, vol. 3 1962, p. 279, and in an article of the same name in Ashley Montagu, ed., *The Concept of Race*, pp. 46–60 (New York: Free Press, 1964).

idea of pastoralism current in Europe in the eighteenth century, that nomadism comes before and gives rise to agriculture, as a later and more complex stage of development. We now know that this idea is incorrect, and to the contrary, pure pastoral nomadism develops out of mixed agriculture and stock-breeding, as people practising such an economy move ever deeper into the more arid grasslands of Central Asia where agriculture becomes increasingly poorer and finally impossible. Moreover, pastoral nomadism always exists in some kind of connection with agricultural settlements through trade relations, for example, or raiding, so that nomads can get cereals and other products of sedentary settlements. The Aryans were not pure pastoral nomads, and did not follow the pattern of the Huns and the Mongols in their warfare. That does not preclude a rapid military invasion, but it gives less reason to think that the Aryan entry into India was as sudden and brief as the military invasions of Huns and Mongols against their agrarian neighbours.

Unfortunately, this backing away from the invasion idea has created some confusion over what it means to speak of 'the myth of the Aryan invasion'. For adherents of the standard or Aryan immigrant view, it means only that the Aryan entry into India did not take the form of a short, swift military invasion, while for adherents of the alternative or indigenous Aryan view, it means that that the Aryans did not originate outside of India. The 'myth of the Aryan invasion' means quite different things to the two sides of the Aryan debate, and readers need to look out for this difference of the senses in which it is used.

The heart of the standard view is the belief that the Aryans came to India from outside it. This conception was first stated by Jones himself, who argued that, from a central point of dispersion somewhere in Iran, straight lines could be drawn to the various destinations of what we now call the Indo-European language family without any two lines crossing. Jones' view was a rationalized version of the Tower of Babel narrative in the Bible, according to which God confused the languages of the nations in Babylon, and they dispersed from there in different directions. Later Western scholars favoured Central Asia as the homeland from which the Indo-European languages spread, but many other possible homelands have been proposed over the years and there is no scholarly consensus on its location, except that it is somewhere to the north or west of India. This lack of precision follows from the nature of the evidence. The ancestor language that is now lost—the Proto-Indo-European language—is known by pure inference from the daughter languages of Indo-European, and there is no reason to think that we will ever find a written text in this language. It is impossible to determine from the material remains of archaeological sites that an unwritten language was spoken there. The coordination of archaeological and linguistic evidence is inherently difficult, and can only achieve certainty where the languages in question leave traces in writing on material objects that survive the ages, or the writings speak unambiguously of distinctive physical objects. This lack of precision is an inescapable weakness of the standard view.

That being so, while the patterning of the linguistic evidence supports the argument that Sanskrit encountered Dravidian languages in India and was influenced by them, it might be possible to respect the linguistic evidence and still argue that the Indo-European languages spread out from a centre within India itself. Since Sanskrit is not the mother of the other languages but their sister, and the oldest Sanskrit we know cannot be dated to the times of the Indus Civilization, it would follow that the language of the Indus Civilization could not have been Sanskrit itself, but could have been Proto-Indo-European, a point not always observed by proponents of the alternative view. Any other position would be in conflict with the findings over which the community of linguists has reached consensus.

The strongest evidence favouring the 'out of India' aspect of the standard view has to do with the importance of horses and chariots in the Vedic evidence, about which I will speak in the next section.

The Alternative or Indigenous Aryan View Examined

The alternative or indigenous Aryan view seeks to overturn the standard view which, as I have said, has been built up over the last two centuries and subjected to continuing debate and refinement. Again, the standard view could still be wrong, and is in any case subject to future discoveries that may affect it adversely. However, because it has been tested by the criticisms of scholars of many countries over a very long time, the consensus of the community of scholars deserves respect and credence. The burden of proof, as the lawyers say, must be on the shoulders of those who are urging us to abandon the standard view. To overturn the standard view, they need to reinterpret the facts in a new way, and their argument must be a powerfully convincing one for them to succeed. Here are the obstacles they face.

First, advocates of the alternative view must argue that Indo-European languages come from a homeland in India. These languages could have spread from India, but Sanskrit is not the mother of Greek, Latin, Old Persian, and so forth but the sister, and the language of the Veda cannot be much older than about 1200 BC, even if the Aryans were indigenous to India. Thus, under the alternative view, the language of the Indus Civilization would have to have been a precursor of Sanskrit, namely Proto-Indo-European or something close to it. The proponents of the alternative view have to show not that the pattern of evidence *can* be read to support that conclusion, but must give compelling reasons why the evidence *must* be read that way.

Second, the alternative view must also account for the existence of Dravidian languages in this hypothetical Indian homeland of the Indo-European language family and explain the history of the encounter between the two language families. It would have to explain why both Dravidian and the Indo-Aryan branch of the Indo-European language family have retroflexion, but not the other Indo-European languages which are also, in this view, supposed to have come from India. This is a very serious obstacle to the alternative view. It is not at all evident that the proponents of the alternative view recognize this problem, let alone provide a plausible answer to it.

The third problem is the horse and chariot. The Rig Veda largely consists of poetic addresses to the gods, and in their nature there is little reference to material objects that will leave an unambiguous archaeological trace. However, the abundant references to horses and spoke-wheeled chariots are one feature of the Veda for which we can expect archaeological confirmation. Indeed, other chariot and horse-using societies, such as early China, Greece, and Egypt, have yielded abundant evidence of them, and Indian sculpture of a later period has many representations of horses and chariots.

There are two aspects to this matter. On the one hand, the Veda and other early Sanskrit texts make it abundantly clear that the warrior class of Vedic society, the Kshatriyas, had a mode of warfare based upon the horse and spoke-wheeled chariot. The warrior class identified strongly with their horses and chariots, even taking names formed with words for horse (*ashva*) and chariot (*ratha*) such as Brihadashva and Brihadratha. On the other hand, the Indian environment is not especially favourable to horses, and horses are not abundant in India. Horses are not found in the wild in India, although there are wild relatives of the horse such as the *khur* of Kutch. Horses had continually to be imported to keep the armies of India adequately stocked, from points to the north and west of India, throughout most of its history—the probable directions of Aryan arrival in the standard view. It is notable that while horses were plentiful in Europe, to the degree that the peasantry owned horses and ploughed with them, in India horses were rare and expensive, ownership was largely confined to the nobility, and agriculture used and still uses oxen or buffaloes to draw ploughs, but not horses. The horse culture of the Kshatriyas that is so noticeable in the Veda, the Mahabharata, and the Ramayana was maintained at great expense and under unfavourable conditions.

The proponents of the alternative view have come up with some bits of evidence which they argue support the claim that horses were known to the people of the Indus Civilization. But if the Vedic texts belonged to the time of the Indus Civilization or the people of the Vedic texts were the immediate descendants of the people of the Indus Civilization we would expect the material evidence of horses and chariots in the Indus Civilization sites to be very, very plentiful. So far the evidence is that horses were not used in the Indus Civilization. For example, we find many instances of toy ox-carts with solid wheels and oxen in sites of the Indus Civilization, but we do not find toy chariots with spoked wheels and horses. An argument from absence, of course, is not as strong as an argument from presence, but the burden of proof lies on those who wish to overturn the standard view, and to meet it they need to come up with lots of evidence. So far, precious little evidence of Indus Civilization horses and chariots has been adduced by proponents of the alternative view, and the evidence adduced is doubtful.

These, then, are the main obstacles which the alternative view must overcome. Has the alternative view met its burden of proof, as it must to overturn the standard view, that the Aryans came to India in about 1500 BC from somewhere to the north-west, after the high period of the Indus Civilization? Readers of this book must decide that question for themselves. The debate will continue. Time will tell whether scholarly opinion worldwide will find the evidence and arguments of the alternative view persuasive, and will form a new scholarly consensus.

The Aryan debate would be very greatly advanced by a successful decipherment of the Indus script. If the script were deciphered, the language of the Indus Civilization would have been identified, which is the crux of the Aryan debate. Many decipherments have been proposed, perhaps as many as a hundred, some presuming the language to be Dravidian and others presuming it to be Sanskrit, but none of them have won the approval of the community of scholars. It appears that the Indus script completely died out, and that, some time before Asoka, writing was reinvented in India, on a new basis, as an alphabetic script rather than a largely pictographic one, with a very much smaller number of signs, proportional to the fifty or so distinct sounds in Sanskrit words, as opposed to more than 300 signs in the Indus script. S.R. Rao, who proposed a decipherment of the Indus script on the assumption that the language was Sanskrit, attempted to show that the Brahmi script evolved out of successive changes and simplifications of the Indus script.[12] The existing explanation, going back to the work of Georg Bühler, goes to show that the Brahmi script is modelled on a Semitic script, though it is much improved by the phonological analysis of the ancient Vedic linguistic science.[13] Rao's argument for continuity is not very compelling. As to the decipherment of the script, we must agree

[12] S.R. Rao, *The Decipherment of the Indus Script*. (Bombay: Asia Publishing House, 1982).

[13] Georg Bühler, *Indian Palaeography* (Calcutta: Firma K.L. Mukhopadhyay, 1962), first published 1896, in German.

with B.B. Lal, Kamil Zvelebil, and other scholars who conclude that none of the decipherments proposed so far is successful.[14]

We need not despair and conclude that the Aryan debate will continue unresolved forever. The Indus Civilization was in communication with other early civilizations that had writing systems. What has hitherto impeded the decipherment of its script is that we are dealing with two unknowns rather than just one—an unknown language written in an unknown script. What is needed is a bilingual inscription, giving a parallel version in a known language. It was such a text—the *Rosetta Stone*—that enabled the decipherment of the Egyptian hieroglyphics. And it was such texts, in the form of the bilingual coins and other texts of the Indo-Greek kings of the Punjab in the second century BC and their successors, with Greek legends on one side and Prakrit ones on the other, that enabled H.T. Prinsep and his team to crack the code that opened up the inscriptions of Asoka. Because the Indus Civilization engaged in trade with other literate civilizations, there is every reason to hope that such a text will be found in the remains of the Indus Civilization or one of its trading partners. A convincing decipherment of the Indus script might end the Aryan debate, but it might not, because facts and interpretations are always open to challenge and the results of historical investigation are always provisional. But it would certainly be a major contribution and move the debate to a higher plane.

[14] B.B. Lal, 'Script and language', Ch. 9 in *The Earliest Civilization of South Asia* (New Delhi: Aryan Books International, 1997) and Kamil Zvelebil, this volume.

PART 1

Starting Points

The Three Discoveries

The articles in this section consist of the first published announcements of the three discoveries that are fundamental to the Aryan debate: that of the Indo-European language family, the Dravidian language family, and the Indus Civilization.

The first article is a short extract from the 'Third anniversary discourse', by Sir William Jones, in 1786, delivered before the Asiatic Society, which he had founded and whose anniversary each year he marked by a lecture. Those lectures, taken together, survey the antiquities, arts, and sciences of the nations of Asia. In the third discourse, 'On the Hindus', Jones identifies the leading ancient languages of what we now call the Indo-European language family, inferring their descent from a common ancestor-language. The passage also speaks of a pre-Sanskritic element in Hindi, a 'substratum' language as linguists would say. These few sentences give in brief outline the views, which prevail among linguists today.

The sketch of the Indo-European language family was consolidated by Franz Bopp in 1816, when he formulated the comparative philology of Indo-European. At the same time, in Chennai, Francis Whyte Ellis published the first demonstration that the languages of South India (those which linguists call Dravidian) are related to one another by common descent, and that they are not descended from Sanskrit. A long extract of this demonstration is given in the second article. While the piece from Jones is no more than a brief assertion without demonstration—because it was part of an annual lecture—the Ellis piece gives abundant supporting evidence for his assertion, and we can see in it the interactions of European and Indian linguistic analyses.

The third discovery, that of the Indus Civilization, was announced over a century later, in 1924, by Sir John Marshall, the Director-General of the Archaeological Survey of India, in a work reprinted here as the third article. The discovery was based upon new excavations undertaken by the Archaeological Survey, led by R.D. Banerji and Daya Ram Sahni. These excavations fortified a growing appreciation of the great antiquity of these sites, and that they belonged to the Bronze Age, long before the iron-using sites of the historic cities of ancient India familiar to us through ancient texts. Thus the discovery of the Indus Civilization came about through a combination of new excavations and reinterpretation of existing finds.

1

Indo-European

Sir William Jones

Sir William Jones' 'Third anniversary discourse' on the Hindus was delivered to the Asiatic Society, Kolkata, in 1786 and published in the first volume of the Society's journal, *Asiatic Researches*, in 1788. In this short extract, the last paragraph gives a list of the ancient languages comprising what we have come to call the Indo-European language family (Sanskrit, Greek, Latin, Gothic, Celtic, and Old Persian). Jones infers that they are derived from a nameless ancestor language, 'which, perhaps, no longer exists', a hypothetical source language, which linguists now call Proto-Indo-European. This famous passage is much quoted in histories of linguistics as a breakthrough to a modern, scientific understanding of historical linguistics, as indeed it is, although the breakthrough was only consolidated later by the more systematic analyses of Franz Bopp and others. Jones believed that these and other languages dispersed from 'some central country' following the Biblical flood of Noah, some four thousand years ago, and he suggested that it might be located in Iran, since lines of dispersal to the locations of the early civilizations would not cross if it were located there. Moreover, it was near the location of the Tower of Babel from which, according to the Bible, the nations dispersed when God confused their languages. Thus Jones' approach uses rationalist means but assumes the truth of the Bible narrative of world history. In the passage preceding this famous paragraph on what we now call the Indo-European languages, Jones detects a non-Sanskritic element in Hindustani, mainly in its inflections, that he believes is more ancient than Sanskrit and is primeval to India. This would now be called a 'substratum' language. The positing of a non-Sanskritic substratum in North India creates a space for the discovery of Dravidian and Munda language families as separate from Sanskrit and the other Indo-Aryan languages and prior to them in India.

[From 'Third anniversary discourse', *Asiatic Researches*, vol. 1, 1788, pp. 415–31.]

It is much to be lamented, that neither the *Greeks,* who attended Alexander into *India,* nor those who were long connected with it under the *Bactrian* Princes, have left us any means of knowing with accuracy, what vernacular languages they found on their arrival in this Empire. The *Mohammedans,* we know, heard the people of proper *Hindustan*, or *India* on a limited scale, speaking a *Bháshá*, or living tongue of a very singular construction, the purest dialect of which was current in the districts round *Agrà*, and chiefly on the poetical ground of *Mat'hurà*; and this is commonly called the idiom of *Vraja.* Five words in six, perhaps, of this language were derived from the *Sanscrit,* in which books of religion and science were composed, and which appears to have been formed by an exquisite grammatical *arrangement*, as the name itself implies, from some unpolished idiom; but the basis of the *Hindustánì*, particularly the inflexions and regimen of verbs, differed as widely from both those tongues, as *Arabick* differs from *Persian*, or *German* from *Greek.* Now the general effect of conquest is to leave the current language of the conquered people unchanged, or very little altered, in its ground-work, but to blend with it a considerable number of exotick names both for things and for actions; as it has happened in every country, that I can recollect, where the conquerors have not preserved their own tongue unmixed with that of the natives, like the *Turks* in *Greece,* and the *Saxons* in *Britain*; and this analogy might induce us to believe, that the pure *Hindı* whether of *Tartarian* or *Chaldean* origin, was primeval in Upper *India,* into which the *Sanscrit* was introduced by conquerors from other kingdoms in some very remote age; for we cannot doubt that the language of the *Véda's* was used in the great extent of country, which has before been delineated, as long as the religion of *Brahmā* has prevailed in it.

The *Sanscrit* language, whatever be its antiquity, is of a wonderful structure; more perfect than the *Greek*, more copious than the *Latin*, and more exquisitely refined than either, yet bearing to both of them a stronger affinity, both in the roots of verbs and in the forms of grammar, than could possibly have been produced by accident; so strong indeed, that no philologer could examine them all three, without believing them to have sprung from some common source, which, perhaps, no longer exists: there is a similar reason, though not quite so forcible, for supposing that both the *Gothick* and the *Celtick*, though blended with a very different idiom, had the same origin with the *Sanscrit*; and the old *Persian* might be added to the same family, if this were the place for discussing any question concerning the antiquities of *Persia*.

2

The Dravidian Proof

F.W. Ellis

F.W. Ellis was the first to publish a proof of the Dravidian language family. It appeared as a 'Note to the Introduction' of a Telugu grammar text written by A.D. Campbell for the instruction of junior civil servants. It was published by the College of Fort St. George, Chennai, in 1816. The article refutes the belief of early British Orientalists that Telugu is descended from Sanskrit. The demonstration is beautifully constructed. First, Ellis shows that Telugu has many roots not traceable to Sanskrit, by listing the first ten roots of a selection of starting letters, taken from the *dhātumalas* (lists of roots) of each language. Second, he juxtaposes roots of Telugu to corresponding ones in Kannada and Tamil, showing that most of them are common to the three. Third, he gives a translation of a lengthy passage from the grammar of Telugu recently composed by Mamadi Venkayya, a Komati trader and scholar of Masulipatam on the coast of Andhra Pradesh. Mamadi's text identifies words traceable to Sanskrit roots using the technical terminology of *vyakarana* analysis, *tatsama* (identical to Sanskrit) and *tadbhava* (similar to Sanskrit, but with modifications), *deshya* (regional words not traceable to Sanskrit roots), and other categories. The analysis leads to a list of 'pure Telugu' words and Ellis goes on to show, by juxtaposing this list of Telugu words with cognate words in Kannada and Tamil, that the words are found in the three South Indian languages and not in Sanskrit. This shows that the three languages are historically related and not derived from Sanskrit. Ellis correctly extends the scope of this language family to Malayalam, Tulu (of the Mangalore region), Kodagu (of Coorg), and Rajmahal, that is, Malto, spoken far to the north in the basin of the Ganga, and he rightly notes that Sinhalese, Marathi, and Oriya, 'though not of the same stock' (that is being of the Indo-Aryan group) have many borrowed words from the South Indian language family. The family was given the name Dravidian by Robert Caldwell, whose masterful *Comparative Grammar of the Dravidian or South-Indian Languages* was published in 1856, forty years after Ellis.

I have abridged this article considerably to make it easier to follow, eliminating many lists of words and modernizing the transliteration slightly.

> [From 'Note to the introduction', in A.D. Campbell, *A Grammar of the Teloogoo Language*, 1816 (reprint New Delhi: Asian Educational Services, 1991), pp. 1–31 (abridged).]

The real affiliation of the Telugu language appears not to have been known to any writer, by whom the subject has been noticed. Dr Carey in the preface to his Sanscrit Grammar says, 'The Hindoostanee and *the Tamil*, with the languages of Gujarat and *Malayala, are evidently derived from the Sanscrit, but the two former are greatly mixed with foreign words.* The Bengalee, Orissa, Maratta, *Kurnata, and Telinga* languages *are almost wholly composed of Sanscrit words.*' In the preface of a Grammar of the Telugu lately published by him he, also, says, 'The languages of India are principally derived from the Sanscrit' and 'The structure of most of the languages in the middle and north of India, is generally the same, the chief difference in them lies in the termination of the nouns and verbs, and in those deviations from Sanscrit orthography which custom has gradually established in the countries where they are spoken. The languages of the south of India, i.e. *The Telinga, Karnatic, Tamil, Malayala,* and Cingalese, *while they have the same origin with those of the north,* differ greatly from them in other respects: and especially in having a large proportion of words, the origin of which is unascertained.'[1] To this testimony Dr Wilkins adds the weight of his authority, when he says in the preface to his *Grammar of the Sanscrit*: '*The Tamil, the*

[1] In this passage Ellis puts in italics the passages with which he disagrees. Thus all the names of the Dravidian languages are in italics, because he denies that they are derived from Sanskrit, while all the names of Indo-Aryan or Indo-European languages are in Roman, because he accepts their derivation from Sanskrit. [ed.]

Telugu, the Carnatic, the Malabar, together with that' (the idiom) 'of the Marratta states and of Gujarat so abound with Sanscrit, that *scarcely a sentence can be expressed in either of them without its assistance.*' Mr Colebrooke, also, in his dissertation on the Sanscrit and Pracrit languages in the *7th Volume of the Asiatick Researches,* though he has not given so decided an opinion, yet, by including these under the general term Pracrit, appropriate only to dialects of Sanscrit derivation and construction, and by the tendency of his remarks, appears to favour the received notion of their origin; he states indeed in express terms that the *Tamil* (which word he writes Tāmla, deducing it from Támraparnȧ, the Sanscrit name of the river of Tirunelveli) is written in a character which is greatly corrupted from the present Devanagari, and that both the '*Carnata*' and '*Telingana*' characters are from the same source. In arrangement, the two latter, which are nearly the same, certainly follow the Nagari, but in the form of the letters, mode of combination, and other particulars, there is no resemblance; and the *Tamil is totally different,* rejecting all aspirates, and having many sounds which cannot be expressed by any alphabet in which the Sanscrit is written.

It is the intent of the following observations to shew that the statements contained in the preceding quotations are not correct; that neither the Tamil, the Telugu, nor any of their cognate dialects are derivations from the Sanscrit; that the latter, however it may contribute to their polish, is not necessary for their existence; and that they form a distinct family of languages, with which the Sanscrit has, in latter times especially, intermixed, but with which it has no radical connection.

The members, constituting the family of languages, which may be appropriately called the dialects of southern India, are the high and low Tamil; the Telugu, grammatical, and vulgar; Carnataca or Cannadi, ancient and modern; Malayalma or Malayalam, which, after Paulinus a St. Bartholoméo may be divided into Sanscrit (Grandonico-Malabarica) and common Malayalam, though the former differs from the latter only in introducing Sanscrit terms and forms in unrestrained profusion; and the Tuluva, the native speech of that part of the country to which in our maps the name of Canara is confined.

Besides these, there are a few other local dialects of the same derivation, such as the Codugu, a variation of the Tuluva spoken in the district of that name called by us Coorg; the Cingalese, Maharastra and the Oddiya, also, though not of the same stock, borrow many of their words and idioms from these tongues. A certain intercommunication of language may indeed, always be expected from neighbouring nations, however dissimilar in origin, but it is extraordinary that the uncivilized races of the north of India should in this respect bear any resemblance to the Hindus of the south; it is, nevertheless, the fact, that, if not of the same radical derivation, the language of the mountaineers of Rajmahal abounds in terms common to the Tamil and Telugu.

The Telugu, to which attention is here more specially directed, is formed from its own roots, which, in general, have no connexion with the Sanscrit, nor with those of any other language, the cognate dialects of southern India, the Tamil, Cannadi, etc. excepted, with which, allowing for the occasional variation of consimilar sounds, they generally agree; the actual difference in the three dialects here mentioned is in fact to be found only in the affixes used in the formation of words from the roots; the roots themselves are not merely similar, but the same.

To shew that no radical connexion exists between the Sanscrit and Telugu, ten roots in alphabetic order, under the letters *A*, *K*, *P*, and *V*, have been taken from the common *dhatu-mala* or list of roots, and with them have been compared ten Telugu roots, under the same letters taken from a Telugu *dhatu-mala* compiled by Patabhi-rama Sastri, the Head Sanscrit and Telugu Master at the College; these will be found in the following lists, the mere inspection of which will shew, that, among the forty Telugu roots, not one agrees with any Sanscrit root. To facilitate a comparison of the several languages treated on, each of which has a distinct alphabet, the roman character is used throughout: the orthography is generally that of Sir Jones, as explained in the *lst Volume of the Asiatic Researches*, but the grave accent is used instead of the acute, to mark a naturally long syllable when final or formed by *Sandhi*, and *K*, is occasionally substituted for *C*, before *i* and *e* in words belonging to the southern dialects only: other variations of trifling importance will be observed.

[The author then gives parallel columns of roots of Sanskrit and Telugu, not printed here, taking the first ten in the list of roots for each, for roots beginning with the letters A, K, P, and V, showing that the roots are completely different between the two languages.]

To shew that an intimate radical connection exists between the Telugu and other dialects of southern India, fifteen roots have been taken in alphabetical order from the *Dhatu-mala* mentioned above, under the first vowel [A] and first consonant [K], with which the correspondent roots of the Tamil and Cannadi are compared: the Tamil roots are from a list compiled by the Head Tamil Master at the College, compared with the Sadur Agaradi and other dictionaries and the Cannadi roots are from an old list explained in Sanskrit.

[The author then gives three columns of words, in Telugu, 'Cannadi', and Tamil, showing cognate words having a single root in the three languages, not printed here.]

But though radial connection may bc proved to exist between languages, their actual connection, as regards terms used for the expression of ideas, may not be intimate and it becomes necessary, therefore, to establish this point, to enter further into detail and compare the words of the three cognate dialects, as well as the roots whence they are derived. Mamidi Vencaya, the author of the *Andhra Dipaca*, an excellent dictionary of the Telugu, has, in the preface to this work, introduced a concise analysis of the language, the substance of which, as affording the means of making this comparison, is translated in the following paragraphs.

'The modes of derivation in the Andhra language are four; they are *tatsaman*, *tadbhavan*, *desyam*, and *gramyam*.

Of Pure Sanscrit Terms Received in Telugu

Tatsamam consists of Sanscrit terms, pure as spoken in heaven, the Telugu terminations being substituted for those of the original language, of which the following are examples.

Sanscrit	*Tatsamam*	
Ramah	Ramandu	*a proper name*
Vanam	Vanamu	*a forest*
Ganga	Ganga	*the river*

(Contd)

(Contd from previous page)

Sanscrit	*Tatsamam*	
Harih	Hari	*a proper name*
Bhagavati	Bhagavati	*a goddess*
Srih	Sri	*prosperity*

...

Of Terms Derived from the Sanscrit

Tadbhavam consists of terms formed, either from the Sanscrit direct, or through one of the six Pracrits, varied by the interposition of syllables, and by the substitution, increment, and decrement of letters, as explained in the *Vaicruta-chundrica*: the several modes of derivation, here indicated, are exemplified in the following lists.

Tadbhavam Terms Derived Immediately from Sanscrit

Sanscrit	*Tadbhavam*	
Samudrah	Sandaramu	*the sea*
Chandrah	Tsandurundu	*the moon*
Kananam	Kana	*a forest*
Kudyam	Goda	*a wall*
Yatra	Dzatara	*pilgrimage*
Aturam	Atramu	*hurry*
Pangtih	Banti	*a line or row*
Churali	Garidi	*a fencing school*

[The author then gives lists of *tadbhavam* loanwords in Telugu derivable from the Prakrit languages Maharashtri, Shauraseni, Magadhi, two varieties of Paishachi, and Apabhramsha, not printed here.]

Verse

All those words which are in use among the several races who are aborigines of the Country of Andhra, which are perfectly clear and free from all obscurity, these shine forth to the world as the pure native speech of Andhra (Suddha Andhra Desyam).

Of These the Following are Examples

Palu	*milk*	Nela	*the moon, a month*
Perugu	*curdled milk*	Vesavi and Vesungi	*sultry weather*
Ney	*clarified butter*		
Rolu	*a mortar*	Gudi	*a temple*
Ronkali	*a pestle*	Madi	*a field*
Utti	*a long net for holding pots, etc.*	Puli	*a tyger*
		Tsali	*cold*
Pudami	*the earth*	Madugu	*a natural pool or lake*
Padatuka	*a woman*	Uru	*a village*
Pasidi-paindi	*gold*	Magavandu	*a man*
Bangaru	*gold*	Andadi	*a woman*
Koduku	*a son*	Aluka	*vexation; displeasure*
Kodalu	*a daughter-in-law*		
Tala	*the head*		

...

Of Terms and Forms of Rustic or Vulgar Speech

Terms which cannot be subjected to the rules of grammar, and in which an irregular increment or decrement of letters occur, are called Gramyam; they are corruptions.

In the preceding extracts, the author, supported by due authority, teaches that rejecting direct and indirect derivatives from the Sanscrit, and words borrowed from foreign languages, what remains is the *pure native language of the land*: this constitutes the great body of the tongue and is capable of expressing every mental and bodily operation, every possible relation and existent thing; for, with the exception of some religious and technical terms, no word of Sanscrit derivation is *necessary* to the Telugu. This pure native language of the land, allowing for dialectic differences and variations of termination, is, with the Telugu, common to the Tamil, Cannadi, and the other dialects of southern India: this may be demonstrated by comparing the *Desyam* terms contained in the list taken by Vencaya from the Appacaviyam, with the terms expressive of the same ideas in Tamil and Cannadi. It has been already shewn that the radicals of these languages, *mutatis mutandis*, are the same, and this comparison will shew that the native terms in general use in each, also correspond.

It would have been easy to have selected from the three dialects a far greater number of terms, than these, exactly agreeing with each other; but it is considered preferable to follow a work of known authority, and to which no suspicion of bias to any system can attach: the author, though a good Sanscrit scholar, was ignorant of all the dialects of southern India, his native tongue excepted.

[The author then gives three columns of words, Telugu, 'Cannadi', and Tamil, not printed here, showing that each of the words in the previously-given list illustrating the 'pure native speech of Andhra' has a cognate word in the other two languages. Thus Telugu *palu*, 'milk', corresponds to *halu* in 'Cannadi' or Kannada and *pal* in Tamil. (Ellis notes, of the Kannada word *hal*, that it is due to a regular sound change: 'When P begins a word in Tamil or Telugu, it is in Cannadi changed to H, as Tamil Palli, Tel. Palle, Can. Halli, a small village.']

With little variation, the composition of the Tamil and Cannadi are the same as the Telugu and the same distinctions, consequently, are made by their grammatical writers. The Telugu and Cannadi both admit of a freer adoption of *Tatsamam* terms than the Tamil: in the two former, in fact, the discretion of the writer is the only limit of their use; in the high dialect of the latter those only can be used, which have been admitted into the dictionaries by which the language has long been fixed, or for which classical authority can be adduced; in the low dialect the use of them is more general—by the Brahmans they are profusely employed, more sparingly by the Sudra tribes. The Cannadi has a greater and the Tamil a lesser proportion of *Tadbhavam* terms than the other dialects; but in the latter all Sanscrit words are liable to greater variation than is produced by the mere difference of termination, for, as the alphabet of this language rejects all aspirates [e.g. *kh, gh*], expresses the first and third consonant of each regular series [e.g. *k, g*] by the same character, and admits of no other combination of consonants than the duplication of mutes or the junction of a nasal and a mute, it is obviously incapable of expressing correctly any but the simplest terms of the Sanscrit; all such, however, in this tongue are accounted *Tatsamam* when the alteration is regular and produced only by the deficiencies of the alphabet.

3

The Indus Civilization

Sir John Marshall

Sir John Marshall's 'First light on a long-forgotten civilization' is the first published recognition of the Indus Civilization as a distinct entity with a Bronze Age date. It was published in the *Illustrated London News*, a weekly magazine that often included articles on important archaeological finds. The discovery came out of excavations at Mohenjo-daro conducted by R.D. Banerji and at Harappa by Daya Ram Sahni. Cunningham had earlier published finds from the Indus Civilization, but he attributed them to more recent times. The new excavations made it clear that the remains of this distinctive civilization preceded the Buddhist monuments of the historic period to which Cunningham's work had been devoted. Marshall's attention focused on the seals, both the images which seemed unlike any hitherto unearthed in India, and the pictographic script, bearing no resemblance to known Indian scripts but, as he suggested, 'They do bear a certain general affinity to pictographs of the Mycenaean age in the Mediterranean area'. Marshall located the Indus Civilization before the Aryans, and tentatively suggested a Dravidian identity. The seals were prominently displayed in the three plates of photographs accompanying the article (not included here).

Marshall's article was published in the issue of 20 September. On October 4, a mere two weeks later, G.J. Gadd and Sidney Smith brought out an article, 'The new links between Indian and Babylonian Civilizations', in the same magazine. The article briefly reviewed the similarities of script and material culture that show a close resemblance, leading the authors to suppose that the makers of the Indus seals 'must have been in very close contact with Sumerian civilization, and have borrowed their artistic style and the basis of their writing from the Sumerians'. The authors thought that much of the evidence suggested a dating between 3000 and 2800 BC for the close contacts between the people of the Indus Civilization and the

Sumerians, which was much earlier than the prevailing date of the Aryan entry into India, at about 1500 BC.

Between Marshall's article and the latter one, in the space of two weeks, the existence of a hitherto unknown civilization in the valley of the Indus, and a time horizon for it going back to c. 3000 BC, had been established, and with it the question of the relation of this newly-discovered civilization to the Veda and all of Indian history that followed. A non-Aryan, specifically Dravidian, identity had been proposed, and seemed to fit the already established Aryan/Dravidian difference.

[From 'First light on a long-forgotten civilization', *Illustrated London News*, 20 September 1924, pp. 528–32 and 548.]

Not often has it been given to archaeologists, as it was given to Schliemann at Tiryns and Mycenae, or to Stein in the deserts of Turkestan, to light upon the remains of a long-forgotten civilization. It looks, however, at this moment, as if we were on the threshold of such a discovery in the plains of the Indus.

Up to the present our knowledge of Indian antiquities carried us back hardly further than the third century before Christ. Of the long ages before the coming of the Greeks and the rise of the Maurya dynasty; of the birth and growth of civilization in the great river basins; of the cultural development of the races who one after another poured into the peninsula from the north and west—of these and other problems relating to that dim and remote past, archaeology has given us but the faintest glimmerings; for almost the only remains of those early times that have come down to us have been rough implements of the Stone and Copper Ages, groups of prehistoric graves in the south of the peninsula, and some rude cyclopean walls at Rajagriha in Bihar. On the other hand, from the third century BC onwards, we have, on the whole, a fairly clear idea of man's handiwork in general: of his religious and domestic architecture, of his formative arts, of his weapons and utensils, of his personal ornaments and his jewellery, of his coins and gems, and of the scripts which he used in his writing. And whenever it happens that new antiquities come to light—no matter to what race or religion they may belong—it is invariably possible to assign them with confidence and within relatively narrow limits to their respective age or class.

Now, however, there has unexpectedly been unearthed, in the south of the Punjab and in Sind, an entirely new class of objects which have nothing in common with those previously known to us, and which are unaccompanied by any data that might have helped to establish their age and origin.

The two sites where these somewhat startling remains have been discovered are some 400 miles apart—the one being at Harappa in the Montgomery district of the Panjab; the other at Moheno-daro, in the Larkana district of Sind. At both these places there is a vast expanse of artificial mounds, evidently covering the remains of once flourishing cities, which, to judge from the mass of accumulated debris, rising as high as 60 ft above the level of the plain, must have been in existence for many hundreds of years. Such groups of mounds abound in the plains of the Indus, just as they do in Mesopotamia and the valley of the Nile; and they are specially conspicuous along the banks of the old, dried-up beds of the main stream and its tributaries, not only in Sind, but in Bahawalpur State and in the Panjab.

The opportunities for excavation, therefore, in this part of India may be regarded as almost limitless; and, when it can be carried out on thorough and systematic lines, there is no doubt that the field will prove a peculiarly fertile one. Up to date, however, the meagre resources at the disposal of the Archaeological Department have permitted it to undertake little more than preliminary trial-digging on these two sites: and it goes without saying that the remains disclosed are correspondingly limited. Yet, such as they are, they are full of promise.

At Mohenjo-daro, the main street of the old city can still be discerned as a broad highway running from the south bank of the river towards the south-east, with houses fringing it on either side. What is surmised by the discoverer, Mr Banerji, to have been the royal palace, stood at the point where this road emerged on to the quays of the riverside. Opposite to it, in the now dry bed of the river, are several islands from which rose the principal shrines of the city, the highest and, no doubt, the chief of them all, being a massive

Buddhist *stupa* raised on a high oblong platform, and surrounded by subsidiary shrines and monastic quarters. These remains belong to about the second century AD when the Kushans were paramount in the north-west of India; and, judging by the finds already made—particularly the urn burials, remnants of painted frescoes inscribed in Brahmi and Kharoshthi characters, new types of coins and other novel objects—there can be no doubt that their further exploration will result in welcome light being thrown on this very obscure period of Indian history.

Valuable, however, as these remains are likely to prove, it is not in them that the real interest of Mohenjo-daro centres at the moment. Deep down below the Buddhist monuments described above, or at other parts of the site appearing close to the surface itself, there are at least two other strata of buildings belonging to much earlier epochs, and containing a variety of brick structures—the character and antiquity of which can at present only be surmised. Among these older structures one group is especially worthy of mention. Besides various halls and passages and chambers, it includes a massive structure—apparently a shrine—with walls seven or eight feet thick, pierced by several conduits which, in the opinion of the excavator, served for carrying off the lustral water when the shrine or image within it was washed. In another part of the same group is what appears to be an altar built of small glazed bricks, and provided with a drain of similar brickwork. Some idea of the appearance of these early buildings, and of their present state of preservation, is afforded by two of the photographs reproduced (Plate 1), the one showing a staircase to the south-west of the shrine referred to, with a conduit in the foreground from which the covering of marble slabs has been removed; the other, illustrating the glazed-brick flooring in a bay on the western façade of the same shrine.

At Harappa, Mr Daya Ram Sahni's excavations disclosed as many as seven or eight successive levels, demonstrating the long and continuous occupation of the site during many hundreds of years prior to the third century BC; and throughout most, if not all, of this long period, burnt brick of a good quality was used for building purposes. The site at Harappa, however, has suffered much from the depredations of railway contractors and others, and the structures brought to light are in a more fragmentary condition than at Mohenjo-daro. On the other hand, the smaller antiquities are generally identical in character with those from Mohenjo-daro, and some of them even are better preserved. These smaller antiquities from the two sites comprise new varieties of potteries both painted and plain, some fashioned by hand and some turned on the wheel: terracottas; toys; bangles of blue glass, paste and shell; new types of coins or tokens; knives and cores of chert; dice and chessmen; a remarkable series of stone rings; and, most important of all, a number of engraved and inscribed seals. Iron does not occur at all, except in the latest deposits, and metal objects of any kind are scarce, particularly at Harappa.

Of all these antiquities the most valuable are the stone seals, not only because they are inscribed with legends in an unknown pictographic script, but because the figures engraved on them, and the style of the engraving, are different from anything of the kind hitherto met with in Indian art. Some of them are of steatite, others of ivory, and others of stone and paste. In shape most are square, and provided at the back with a boss pierced with a small hole from suspension. The animals engraved on them are in some instance bulls; in other unicorns; but it is to be observed that neither the Indian humped bull nor the water-buffalo occurs among them.

As to the strange pictographs which do duty for letters, three points are worth of remark: first, that the marks (apparently vowel signs) attached to many of the pictographs indicate a relatively high stage of development; secondly, that some of the inscriptions from Mohenjo-daro betray a later stage in the evolution of this script than those from Harappa; thirdly, that they bear no resemblance whatever to any ancient Indian alphabet known to us; but, on the other hand, they do bear a certain general affinity to pictographs of the Mycenaean age in the Mediterranean area, though it is not possible to point to any of the symbols as being actually identical.

Examples of the pictographic writing are found not only on the seal dies, but also (at Mohenjo-daro) on certain oblong bars of copper which their discoverer assumes to have been coins, since they are similar in shape to the early Indian oblong coins known as 'punch-marked', though they do not correspond in weight with any recognized standards used in ancient India. Should this assumption of Mr Banerji's prove correct, it would mean that these coins may turn out to be the earliest, since the first coins hitherto known to have been struck in any other country are the Lydian pieces of the seventh century BC.

Notwithstanding that the curious ring stones mentioned above have been found in large numbers on both sites, the purpose to which they were put has hitherto quite baffled the ingenuity of the excavators; though, for reasons into which it would take too long to enter here. Mr Banerji believes that they were in some way connected with the *Bhartaris*, or shrines of eternal fire. They are of all sizes, from that of a small napkin ring up to fifty pounds in weight, and are made of various coloured stones or marble; but what is particularly curious about them is that in many specimens the upper and lower surfaces are undulating.

Another remarkable and significant feature at the Mohenjo-daro site is the character of the burial customs. In the earliest period the practice was to bury the body in a hunched position in a brick tomb, generally of square or oblong form. Later on (it may be very much later), the custom obtained of burning the body, as is commonly done in India to-day, and depositing the ashes in a small urn, which, along with two or three others, was placed inside a larger round jar, accompanied by several miniature vessels containing food, raiment, and so on.

To what age and to what people do these novel antiquities belong? Those are the two questions which will naturally occur to the reader, and to which a score of different answers may perhaps suggest themselves. As to the first question, all that can be said at present is that the period during which this culture flourished in the Indus valley must have extended over many centuries, and that it came to an end before the rise of the Maurya power in the third century BC. So much may be inferred, on the one hand, from the many successive strata of habitation, particularly on the Harappa site: on the other, from the presence of copper weapons, and the total absence of any iron on either site, as well as from the fact that none of the objects, except the bricks and a few toy terracottas, can be paralleled among the known antiquities of the Mauryan or subsequent epochs; while the pictographic writing is totally distinct from the early Brahmi script which the Emperor Asoka employed throughout the greater part of India, or from the Kharoshthi script which he used in his inscriptions on the North-Western Frontier.

As to the second question, it is possible, though unlikely, that this civilization of the Indus valley was an intrusive civilization emanating from further west. Painted pottery and other objects somewhat analogous to those from Mohenjo-daro and Harappa have been found in Baluchistan; and there are linguistic reasons for believing that it was by way of Baluchistan that the Dravidian races (thought by some writers to have been originally connected with the Mediterranean) entered India. Mr Banerji himself is inclined to connect this culture of the Indus valley directly with the Aegean culture of the Eastern Mediterranean, and holds that distinct affinities are traceable between the Minoan antiquities of the Crete, and those unearthed by him at Mohenjo-daro—especially in regard to the painted ceramic wares and pictographic inscriptions. But the resemblances referred to are, at the best, problematical, and, in case too slight the intangible to warrant any inference being drawn as to a cultural connection between the two areas.

What seems prima facie more probable is that this forgotten civilization, which the excavations of Harappa and Mohenjo-daro have now given us a first glimpse, was developed in the Indus valley itself, and just as distinctive of that region as the civilization of the Pharaohs was distinctive of the Nile. In the marvellous forward progress which mankind made during the Neolithic, Copper, and Bronze Ages, the great river tracts of the then inhabited parts of the world played a most important part; for it was in these tracts that conditions were found most favourable from supporting a dense and settled population—namely, fertility of the soil, an unfailing water supply, and easy communications; and it was, of course, among such large and settled populations that civilization had the best chance of making progress. The debt which, in the early stages of its development, the human race owed to the Nile, to the Danube, to the Tigris, and to the Euphrates, is already well known. But how much it owed to the Indus and to the Ganges has yet to be determined. In the case of the Indus, it is probably true that successive migrations from outside had a useful effect, as they did in

Mesopotamia and in Egypt, in promoting the development of indigenous culture; but there is no reason to assume that the culture of this region was imported from other lands, or that its character was profoundly modified by outside influences.

PART 2

Aryans and Dravidians

The five pieces of this section (articles 4–8) are a sampling of the scholarly literature on Aryans and Dravidians, both technical linguistic studies and historical studies of racial ideas and political appropriations.

The first three articles are by linguists. M.B. Emeneau's article on the linguistic prehistory of India is a classic, giving a broad overview of its topic, with argumentation that is widely accepted today, many decades since its first publication, in 1954. The next article, by M.A. Mehendale, gives an elegant, concise analysis of the linguistic evidence by which the interrelations of the linguistic groupings is determined: Indo-Aryan (languages of India and its neighbours), Indo-Iranian (the larger, inclusive grouping of Indo-Aryan and Iranian languages), and Indo-European (the even larger, more inclusive grouping containing all the foregoing language branches and those of Europe). Madhav M. Deshpande, in the third article of this section, completes the picture of linguistic analysis bearing on the Aryan debate by examining the Vedic Aryans and those outside the Veda, that is, both non-Vedic Aryans who do not perform the Vedic sacrifice and various peoples identified by the Veda as non-Aryan.

In the last two articles of this section, historians examine ways in which ideas of race have coloured the interpretation of the evidence and contributed to political appropriations of the Aryan idea. In the first of these, Thomas R. Trautmann shows how, in the late nineteenth century, a theory arose that Indian civilization was formed by a clash of civilized and uncivilized races, by overinterpreting the Vedic evidence. Romila Thapar examines the roots of two very different interpretations of the idea of the Aryans in India. The first of these is a Dalit one, which takes the Aryans to be foreign invaders and oppressors of the indigenous inhabitants after the golden age of the Indus Civilization; the second is a Hindutva one, stressing the oneness of the Indian people, positing the indigenous origin of the Aryans and asserting the identity of the Indus and Vedic civilizations.

4

Linguistic Prehistory of India

M.B. Emeneau

M.B. Emeneau's classic article on the linguistic prehistory of India, first published in 1954, gives a good overview of the topic as it stood at that time among philologists of the West. In this argument what he calls the non-Indo-European elements in Sanskrit is the central issue, that is, features of Sanskrit that it does not share with the Iranian languages, to which it is most closely related, and with the other branches of the Indo-European family (Greek, Germanic, etc.) to which it is more distantly related. These include retroflexion, that is, the sounds *ṭ*, *ṭh*, *ḍ*, *ḍh*, *ṇ* (in Nagari: ट ठ ड ढ ण) which are found in most Indian languages, Indo-Aryan, Dravidian, and Munda, and which are ancient in the Dravidian languages because they can be reconstructed for their inferred ancestor language, called Proto-Dravidian. They also include a number of borrowed Dravidian words in Sanskrit, of which the article gives a sampling. Emeneau, along with Thomas Burrow and F.W. Kuiper, is one of the pioneers of this line of scholarship, and he subsequently teamed up with Burrow to compose the massive *Dravidian Etymological Dictionary*, which consolidated the arguments made in this paper.

[From *Collected Papers*, Art. 10, pp. 155–71 (Annamalainagar: The Annamalai University, 1967). First published in *Proceedings of the American Philosophical Society*, Vol. 98 (1954), pp. 282–92.]

At some time in the second millennium BC, probably comparatively early in the millennium, a band or bands of speakers of an Indo-European language, later to be called Sanskrit, entered India over the north-west passes. This is our linguistic doctrine which has been held now for more than a century-and-a-half. There seems to be no reason to distrust the arguments for it, in spite of the traditional Hindu ignorance of any such invasion, their doctrine that Sanskrit is 'the language of the gods', and the somewhat chauvinistic clinging to the old tradition every today by some Indian scholars. Sanskrit, 'the language of the gods', I shall therefore assume to have been a language brought from the Near East or the Western world by the nomadic bands.

These invaders did not penetrate into a linguistic vacuum. What did they find to the east of the passes? If the archaeologists' reconstruction and chronology of the events are at all well-founded, they found over the whole of the Indus valley a high culture (the Harappā culture of the archaeologists, which was a sibling or a remote cousin of the high cultures of the Near East—Egypt, the Fertile Cresent, Mesopotamia.[1] Here were great and small cities, whose life was based on the riverine agriculture permitted by a great river and its tributaries in a vast, irrigable, alluvial valley. The probabilities are that the culture was as rigidly regimented and as firmly based on a system of serfdom or slavery as were the Near Eastern cultures.[2] So far the excavations have not yielded, and it seems improbable that they will in future yield, evidence of a material brilliance such as that of Egypt and Mesopotamia. It may be that the Harappā

[1] See, e.g., Mackay, Ernest, *Early Indian Civilizations*, (London: Luzac and Co., 1948); Wheeler, R.E.M. (now Sir Mortimer), in various places, esp. *Ancient India* 3: 74–6, January 1947, and *The Cambridge History of India*, supp. vol. *The Indus Civilization* (Cambridge: Cambridge University Press, 1953); Piggott, Stuart, *Prehistoric India to 1000 B.C.* (Harmondsworth, Middlesex: Pelican Books, 1950), with good select bibliographies.

[2] Wheeler, *Ancient India, loc. cit.*

culture was the 'repellent' thing that one of its interpreters[3] has called it—'drab' or 'dull'[4] might be a better, because a less subjective, word.

For our present interest, however, it is to be recalled that this culture was literate. The many short inscriptions on seals are written in a script that is non-identical in its forms with either the Egyptian hieroglyphs or the Mesopotamian cuneiform, but that is somewhat similar to the early stages of both in that it probably developed from a picture-writing, rebus-like in nature, and was apparently, like both, syllabic in its strucure.[5] The unknown script and subject matter combined with the shortness of the inscriptions, have so far defied convincing decipherment.

The most ambitious attempt up to date, that of Father Heras,[6] has posited that the language is an old member of the Dravidian family which is now located chiefly in South and Central India, but which still has an outlying member, Brahui, in the highlands of Baluchistan to the west of the Indus valley. There is nothing a priori against this assumption. Speakers of Dravidian languages now number about 90 million or just under one-quarter of the population of the Indian subcontinent (making the family the fifth or sixth largest in the world). The geographical distribution, and the nature of the boundary in Central India between Dravidian speakers and the speakers of the Indo-Aryan languages that descend from the invader language Sanskrit, are good evidence that Dravidian has been steadily retreating before Indo-Aryan. The Dravidian-speakers of the farthest South, the Tamil-speakers, early acquired a high culture with all the features of the North Indian culture that was framed in Sanskrit. Even the grammar and the literary criticism of the Sanskritic culture were

[3] Piggott, *op. cit.*, 201.

[4] 'Dull' is Wheeler's word in *Tamil Culture*, 2: 20, 1953: he declares, however, in *The Indus Civilization*, 63 f. that the remains suggest 'an aesthetic capacity more broadly based than the recovered examples of it alone would indicate', an aesthetic capacity perhaps expended in part on the perishable art of wood-carving.

[5] Piggott, *op. cit.*, 178–81. Kroeber's term 'stimulus diffusion' must be called to mind.

[6] Many articles in Indian journals have been devoted to this 'decipherment'. It seems unnecessary to list them.

among the early borrowings and are the subjects of the earliest extant Tamil text. As is usual in India, no exact dating of this early literature is possible, but it is clearly no later than the earliest centuries of the Christian era and may well be pre-Christian. Tamil script is known from the Arikamedu finds of the first century AD. And the presence of Aśokan inscriptions in the Middle Indo-Aryan dialects as far south as Mysore state in the third century BC is witness to the spread of Sanskritic culture southwards prior to this period—for who could have been addressed by Aśoka in Indo-Aryan dialects if not literate Brahmans who had settled in the South in some numbers on their missionary occasions?

Be that as it may, it has been claimed that the far southern, Tamil form of the Brahmanical Sanskritic culture of India shows in its earliest remains so many specific high features that are not North Indian, that we must posit a high culture in South India prior to the spread of the brahmanical culture there. Archaeological evidence to substantiate these claims, however, is still lacking.[7] Yet, taking all together, the assumption that the language of the Indus valley documents was Dravidian is clearly not fantastic.

In spite of this, the attempts at interpretation have not been convincing. Since the subject matter of the documents is unknown, any subject matter, that is, meaning, that is assigned to any element of the script, is arbitrary. A succession of arbitrary meanings thus assigned to the symbols (with, to be sure, a little aid from Sumerian texts) may, in fact, be made to coincide with a Dravidian-like succession of phonemes, but only for short stretches of the material. The Indus valley material is made up of a fairly large number of short inscriptions, but it is only by positing numerous arbitrary variations of sound and of meaning for the same symbols that anything like a coherent system can be made to run through the total corpus. It is this necessity to vary, or, in other words, this self-given permission to vary in the sound and meaning that are attached to the smallish number of different symbols, plus the impossibility of checking the arbitrary meanings, that has convinced the interested

[7] Wheeler, *Ancient India*, 4: 89, July1947–January 1948, with some bibliography.

scholars that the method used has been an unconvincing one—that, to put it more crudely, by this method one can give the inscriptions any interpretation one wishes.

In fact, promising as it has seemed to assume Dravidian membership for the Harappa language, it is not the only possibility. Professor W. Norman Brown has pointed out (*The United States and India and Pakistan*, pp. 131–2, [Cambridge: Harvard University Press, 1953] that North-west India, that is the Indus valley and adjoining parts of India, has during most of its history had Near-Eastern elements in its political and cultural make-up at least as prominently as it had true Indian elements of the Gangetic and Southern types. The passage is so important that it is quoted in full:

More ominous yet was another consideration. Partition now would reproduce an ancient, recurring, and sinister incompatibility between the Northwest and the rest of the subcontinent, which, but for a few brief periods of uneasy cohabitation, had kept them politically apart or hostile and had rendered the subcontinent defensively weak. When an intrusive people came through the passes and established itself there, it was at first spiritually closer to the relatives it had left behind than to any group already in India. Not until it had been separated from those relatives for a fairly long period and had succeeded in pushing eastward would it loosen the external ties. In period after period this seems to have been true. In the third millennium BC the Harappa culture in the Indus Valley was partly similar to contemporary western Asian civilizations and partly to later historic Indian culture of the Ganges Valley. In the latter part of the next millennium, the earliest Aryans, living in the Punjab and composing the hymns of the Rig-Veda, were apparently more like their linguistic and religious kinsmen, the Iranians, than like their eastern Indian contemporaries. In the middle of the next millennium the Persian Achaemenians for two centuries held the Northwest as satrapies. After Alexander had invaded India (327/6-325 BC) and Hellenism had arisen, the Northwest too was Hellenized, and once more was partly Indian and partly western. And after Islam entered India, the Northwest again was associated with Persia, Bokhara, Central Asia, rather than with India, and considered itself Islamic first and Indian second.

The periods during which the Punjab has been culturally assimilated to the rest of northern India are few if any at all. Periods of political assimilation are almost as few; perhaps a part of the fourth and third centuries BC under the Mauryas; possibly a brief period under the Indo-Greek king Menander in the second century BC; another brief period under the Kushanas in the first and second century AD; an even briefer period under the Muslim Kingdom of Delhi in the last quarter of the twelfth century AD; a long one under the great Mughals in the sixteenth and seventeenth centuries AD; a century under the British, 1849–1947.

Though this refers to cultural and political factors, it is a warning that we must not leap to linguistic conclusions too hastily. The early, but probably centuries-long condition in which Sanskrit, a close ally of languages of Iran, was restricted to the north-west (though it was not the only language there) and the rest of India was not Sanskritic in speech, may well have been mirrored earlier by a period when some other language invader from the Near East—a relative of Sumerian or of Elamitic or what not—was spoken and written in the Indus valley. It is not ruled out, of course, that this anonymous Near Easterner might have been only one of the languages spoken in the Indus valley—perhaps that of invaders and conquerors—while the indigenous population spoke another language—perhaps one of the Dravidian stock, or perhaps one of the Munda stock, which is now represented only by a handful of languages in the backwoods of Central India.

On leaving this highly speculative question, we can move on to an examination of the Sanskrit records, and we find in them linguistic evidence of contacts between the Sanskrit-speaking invaders and the other linguistic groups within India.

Whenever two language communities come in contact and remain in contact for any appreciably long period, the languages have some effect upon each other's structure. Borrowing of words in one or the other direction or in both is the most obvious effect. But there may also be a shift of sound systems, borrowing of derivational or inflectional morphemes, or borrowing of syntactical traits.

Sanskrit scholarship in the West soon saw that some of the non-Indo-European features of Sanskrit were Dravidian (or possibly Munda) in type. The retroflex (domal or cerebral) consonants in Sanskrit may be explained for some of their occurrences as being the reflexes of Indo-European consonant clusters of certain types. The fact, however, that the later in Indo-Aryan linguistic history we go, the greater is the incidence of retroflex consonants, and the further fact that most of the Dravidian languages and Proto-Dravidian itself have this type of consonant in abundance (the case is not so clear for Munda, but is in all probability similar), can only lead to the conclusion that the later Indo-Aryan developments are due to a borrowing of indigenous speech habits through bilingualism, and to the well-grounded suspicion that even the early development of retroflexes from certain Indo-European consonant clusters results from the same historic cause.[8] The same argument applies also to the development of absolutives (otherwise called gerunds) in Sanskrit; this non-finite verb form and its syntactic use are so closely parallel to a feature of Dravidian and so unlike what is found in the other old Indo-European languages that we must certainly posit Dravidian influence here.[9]

Prima facie, it should have been easy to examine the Sanskrit dictionary for possible borrowings from Dravidian. There were, however, several blocking factors. First, and perhaps most important, was the assumption, usually but not always only implicitly made and seldom argued or supported by evidence, that the Sanskrit-speaking invaders of North-west India were people of a high, or better, a virile, culture, who found in India only culturally feeble barbarians, and that consequently the borrowings that patently took place from Sanskrit and later Indo-Aryan languages into Dravidian were necessarily the only borrowings that could have occurred. Indian civilization itself, with its enthronement of Sanskrit at the expense of other languages, taught Western scholars to think this way about Sanskrit. Moreover, the early days of Indo-European scholarship were without benefit of the spectacular archaeological discoveries that were later to be made in the Mediterranean area, Mesopotamia, and the Indus Valley. It was but natural to operate

[8] This doctrine is held by, e.g., Bloch, Jules 'Sanskrit et dravidien', *Bull. Soc. Ling.*, Paris, 1925, 25: 1–21, esp. 4–6; 'Some problems of Indo-Aryan philology', *Bull. School Orient. Stud.*, 1930, 5: 731–3; *L'Indo-aryen du Veda aux temps modernes*, 53 ff., 325, Paris, 1934; Katre, S.M., *Some Problems of Historical Linguistics in Indo-Aryan*, 135 ff., Bombay, 1944; Prokosch, E., *A Comparative Germanic Grammar*, 39, Philadelphia, 1939; Wackernagel, Jackob, *Altindische Grammatik*, 1: 165, §144 (a) Anm. Göttingen, 1896, with earlier bibliography, Gundert, in 1869, *Ztschr. Deutsch. morgenländischen Ges.*, 23: 517 ff., having apparently the earliest suggestion.

[9] *Cf.* Bloch, *Bull. School Orient. Stud.*, 1930, 5: 733–5.

with the hidden, but anachronistic, assumption that the earliest speakers of Indo-European languages were like the classical Greeks or Romans—prosperous, urbanized bearers of a high civilization destined in its later phases to conquer all European and then a great part of the earth—rather than to recognize them for what they doubtless were—nomadic, barbarous looters and cattle-reivers whose fate it was through the centuries to disrupt older civilizations but to be civilized by them. This was in all probability the event in India as it was in Greece or in the later Roman empire.[10]

This assumption led in the long run to another block—the methodological tendency of the end of the nineteenth and the beginning of the twentieth century to attempt to find Indo-European etymologies for the greatest possible portion of the vocabularies of the Indo-European languages (see also note 10), even though the object could only be achieved by flights of phonological and semantic fancy. Latin perhaps was the greatest sufferer from this urge,[11] but none of the languages was exempt, and Sanskrit was no exception. It was the less pardonable in dealing with a language spoken and written in India, where even casual inspection of the Dravidian languages would have suggested some borrowings, at least, from Dravidian into Sanskrit.[12]

[10] Mingled with this essentially Europe-centred attitude was that other strand in late eighteenth century thinking, the 'romantic' one stressed by Mayrhofer, Manfred, *Saeculum*, 1951, 2: 54 ff. It led to Sanskrit being regarded (to use Mayrhofer's phrase) as 'die ur-ste aller Ursprachen', as an exemplar of purity and freedom from all non-Indo-European influence. The Indo-European savages, in short, were the noblest of all noble savages. But this, of course, is ethnocentrism all over again.

[11] *Cf.* Lane, George S., *Lang.*, 1949, 25: 335–7.

[12] The borrowings from the vernacular Middle Indo-Aryan into Sanskrit, when the latter became, as it early did, a hieratic and then a dead language in which speakers of Middle Indo-Aryan languages composed freely, form another portion of the Sanskrit lexicon which must be identified and not subjected to fantastic Indo-European etymologizing. Paul Tedesco had made many notable contributions here, but he also is willing to operate with a methodology in which the Dravidian languages do not exist except as borrowers from Indo-Aryan. One example of this is his treatment of words for 'belly, stomach' in Sanskrit piṭaka- 'basket', *Archaeologica orientalia in memoriam Ernst Herzfeld*, 218, Locust Valley, N.Y., 1952. Whatever may be the etymology of Br. piḍ 'belly,

The third blocking factor has been for long the general ignorance of and indifference to the Dravidian languages, even among professed Indological linguistic scholars. They must not, of course, be judged too harshly. The Dravidian languages are not easy; most of them are languages spoken by backwoods 'primitives' and are badly reported; the four literary languages have enormous literatures; *ars* (*et scientia*) *long, vita brevis.*

Finally, fourth blocking factor has been the general caution of Indo-European scholars when confronted with a substratum situation. In this they were justified, for apart from Basque, the substrata that have been operated with in the study of the history of European languages have been languages that are fragmentarily recorded and badly known (for example, Gaulish Celtic), not really on record (for example, Illyrian), or not understood (for example, Etruscan). In the case of Sanskrit, however, the Dravidian substratum is easily accessible in its dozen or more living languages and in that a Proto-Dravidian can be worked out, given enough scholars interested in the matter.

The end result of the block, however, was that very few scholars attempted to identify borrowings from Dravidian into Sanskrit; those who were interested worked unmethodically and without establishing criteria for recognition of probable, possible, and unlikely examples, and their results were universally ignored. The Sanskrit etymological dictionary of Uhlenbeck (1898–9)[13] and the

stomach' (so with Bray, rather than p[h]īḍ with *Linguistic Survey of India*), the Go. pīr id. is rather to be interpreted as going with Te. pēgu, prēgu 'entrail, gut, bowel' than as borrowed from as Indo-Aryan *petta-*. More striking is the Sanskrit word mālā- 'garland, wreath', which can be provided with an Indo-Aryan etymology only with the utmost ingenuity (*Jour. Amer. Soc.*, 67: 85 ff., 1947). The 'rope' meanings in modern Indic vernaculars may belong to homonyms, to be etymologized as Tedesco does. But the Sanskrit 'garland' word may well be borrowed from the Dravidian group of words given in Appendix 1, etym. 13, which may be seen for details.

[13] Uhlenbeck, C.C., *Kurzgefasstes etymologisches Wörterbuch der altindischen Sprache*, Amsterdam, 1898–9. He mentions non-Sanskritic languages, though without any detail, s.vv. drāviḍī, pallī. Mayrhofer has apparently found several more such instances; *Saeculum* 2: 55, 1951: 'verzeichnet kaum fünf Wörter einheimischer Abkunft'.

Indo-European etymological dictionary of Walde and Pokorny (1930–2)[14] completely ignore the work of Gundert (1869),[15] Kittel (1872, 1894),[16] and Caldwell (1856, 1875).[17]

More recent work by Jules Bloch (1925, 1930, 1934)[18] attempted to salvage some items from the early attempts, and in the 1940s T. Burrow in an important series of articles (1945, 1946, 1948)[19] attempted to set up methodological principles (see Appendix 1) and suggested Dravidian sources for some Sanskrit words. Collaborative work by Burrow and myself on a Dravidian etymological dictionary will add more items. The Sanskrit etymological dictionary that Manfred Mayrhofer has begun to publish in Germany (1953)[20] takes account of this recent work.

It is clear that not all of Burrow's suggested borrowings will stand the test even of his own principles.[21] Much labour will have to be expended by qualified scholars on methods and on the individual

[14] Walde, Alois, and Julius Pokorny, *Vergleichendes Wörterbuch der indogermanische Sprachen*, 3 v., Berlin, 1930–2.

[15] Gundert, H., *Ztschr. Deutsch. morgenländischen Ges.*, 23: 517–30, 1869.

[16] Kittel, F., *Indian Antiquary*, 1: 235–9, 1872; *A Kannaḍa–English Dictionary*, xiv-x1v, Mangalore, 1894.

[17] Caldwell, Robert, *Comparative Grammar of the Dravidian Languages*, 565–79, 2nd ed., 1875. I have no access to the 1st ed. of 1856.

[18] Bloch, Jules 'Sanskrit et dravidien', *Bull. Soc. Ling.*, 1925, Paris, 25: 1–21; 'Some problems of Indo-Aryan philology: II. Indo-Aryan and Dravidian', *Bull. School Orient. Stud.*, 1930, 5: 730–44; *L'Indo-aryen du Veda aux temps modernes*, 322–8, Paris, 1934.

[19] Burrow, T., 'Some Dravidian words in Sanskrit', *Trans. Philol. Soc.*, 1945: 79–120; 'Loanwords in Sanskrit', ibid., 1946: 1–30; 'Dravidian studies VII: Further Dravidian words in Sanskrit', *Bull. School Orient. and African Stud.*, 1948, 12: 365–96.

[20] Mayrhofer, Manfred, *Kurzgefasstes etymologisches Wörterbuch des Altindischen*, 1 und 2. Lieferung, Heidelberg, Carl Winter, 1953, 1945.

[21] One should certainly rule out the Dravidian etymologies given for kúṇāru- and vríś-, which occur in one passage each in the Rig-Veda and nowhere else in the whole of Sanskrit literature and are of highly uncertain meaning (*Trans. Philol, Soc.* 1946: 22–3). To provide these with Dravidian etymologies is as futile as to provide them with Indo-European etymologies, which Uhlenbeck did for the former (following Roth, presumably).

items, but it can be safely predicted that the work of these modern scholars will yield an acceptable residue that will at long last be available for studies of Indic linguistic prehistory.

It is possible already to take some tentative steps.

As was to be expected, many of the borrowed items are names of flora and fauna indigenous in India and not elsewhere in the old Indo-European territory, for example, the fragrant screw-pine, *Pandanus odoratissimus* (App. 1, etym. 1), the cardamom (etym. 2), the house lizard, *Lacerta gecko* (etym. 3), perhaps the peacock (etym. 4), and certainly the white ant or termite (etym. 5). Some of these words occur in Sanskrit literature from the epic on; others are hardly more than items in the lexica (perhaps intended as etyma from which the Dravidian words were to be derived). But words of much more general semantic range also occur, some (for example, nīra- 'water', etym. 6) as early as the epic. We can be sure of Dravidian origin for a few proper names; for example, the late Vedic and epic hero Nala seems to have a Dravidian name 'the good (or handsome) man', and the southern Malaya mountains have a name derived from the Dravidian **malay* 'mountain' (etymologies 7 and 8). Even the interjection aye of the dramas probably has a Dravidian origin (etym. 9). It is unexpected to find that kalā- 'an art' (epic and later), which has not been provided with an Indo-European etymology, is probably derived from the Dravidian verb kal- 'learn', but the suggestion cannot be rejected out of hand and in fact is not unattractive when we remember that India had a high culture before the Sanskrit speakers arrived.

The greatest interest attaches to the items that occur in the earliest Sanskrit recorded, the Rig-Veda. Burrow finds some twenty words, a very mixed lot including the 'peacock' word mentioned before and one or two other labels for specifically Indian phenomena. Most of them, however, are much more general; for example, khála- 'threshing floor' (etym. 10) and phála- 'fruit' (etym. 11); káṇa- 'one-eyed' is very obviously derived from the negative adjective ('who does not see') of the Dravidian verb *kāṇ-* 'see'.[22] Most strikingly,

[22] The word occurs in the Ṛig Veda, 10.155.1, an Atharavanic charm. It is common in later Sanskrit and has an abundant progeny ('blind' and 'blind of one eye') in the Indo-Aryan vernaculars; see Turner, Ralph Lilley, *A Comparative*

bála- 'strength',[22] which has been one of the more certain examples given in the handbook for the rare Indo-European phoneme **b* (though the meanings of the cognates are not really identical), may be derived from the very widespreading and ramifying Dravidian family of val- 'be strong, strong, strength' (etym. 12); one of the languages in which Proto-Dravidian **v* becomes *b* will have to be involved here. Indo-Europeanists may be inclined not to accept this, unless they are already desirous of getting rid of all examples of the rare Indo-European **b*.

If the Rig Vedic examples, or any of them, are accepted, this is evidence for the presence of Dravidian speakers as far toward the north-west as the Punjab, that is, the upper Indus valley, in the first centuries (it is uncertain how many) of the presence of Sanskrit-speakers on Indian soil. It is not entirely clear evidence for the Dravidian nature of the Harappa language or of one of the Harappa languages; it does, however, lead towards that hypothesis.

If the Munda languages have been mentioned only in passing, it is not because there were no contacts between Munda speakers and those of the other two language families. The reason is that we know so little that is certain about the Munda family, either descriptively or comparatively. Even the most ambitious attempts at demonstrating borrowings from Munda into Sanskrit have been based on fantastically unsound methods. Although certain Sanskrit words with no Indo-European or Dravidian etymologies might be borrowings from Munda, it seems sounder to ignore the suggestions that have been made, until clear criteria for judging them are at hand (see further Appendix 2).

---

and Etymological Dictionary of the Nepali Language (London, 1931), s.v. kānu. Connection with an Indo-European root (s)qer- 'to cut' or with qel- 'to stick' is not obviously convincing. The Dravidian etymology is in Burrow, *Trans. Philol. Soc.*, 1946: 22; earlier Gundert, *Ztschr. deutsch. morgenländischen Ges.* 23: 521. Not to be derived with Kuiper, F.B.J., *Proto-Munda Words in Sanskrit*, 52, from a Proto-Munda *ga-ḍa 'defective'.

Appendix 1

Sanskrit Borrowings from Dravidian[23]

T. Burrow in *Trans. Philol. Soc.*, 1946: 13–18 set forth criteria for identifying Dravidian words borrowed into Sanskrit. I summarize them, with some comment, as follows: (1) the Sanskrit word should have no Indo-European etymology—it should rather be: no certain or obvious Indo-European etymology; (2) there should be a wide currency of the etymon in the Dravidian languages and it should be a basic element in the vocabulary; (3) 'a word is shown to be Dravidian in origin if it is clearly to be derived from some Dravidian root' (e.g. candana- 'sandalwood tree, ointment' is Dravidian in origin since the corresponding Dravidian nouns cāntu, etc. are specialized derivatives of a verb meaning 'to rub into a paste'); (4) the word should be of some antiquity in Dravidian (e.g. occurring in the earliest Tamil texts); (5) comparative lateness of appearance of the word in Sanskrit (or, one may add, appearance only or first in Sanskrit lexica) increases the probability of its being a borrowing; (6) in each case possible phonetic criteria should be looked for; (7) likewise, semantic developments can sometimes be taken as criteria. There should be added, possibly as a corollary to (2), that if the word denotes something peculiar to the Indian geographical or social scene, a Dravidian origin is more probable than an Indo-European one.

Not all these criteria can be brought to bear in all cases. Comparative simplicity and avoidance of the assumption of tortuous

[23] Abbreviations used in this Appendix:

Br.	Brahui	Nk.	Naiki
Go.	Gondi	Oll.	Ollari dialect of Gadba
Ka.	Kannada	Pa.	Parji
Ko	Kota	Skt.	Sanskrit
Kod	Kodagu	Ta.	Tamil
Kol	Kolami	Te.	Telugu
Kur.	Kurukh (Oraon)	To	Toda
Ma.	Malayalam	Tu.	Tulu
Malt.	Malto		

phonological and semantic developments should be aimed at, following the general practice of all disciplines ('Occam's razor'), and may well at times tip the scales for borrowing from Dravidian rather than for an Indo-European etymology that has been suggested.

The etymologies that follow have been referred to in the body of the paper:

1. Ta. kaital, kaitai; Ma. kaita; Ka. kēdage, kēdige; Tu. kēdai, kēdayi, kēdāyi; Te. gēdãgi 'the fragrant screw-pine, *Pandanus odoratissimus*': Skt. ketaka-, ketakī- id. Burrow, T., *Trans. Philol. Soc.*, 1946: 16 'the diphthong *ai* in the Tamil and Malayalam words is an indication that the word is originally Dravidian'; so also the suffix- *ai* in Ta.-Ma. and Tu.
2. Ta. ēlam 'cardamom plant, *Elettaria cardamomum*'; ēlā-varici 'cardamom seed'; Ma. ēlam 'cardamoms'; ēlatt-ari 'cardamom seeds'; Ka. ēl-akki, yāl-akki, yālaki 'large cardomoms'; Koḍ. e·l-akki 'cardamom seeds'; e·la male, e·latï male 'cardamom plantation'; Tu. ēl-akki 'cardamoms'; Te. ēla, ēlaki 'cardamom plant'; ēlakulu 'cardamom seeds': Skt. elā 'cardamom.' Kittel, no. 85.
3. Ta. palli; Ma. palli; Ko. e·paj; To. pas̱y; Ka. palli; Koḍ. palli; Tu. palli; Te. palli, balli 'house lizard, *Lacerta gecko*': Skt. pallī, pallikā id. (lexical); Mar. palli, popular pāl. Kittel, no. 59; Emeneau, M.B., paper 9: 261, fn 31, 1943; Borrow, T., *Trans. Philol. Soc.*, 1946: 10.
4. Ta. mayil, maññai; Ma. mayil; Ko. mi·l; To. mi·s̱; Ka. mayla, maylu; Koḍ. maylï; Tu. mairu, Pa. manjil, mañil; Oll. mañgil; Go. mal; Kui meḍu, melu; Kuwi mellu 'peacock'; Skt. mayūra- id. (in two compounds in Rig-Veda 3.45.1, 8.1.25), mayūrī- 'peahen' (Rig-Veda 1.191.14, an Atharvanic charm). Burrow, T., *Bull. School Orient. and African Stud.* 11: 608–10, 1945. He discusses Przyluski's Austro-Asiatic suggestion (*Bull. Soc. Ling.*, Paris, 26: 99 f, 1925) and shows that Skt. mayūra- is closer in form to the Dravidian series than to the posited Austro-Asiatic **marak* or the like. He notes also that *r* in mayūra- instead of *l* is not entirely unexpected in Rig-Vedic Sanskrit. Further discussion by Jules Bloch,

Bull. Soc. Ling., Paris, 25: 16, 1925. The suggestion (Walde-Pokorny 2: 243) of an Indo-European etymology on the basis of connexion with Skt. mímāti 'bellow, bleat', māyú-n. 'bellowing', Gk. μιμιξω 'neigh,' etc., is not convincing.

5. Ta. pur̲r̲u, pur̲r̲am 'white anthill'; Ma. pur̲r̲u 'ground thrown up by moles, rats, esp. a white anthill'; Ka. putta, putta 'white anthill'; Koḍ. puttï id.; Tu. puñca id., 'snake's hole'; Te. puṭṭa 'anthill, snake's hole, heap, lot, crowd'; Kol. (Kin.) puṭṭa 'white anthill'; Nk. puṭṭa id.; Pa. putkal; (NE) puṭkal id., (S) putta 'nest inside anthill'; Oll. puṭkal 'white anthill'; Go. putti id.; Kui pusi id.; Kuwi [F] pūci 'anthill,' pūnja 'ants' nest (earthen)'; Kur. puttā 'anthill'; putbelō 'white ants' queen' (belō id.); Malt. pute 'anthill'; Skt. puttikā- 'the white ant or termite'; pipīlika- puṭa- 'anthill' (pipīlika- 'ant'). Burrow, T., *Trans. Philol Soc.,* 1945: 111. Skt. puttikā- has been taken to be a meaning development from puttikā- 'doll, puppet' by Boehtlingk-Roth and Uhlenbeck ('das puppenähnliche tier') and Monier-Williams ('so called from its doll-like form'); this is clearly ad hoc. Proto-Dravidian *r̲r̲* survives in Ta.- Ma. but develops in two different ways (tt, ṭṭ) in different languages. Sanskrit has borrowed from two different Dravidian languages, giving puṭa- and *putta-*, both meaning 'anthill' or more specifically 'white anthill', from the latter of which puttikā- is derived by a Sanskrit formative suffix.

6. Ta nīr 'water, sea, juice, liquor, urine, dampness, moisture'; (nīrpp-, nīrtt-) 'become thin or watery (as liquid food in cooking), be wet, moist'; nīrmai 'property of water, as coldness'; īr 'moisture, wetness'; īram 'wet, moisture, freshness, coolness'; īrali (īralipp-, īralitt-), īri (īripp-, īritt-) 'become moist, damp'; īrippu 'dampness'; īriya 'damp, wet, cold'; Ma. nīr 'water, juice, moisture'; īram 'moisture, dirt'; īrikka 'grow damp'; īrmam, īrman, īran 'damp cloth'; Ko. ni·r 'water'; To. ni·r 'water'; i·rm 'dampness'; Ka. nīr 'water'; īra 'moisture, dampness, wetness'; Koḍ. ni·rï 'water'; Tu. nīru 'water'; Te. nīru 'water' (literary); nīḷḷu 'water'; īmiri 'moisture'; Kol.-Nk i·r 'water'; Pa.-Oll. nīr 'water'; Kui nīru 'juice, sap, essence'; Br. dīr 'water, flood-water, juice,

sap': Skt. nīra- 'water' (epic+); 'juice, liquor' (lexical); nīvara- 'water, mud' (lexical). Kittel, no. 157; Bloch, J., *Bull. School Orient. Stud.* 5: 739, 1930; Burrow, T., *Trans. Philol. Soc.* 1946: 9. An old Indo-European etymology, that always required faith both in its phonology and in its semantics, has recently been revived with all the apparatus of the laryngeal hypothesis by Louis H. Gray, *Lang.* 25: 376–7, 1949; it is hardly convincing *vis-à-vis* the general Dravidian word for 'water'.

7. Ta. nal, nar̲-, nalla 'good'; nala (nalapp-, nalant-) 'result in good, take a favourable turn'; nalappu 'goodness, benefit, success'; nalam 'goodness, virtue, beauty, profit, fame, prosperity'; nalavu 'goodness'; nar̲ku 'good'; nar̲pu, nar̲r̲am, nan̲pu, nan̲mai, nan̲r̲i, nan̲n̲ar 'goodness' (some of these also mean 'beauty'); Ma. nal 'good, fine'; nalam, nallam 'goodness, beauty'; nalpu, nalma, nanni, namma 'goodness'; nalla 'good, fine, handsome'; Ko. nal va·yn 'one whose mouth smells good, who enjoys food and prosperity'; na pal 'teeth that grow straight and regular'; To. nas̲, nas̲θ 'beauty'; nas̲o·n n. pr. of a man; Ka. nal, nalme 'goodness'; nalla 'a good man; goodness, excellence, beauty'; Koḍ. nallë 'good'; Tu. nalu, nala 'good, cheap'; nalmè 'goodness, friendship'; Te. naluvu 'beauty, ability; beautiful'; Go. (M) nelā 'good': Skt. Nala- n. pr. of a man. Emeneau, M.B., paper 9, 255–62, 1943; this still seems to me to be a good etymology. Manfred Mayrhofer agrees, *Symbolae Hrozny*, 5: 371, 1950.

8. Ta malai, 'hill, mountain'; Ma. mala 'mountain'; Ko. mal im 'buffaloes of the Nilgiri tribes (i.e. mountain buffaloes)' mal a·ṛ 'high downs on western half of Nilgiri plateau'; To. mas̲ o·ṛ id.; Ka. male 'mountain, forest'; Kod. male 'thick jungle land, cardamom plantation in jungle on mountain'; Tu. malè 'forest, hill overgrown with forest'; Te. mala 'mountain'; Kol. ma·le 'hill'; Pa. malaηg 'forest'; Br. mash 'hill, mountain': Skt. malaya- 'the mountains which border Malabar on the east (i.e., Western Ghats)' (epic +); 'a celestial grove (Nandanavana)' (lexical); 'a garden' (lexical); māla 'forests near a village; field' (lexical). Kittel,

no. 164; also Gundert and Caldwell. The Sanskrit lexicographers derive malaya- from a hypothetical root mal 'hold, possess', since the mountain range 'contains sandalwood'! The commentators are widely at variance about the meaning of māla- in Meghadūta 16, some taking it as a proper name of a field, other as a common noun; certainty seems impossible, but it is in all probability the word that we are dealing with, whatever its specific denotation in Kālidāsa's verse.

9. Ta. aiya excl. of wonder, of pity or concern; aiyakō excl. of pity or sorrow; ai 'wonder, astonishment'; aiy-e̠nal 'uttering ai expressive of wonder, of distress or mental suffering, of assent'; aiyaiyō excl. of pity or grief; aiyō excl. of wonder, of pity or concern, of poignant grief; Ma. ayyā interj. of derision; ayyō, ayyayyō interj. of grief or pain; Ko. aya· excl. of surprise or grief; aya· ava· excl. of grief; To. eya excl of surprise, Ka. ayyō, ayyayyō, ayyayyē interj. of grief or astonishment or compassion; Tu. ayyō, ayyayyō interj. of grief, annoyance, or pain; Te. ayyo, ayyō, ayyayō, ayyayyō, ayayō interj. of sorrow, lamentation, pity, pain, etc.; Kui āige, āigo, āigōna, āike, āiko, āikōna interj. of annoyance, impatience, or disgust; Kuwi (S) ījalijō, ījalesa (j = y) 'alas'; Kur. ayō, ayō ge excl. of pain or surprise; Malt. aya, ayyi, ayyu excl. of wonder, woe, or joy; ay(y)oke, ay(y)okaboke 'alas': Skt. aye excl. of surprise, recollection, or fear (esp. in dramas). In the Dravidian languages these are either vocatives of words for 'father' (all the southern languages) or 'mother' (Kui- Kuwi, Kur., Malt.), or have in a secondary way been equated with or assimilated to such vocatives; note Ko. aya· ava· father! mother!' In Sanskrit there is no such connection. An Indo-European etymology might be suggested with such interjections as Gk. *αἴ*, *αἶ*, *ἆιαῖ*, Lith. aĩ, ái, German ei, and Skt. e, ai (both lexical) *cf.* Walde-Pokorny 1:1), but the Dravidian forms are so much more current than the suggested Indo-European etyma that a borrowing from Dravidian seems more plausible.

10. Ta. kaḷam, kaḷaṉ 'place, open space, threshing floor, battlefield'; Ma. kaḷam 'threshing floor, level space for spreading grains for drying, battlefield'; Ko. kaḷm 'place for threshing or dancing'; To. koḷṇ 'threshing floor'; Ka. kaḷa, kaṇa 'threshing floor, battlefield'; Koḍ. kaḷa 'threshing floor'; Tu. kala 'a square, bed of flowers, etc., place where pariahs combat, (B) threshing floor'; Kol. kalave 'workshed in field, (Kin.) threshing floor'; Nk. kaḷave 'threshing floor'; Pa. kali id.; Oll. kalin id.; Go. kăṛā 'sacred enclosure, threshing floor'; Kui klai 'threshing floor'; Kuwi (F) kṛanū, kalōmi id.; Kur. k̲h̲all 'field, piece of land suitable for tillage'; Malt. qalu 'field on the hills'; Skt. khála- 'threshing floor, granary' (*Rigveda*+); 'place, site' (lexical). Burrow, T., *Bull. Soc. Orient. and African Stud.* 11: 133, 1943; *Trans. Philol. Soc., 1946*: 9. No Indo-European etymology has been plausibly suggested.
11. Ta. paṟu (paṟupp-, paṟutt-) 'ripen (as fruits, grain), grow mature, arrive at perfection, become old, come to a head (boil), change colour by age, become pale or yellowish (as the body by disease), become flexible, pliant'; paṟu, paṟuppu 'ripeness, yellowness (of fruits), leaf turned yellow with age'; paṟunu (paṟuṉi-), paṟuṉu (paṟuṉi-) 'grow ripe, become mellow, mature, be full or perfect'; paṟam 'ripe fruit'; Ma. paṟukka 'grow ripe, become well-tempered, suppurate, decay'; 'a fruit put to ripen'; paṟuppu 'ripening of fruit'; paṟuppikka 'ripen artificially'; paṟam 'ripe fruit, ripe plantains'; Ko. paṛv- (paṛd-) '(fruits) become ripe, (boil, sore) opens'; paṇ 'fruit'; To. pošf- (pošt-) 'ripen'; pum 'fruit'; Ka. paṇ 'be produced (ripe fruit)'; paṇ, paṇṇu 'ripe fruit, ripeness'; Koḍ. paṇṇï 'fruit'; Tu. palkuni, paḷkuni 'be very soft (as an overripe fruit), be pliant, flexible'; parnduni 'be ripe, mature, (hair) turns gray'; parndu 'ripeness, ripe fruit, ripe plantains, ripe, gray'; palu 'ripening (as of fruit), half-ripe'; Te. paṇḍu 'ripen, mature'; 'fruit, berry'; 'ripe, mature'; paṇṭa 'produce, crop, fruit, ripening'; Kol. panḍ- (panḍt-) 'become ripe'; panḍuḍ 'ripe fruit'; (Kin.) pan 'fruit'; Nk. panḍ- 'become ripe'; panḍe 'ripe fruit'; Pa. panḍ- '(plant)

matures'; paṛñ- 'ripen'; pal 'ripe fruit, pus'; Oll. paṛŋ (g)- 'become ripe'; Kuwi (S) panḍu 'ripe fruit'; Kur. pa͂nnā (pañjā) 'ripen, (boil) festers, have a yellowish appearance (as after a prolonged illness)'; pañjkā 'fruits'; Malt. páne 'ripen'; panjek, panjeke 'ripe': Skt. phála- 'fruit' (Rig Veda +); phalati 'bear or produce fruit, ripen' (epic+). Gundert, H., *Ztschr. deutsch. morgenländischen Ges.* 23: 519, 1869; also Caldwell and Kittel; Burrow, T., *Trans. Philol. Soc.*, 1946: 10; Ammer, Karl, *Ztschr. deutch. morgenländischen Ges.* 51: 128, 1948; Mayrhofer, Manfred, *Anthropos* 47: 664, 1952; with some uncertainty Bloch, Jules, *Bull. School Orient. Stud.* 5: 740, 1930; Kuiper, F.B.J., *Acta Orientalia* 16: 305, 1938; the possibility is not even mentioned by Lüders, Heinrich, *Kuhn's Zeitschrift* 42: 198 ff., 1909. This hypothesis of borrowing is much more obvious than the suggested derivations from Indo-European roots meaning 'swell' or 'burst' or than Sturtevant's connection with words for 'leaf; (*Lang.* 17: 6, 1941).

12. Ta. val 'strong, forceful, skilful'; valam, vallam 'strength, power, right side, victory, authority'; vallavaṉ, valavaṉ, vallāṉ, vallāḷaṉ 'strong man, capable man'; vallu (valli-) 'be able'; vali 'strength, power'; (valiv-, valint-; valipp-, valitt-) 'be strong, compel'; valimai 'strength, skill, hardness'; valiya 'strong, big'; valivu 'strength', valu 'strength, skill, ability'; (valupp-, valutt-) 'be strong or hard': valuppu, vaṉpu, vaṉmai, 'strength, firmness'; valumai 'strength, force, violence'; valakkai, valaṅ kai 'right hand'; Ma. val, valu, valiya 'strong, powerful, great'; vallu 'be able, strong'; valippam, valima 'greatness bigness'; valiyē 'forcibly, suddently'; valam 'the right side', valaṅ kai 'right hand'; Ko. val 'powerful, very right'; val kay 'right hand'; val(n) 'man who is clever at cheating'; valc- '(man) becomes stout, (heart) becomes bold, (grain) becomes solid lump when boiled'; To. pas̱ 'right'; pas̱ koy 'right hand'; paly- (pals-) '(child) becomes strong'; Ka. bal, bali 'grow strong or firm, increase'; bal, balu, bolu 'strength, firmness, bigness, abundance'; bala 'right'; bala key/gey 'right hand';

balume, balme, baluhu, balpu 'strength'; Koḍ. bala 'power, strength'; balate 'right (hand)'; ballyë 'great'; Tu. bala 'strength'; balatu 'the right side'; balata kai 'right hand'; balāpini 'gain strength, recover health'; balike 'prowess, strength, hardness'; balimè, balumè, balme 'strength, might'; balu 'very large, great, severe, violent'; Te. valãti 'clever person, expert'; vala 'right'; vala cēyi 'right hand'; valadu 'much'; valanu 'skill, excellence, possibility'; 'right, possible, convenient'; valan 'instrumental postposition'; valamu 'largeness, stoutness'; valũda 'stout, large'; valla 'possible'; vallaḍi 'violence, oppression'; Pa. vela key 'right hand'; Go. wăllē 'much, very'; Kuwi (F) braiyū, (S) blājugatti (j = y) 'strong'; Kur. balē, balēti 'with the help of': Skt. bála- 'power, strength, might' (Rig-Veda +) balena, balatas 'by means of '. The *v*-languages are primary; *v* > *b* in Ka. beginning in the ninth century AD. Sanskrit may then have borrowed from a Dravidian language with secondary *b*. Kittel, no. 398; also Caldwell; Burrow, T., *Trans. Philol. Soc*. 1946: 19.

13. Ta. mālai 'garland, wreath, necklace, anything strung together'; malai (malaiv-, malaint-) 'wear, put on' (Burrow, 'put on as a garland,' based on the old text Puṟanāṉūṟu 12, etc.); Ma. māla 'garland' wreath, necklace, dewlap'; Ka. māle 'wreath, garland, necklace'; Koḍ. ma·le 'necklace, dewlap, jungle cock's ruff or neck feathers'; Tu. mālè 'garland, wreath, necklace'; Te. māla id. Skt. mālā-, mālya 'wreath, garland, necklace' (sūtra, epic +). Burrow, *Bull. Soc. Orient. and African Stud*. 12: 390, 1948. He notes that Ta. has mālai in the oldest literature (Puṟanāṉūṟu 60, 76) and that the verb malai with a short vowel is just as old and related as a derivative from the noun. The Ka. word is classed by the Ka. grammarians as a *tatsama*, i.e. 'a term not borrowed from Sanskrit, but existing in Kannaḍa as well as in Sanskrit' (Kittel's definition); this native analysis always may be taken as speaking in favour of Dravidian origin. The Ma.-Koḍ. meaning 'dewlap' may possibly also be taken as evidence for mālai as a native Dravidian word.

For non-Dravidianists it should be noted that the Dravidian forms are those that a borrowing from Sanskrit would have but are also those proper to a native Dravidian group of etyma.[24]

[24] Appendix 2, 'The Munda Languages', is not printed here [Ed.].

5

Indo-Aryans, Indo-Iranians, and Indo-Europeans

M.A. Mehendale

M.A. Mehendale's paper does not deal with the Dravidian languages, but it is included in this section because it gives a particularly clear and elegant exposition of the relation of the Indo-Iranian group of languages, and its two branches, Indo-Aryan (including Sanskrit and the modern north Indian languages, plus Sinhalese) and Iranian, by one of India's leading scholars of historical linguistics. The three diagrams in the article illustrate the three alternative ways of interpreting the patterning of the evidence, and the article explains why the third diagram best accounts for the evidence. The patterning is complex because there is evidence of Indo-Aryan language in the ancient Near East, far to the west of the present-day locations of the Iranian and Indo-Aryan languages. This evidence appears in a treaty between Hittite and Mitanni leaders and related documents written on clay tablets in cuneiform script, and consists of words that are closer to Sanskrit than to the ancient Iranian languages (Avestan and Old Persian). The author also discusses the original location of the Indo-European family, and the patterning of evidence that shows there were dialect differences within Proto-Indo-European before the splitting up of the population that spoke this inferred ancestor-language. Although the exact location is subject to debate, the evidence points to a region outside of India. Mehendale's *Historical Grammar of Inscriptional Prakrits* (1948) is a major contribution to the historical study of the Indo-Aryan languages.

[From *The Aryan Problem*, eds S.B. Deo and Suryanath Kamath (Pune: The Mythic Society and The Bharatiya Itihasa Sankalana Samiti, 1993), pp. 43–50.]

Indo-Aryans

The term 'Indo-Aryan' is applied to a specific group of languages spoken primarily in North India and in some countries around India, for example, Pakistan, (Sindhi and Lahnda or Western Punjabi), Nepal (Nepali), Bangladesh (Bengali), and Sri Lanka (Sinhalese). The forefathers of the present-day speakers of these languages are supposed to have entered India from Iran along the north-western mountain passes. This event may have happened c. 2000 BC.

The designation 'Indo-Aryan' serves a twofold purpose: in the first instance, it distinguishes this group of languages from Old Iranian together with which it forms the easternmost Indo-Iranian branch of the Indo-European family of languages; and (2) it distinguishes this group of languages from the other three families of languages spoken in India, viz. the Dravidian, the Munda, and the Tibeto-Burman.

The term 'Indo-Aryan' has two components: the former component has its justification in the fact that these languages are spoken mainly in a large part of India (before Partition) as distinguished from Iran, Afghanistan, Central Asia, etc., where other languages of the Indo-European family are spoken. The second component 'āryan' used in the term 'Indo-Aryan' needs clarification. It must be understood that it has nothing to do with any particular race. The use of the word '*ārya*' does not mean that the speakers of these languages belong or belonged to any one race called 'Ārya'. It is well known that the speakers of these languages today represent a mixture of races. And as for the past, we have no justification to assume that the speakers of the languages at the Indo-Iranian stage belonged to a single race. The word *ārya* has its justification in the designation 'Indo-Aryan' in the fact that the speakers of the languages in the oldest attested stage in India (as well as in Iran) called themselves '*ārya*'. But this word refers to certain quality or qualities and not to race.

The word '*ārya*' has left no trace in the name of our country where these languages are currently spoken. The country today, as in the past, is called 'Bhārata (varṣa)' At one time, however, as witnessed by Patañjali, the word *ārya* appeared in the name *Āryāvarta* which was then applied to northern India. In answer to the question *kaḥ punar āryāvartaḥ* 'what is Āryāvarta', Patañjali on Pāṇini 6.3.109 says: the country bounded by Ādarśa[1] in the west, Kālakavana[2] in the east, Himavant in the north, and Pāriyātra (that is, Vindhya) in the south is known as Āryāvarta. According to *Manusmṛti* 2. 21–2 it is the land between the two seas (in the west and east) and between the Himavant and the Vindhya. Today the word *ārya*, through Pāli and the Prākṛits survives only in the words ājā (m.), āji (f.) meaning 'grandfather' and 'grandmother' respectively in some of the North Indian languages.

The story of the word *ārya* is different in Iran. There it continues in the name of the country, Iran, which is derived from *airyanam* (gen. pl. of *airya*) = Sk. *āryāṇām* 'of the Āryas' with the word for 'country' supplied. Iran thus means '(the country) of the Āryas'.

The history of the Indo-Aryan branch of languages in India is conveniently divided into three broad stages—Old, Middle, and the New. The oldest attested stage of the Indo-Aryan is found in the Veda—particularly the Ṛgveda. The text of the mantras as composed by *ṛṣis* has been substantially well preserved except for making some phonetic changes of the type of vowel *sandhi*. Although the mantras of the Ṛgveda have been composed by various authors, we do not find in them dialectal variations. The language of the Ṛgveda gives us an impression of a homogenous language. Later we see successive developments of this language in post-Ṛgvedic texts like the *Brāhmaṇa*s, the *Upaniṣad*s, and the *sūtra*s. This late Vedic stage approaches closely to the *bhāṣā*—'spoken dialect'—described by Pāṇini in his *Aṣṭādhyāyī* and which became the model for the writers of the classical Sanskrit. The old Indo-Aryan has more or less maintained without change its linguistic character since the days of Patañjali (second century BC). In the classical period, the language

[1] *Ādarśa* is probably a mistake for *adarśa* = *adarśana* or *vinaśana* which is identified with Kurukṣetra.

[2] Identified with Allahabad in D.C. Sircar's *Studies in the Geography of Ancient India*, pp. 40, 172, 173, 241 but with Rajmahal hills in Bihar in N.L. Dey's *Geographical Dictionary*.

does not show the types of changes which are seen earlier from the period of the Ṛgveda to that of the sūtras.

This difference between Vedic Sanskrit and classical Sanskrit is not in phonology. The vowel and the consonantal systems are the same except the disappearance of the intervocal *ḷ* and *ḷh* found in the Ṛgveda. The difference lies chiefly in grammar and vocabulary. In grammar, many forms like the nom. pl. in *-asas*, infinitives in *-tavai*, *-dhyai*, etc. are lost. In vocabulary we see some old items like *jalāṣa* (?), *cēru* (?) disappearing, some others being retained with a difference in meaning, cf: *kratu-*, *ram-*, *kup-*. But more important is the addition of many words which are borrowed from languages, either Middle Indo-Aryan, cf. *dohada*, *muktā*, *utsuka*, *akṣauhiṇī*, etc. or non-Sanskritic, cf. *pūjā*, *valaya*, *kuṇḍala*, etc.

The second stage of the development of the Indo-Aryan languages, viz. the Middle Indo-Aryan, is represented by the Pāli and the literary Prākṛts. There is no doubt that certain Middle Indo-Aryan tendencies like the disappearance of the vowel *ṛ* and the emergence of the retroflex sounds had started as early as the Vedic period. This is witnessed by the presence of such words as (vī)kaṭa (already in the *ṚV*) *naṭa*, *bhaṭa* in the late Vedic literature. The spoken languages of those times must have considerably differed from the languages of the educated and the cultured people. The distinction between the standard, the polished, the hieratic and the substandard forms was expressed by the terms *saṁskṛta* and *prākṛta* applied to them. The term *prākṛta* as opposed to *saṁskṛta*, is to be understood either as 'natural, unsophisticated' form of speech as opposed to *saṁskṛta* which is 'refined, polished' form of speech; or it can be understood as the grammarians do it: *Saṁskṛta* language is the *prakṛti* 'basis' and *prākṛta* is the one 'derived from this *prakṛti* (cf. Hemacandra 1.1 *prakṛtiḥ saṁskṛtam* | *tatra bhavam, tata āgataṁ vā prākṛtam*). It must be remembered that this *prākṛta* could not have directly come from the late literary or standard Sanskrit, but from its earlier spoken variety in the Vedic period. This explains why in Pāli we have *ḷ* and *ḷh* in place of *ḍ* and *ḍh* exactly as in the Ṛgveda but not in the classical Sanskrit, or why we have the instr. pl. endings *-ehi* (Pāli) or *ehiṁ* (Pkt) < Vedic *ebhiḥ*, or the nom. pl. ending *-āso* (Pāli), *-āho* (Mg.) < Vedic *-asaḥ*; the classical Skt. does not have these terminations but has *-aiḥ* for instr. sg. and *-as* for nom. pl.

The period of the middle Indo-Aryan stretches roughly from the fifth century BC to AD 100. It could be fairly easily assumed that these languages played a distinct role as means of communication in the everyday life of the people since both Buddha and Mahāvīra favoured the use of these, as against Sanskrit, for teaching their messages. The earliest attestation of this middle Indo-Aryan stage is found in Pāli, the language of the Buddhist canon and in the inscriptions of Aśoka. It is believed that the Buddhist canon was first formulated in the eastern dialect, the dialect of Buddha himself, and that it was later translated into Pāli. The assumed eastern canon is no longer available. The Aśokan inscriptions reflect at least two varieties of the MIA stage, the eastern (with *l* and nom. sg. *-e*) and the western (with *r* and nom. sg. in *-o*), and perhaps a north-western (having three sibilants *s*, *ś*, and *ṣ* and many consonant clusters). The principal languages included in the MIA stage are the *Ardhamāgadhi* the *Śaurasenī*, the *Māgadhī*, the *Paiśācī*, and the *Māhārāṣṭrī*. The *Māhārāṣṭrī* does not represent any regional variety of MIA but a stage of development that lies between the literary *Prākrtis* on the one hand and the *Apabhraṁśa* on the other. The *Apabhraṁśa* of about AD 1000 marks the close of the Middle Indo-Aryan period.

The new Indo-Aryan or the last stage in the development of the Indo-Aryan languages is said to have commenced in the eleventh century AD and is represented in the various standard and sub-standard regional languages of northern India. These languages apparently grew out of the local *Apabhraṁśa*s which, although not attested for different regions, must be assumed to precede and be the starting points of the NIA languages.

Indo-Iranian

The language family designated as 'Indo-Iranian' includes the Old Iranian and the Old Indo-Aryan. It represents that stage in the linguistic development of a branch of the Indo-European which is the source-language for the Avestan and the Old Persian in Iran and the Vedic Sanskrit in India. A certain group of people speaking a certain variety of the Indo-European migrated from the original home of the IE towards the south and east. It is supposed to have settled down for sometime to the north of Iran and Afghanistan from where one branch came down to eastern Iran and after sometime migrated further south through the passes of the Hindukush to reach the north-western frontiers of India. Those who remained behind in the common home to the north of Iran and Afghanistan came later to western Iran and then even occupied the eastern Iran. It is in the common home of the forefathers of the later Iranians and Indians that Indo-Iranian is supposed to have been spoken.

The Old Iranian of the settlers of Iran is represented by the Avestan, the language of the holy texts of the Zoroastrians and the Old Persian found in the inscriptions of the Achaemenian rulers of Iran. The date of oldest portions of the Gāthās of the Avesta is likely to be c. 1000 BC, while the Old Persian inscriptions date from the fifth century BC. The Iranian branch, like the Indian branch, can be conveniently divided into three stages—the old, the middle, and the new. The old Iranian is available in two dialects—the western in the Old Persian inscriptions and the eastern in the Avesta. The middle Iranian is represented by various languages, chief among which is Pahlavi. The new Iranian is represented, among others, by modern Persian in Iran, Pušto in Afghanistan, and Baluchi in Baluchistan.

Some centuries after the forefathers of the Vedic Aryans left eastern Iran, the Iranian prophet Zarathustra introduced certain radical reforms in the traditional religion and gave a new message to the people of Iran. He recognized one god, Ahura Mazda 'the wise Lord', as against the many in the religion inherited by him, and forbade the killing of animals and offerings of flesh together with those of a stimulating drink of *haoma* (Sk. *soma*) in religious worship. The linguistic impact of the revolution is seen in the meaning of the *dāeva* (Sk. *deva*) 'demon, evil spirit' and the establishment of a series of parallel pairs of synonyms, one of which was used in connection with the *ahuras* 'gods' and the other with the *dāevas* 'demons'—witness the use of *uš* 'ear', *vaγδana* 'head', *zasta* 'hand' (Sk. *hasta*), etc. used with reference to Ahuric, that is, divine beings and the use of karəna (Sk. *karṇa*) 'ear', kamərəδa 'head' (Sk. **ku.mūrdhan*) and 'go', 'hand' used with reference to *daevic*, that is, demoniac beings.

That the forefathers of ancient Indians and the ancient Iranians were at one time one people showing common culture and speaking one language is established beyond doubt due to the close affinity between Vedic Sanskrit and Avestan—an affinity so close as is not found in any other two branches of the Indo-European family of languages. If one glances through the pages of the *Altiranisches Wörterbuch*—the extent of which is far smaller than that of a Sanskrit dictionary—one meets with many vocabulary items which have cognates in Sanskrit and hence prove their common origin—examples chosen at random: Sk. *hiraṇya*, Av. *zaranya* 'gold'; Sk. *vṛkṣa*, Av. varəša 'tree'; Sk. *mátsya*, Av. *mašya* 'fish'; Sk. *sénā*, Av. *haenā* 'army'; Sk. *yajñá*, Av. *yasna* 'worship, sacrifice'; Sk. *hótar*, Av. *zaotar* 'priest'; Sk. *Mitrá*, Av. miθra 'name of a deity', etc. The similarity between the two languages is not restricted to the vocabulary items in large number; it is witnessed even more strongly in grammar—that is in the manner of root alternation, cf. Sk. *gam*: *gacch*, Av. *gam*: *jas*, in the use of *vikaraṇas* to form stems, for example, Sk. *su*: *su-nu*, Av. *hu*: *hunu*; and in terminations, for example, Sk. *bhárāmi*, *bhárati*, Av. *barāmi*, *baraiti*. Not only this. Both these branches have made common innovations in the parent Indo-European language, for example, they have merged IE *ā*, *e*, *o* > *ā*, and changed IE *m*, *n* > *ā*; both show palatalization before front vowels as in *ca-kāra, ja-gāma* and the introduction of *n* before gen. pl. term., hence Sk. *devānām*, Av. *daevānam* against Gk. *hippon*, Lat. *deum* = *deorum*, etc. The similarity between Sanskrit and Avesta is best illustrated by showing how an Avestan line like *təm amavantəm yazatəm sūrəm dāmohu səvištəm miθrəm yazāi zaoθrābyo* (Yt. 10.6) can be easily rendered into Sanskrit—*tam amavantam śūram dhāmasu śaviṣṭham mitram yajai hotrebhyaḥ* (for *hotrebhiḥ*) 'that strong, brave, bravest among the creations, Mitra, I worship with oblations'.

It is very likely that the Indo-Iranians, after they left the original home of the Indo-Europeans, came to Iran and Afghanistan from South Russia. The common view regarding their coming to this new land together and the subsequent migration of a part of them to India has to be a little modified on account of certain linguistic evidence brought to light from the Near East. There, in upper Mesopotamia, Mitanni kingdom was established by people who spoke a language very similar to the Indo-Iranian or the Old Indo-Aryan. These people are supposed to have come to Mesopotamia between 1741 and 1600 BC. The Kuneiform inscriptions discovered in this area reveal certain terms and names of deities which are unmistakably of the Indo-Iranian branch. Some of the names of the Mitanni princes also show closeness to Indo-Aryan, for example, *šuvar-data* = Sk. *svar-datta* or *svar-dhāta* 'given or created by the sun'; *Indaruta* = Sk. *Indra-ūta* 'protected by Indra'. In a treaty concluded in 1360 BC by the Hittite king Šuppiluliuma with Mattiwaza of the Mitanni people when the latter was made a king and was given his daughter by the Hittite king, we have the mention of the names of deities as witness to the treaty. In this list of gods we find, by the side of a number of non-Aryan deities, such names as are easily identifiable with the Vedic gods Mitra, Varuṇa, Indra, and Nāsatyā. Then in a Hittite text composed by one Kikkuli on horse-training we find such numerals as *aika* 'one', *tera* 'three', *panza* 'five', *satta* 'seven', *na(va)* 'nine', and such words as *ašu̯a* 'horse' and technical terms like *u̯artana* 'circular course (in which a horse moves when under training)'.

The question raised by this unmistakable Aryan evidence in Asia Minor is from where did the people speaking the language akin to the Indo-Iranian reach there. Did they go there sometime during their migration before or after the Indo-Iranian broke into Iranian and Indian, that is did they go there as Ur-Aryans, or as Iranians or as Indians?

At one time it was felt that some of the speakers of the Indo-Iranian language separated from the others who later became Proto-Indo-Aryans and went to Asia Minor from south Russia along the Caspian Sea. Some of them remained there to establish the Mitanni kingdom in south but others went to Iran. This theory is, however, not acceptable because the Aryan remains in Asia Minor are more akin to Indian than to Iranian or to Proto-Indo-Iranian, for example, we have *s* and not *h* in *satta*, the word for 'seven' (Sk. *saptá*: Av. *hapta*), in *našatya* 'the name of the deity' (Sk. *nāsatyā*, Av. *nāŋhaiθya*), and the word for 'one' is *aika* with *-k-* as in Sk. *éka*, as against Av. *aiva* which has *-v-*. This should force us to admit that those who established the Mittani kingdom were not Iranians but Indians who may have gone to the Near East from India. Between these two extreme theories, a compromise theory is proposed because the Aryan evidence from Mitanni is not exactly identical with Sanskrit either, but occasionally shows an older stage of development as witnessed in the word for 'one' *aika* which shows a diphthong *ai* as opposed to the monophthong *e* in Sk. *eka*. According to the compromise theory, the speakers of the Mittani Aryans went to the Near East after the Proto-Aryans separated from the Indo-Aryans but before the forefathers of the Indo-Aryans came to India. T. Burrow chooses to call this stage of separation as Proto-Indo-Aryan.[3]

Thus we do not imagine the relationship of the Near-Eastern Aryan, Old Iranian, and Old Indo-Aryan as something like that shown in the following diagram.

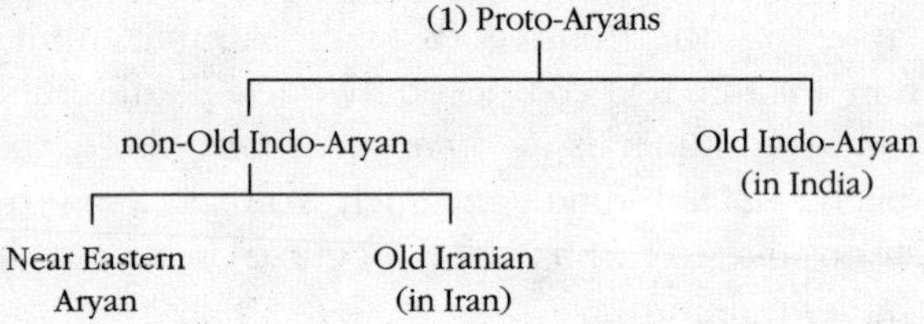

(2) nor as

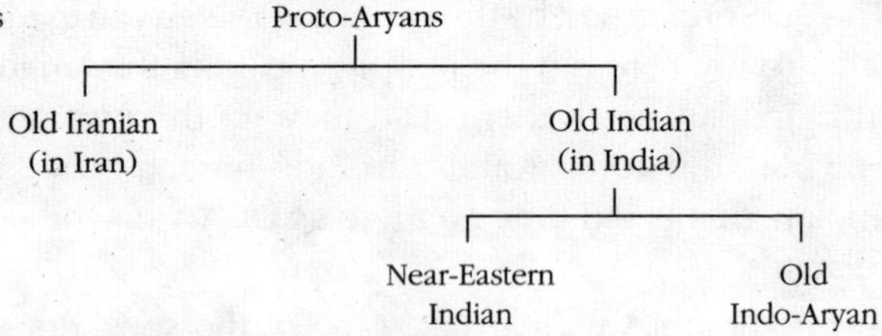

(3) but as

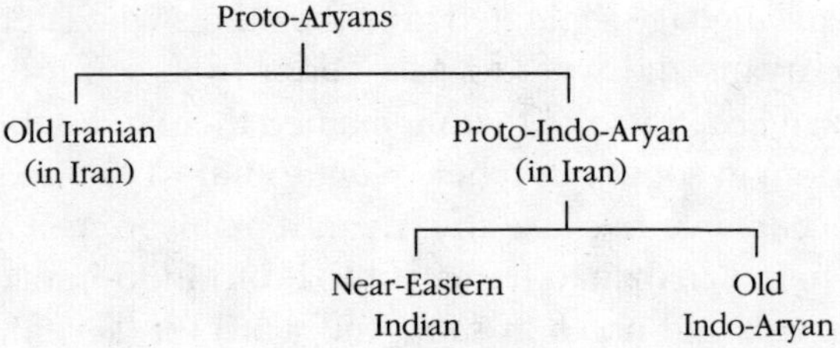

Such a view permits us to say that the cluster pt became tt in Near-East, but was preserved in India; but the diphthong *ai* > *e* in India was preserved in the Near-East. This happened after the branching off of the Near-Eastern from Proto-Indo-Aryan.

[3] 'The Proto-Indoaryans', *JRAS*, 1973, 123–40.

Indo-European

The Indo-Iranian family together with many other languages or language-families like Greek, Latin, Germanic, and which were once spread over large parts of Asia and Europe form a family of languages known as the Indo-European family, as distinct from such other families of languages as Dravidian, Munda, and Tibeto-Burman (in India), and Semitic, and Finno-Ugrian. (in Europe and Asia).

Similarities between the vocabulary items of Sanskrit and some other languages like Latin or Italian were long recognized by the missionaries who arrived in India. But they remained more or less as curiosities. The credit for the formulation of the theory of a common origin for these languages goes to Sir William Jones who made the now famous pronouncement in AD 1786. It was he who for the first time declared that the linguistic similarities between the languages now grouped in the IE family of languages can be explained only on the assumption of their having sprung from a common origin which, perhaps, no longer exists.

Today no one is in doubt that the common source, which was once called Indo-Germanic and which is now known as Indo-European, no longer exists, which means that none of the attested languages like Hittite, Sanskrit, Greek and others, however old they may be, can be looked upon as the 'mother' language of this family.

The languages, or the language families, comprising this large family of languages are: (1) Indo-Aryan, (2) Iranian, (3) Armenian, (4) Albanian, (5) Balto-Slavic, (6) Greek, (7) Latin, (8) Germanic, (9) Celtic, and the two more recently discovered, (10) Hittite and (11) Tokharian.

It is likely that the Indo-European common speech had already started showing dialectal variations within its 'home' before its speakers migrated into different lands. This means that not all the characteristics which distinguish these languages from one another developed after their separation from each other. Thus the augment *a-* in the preterite forms like Sk. *ábharat*, Gk. *éphere*, Arm. *eber* is seen only in these three languages and at one time must have formed a common feature of these three, as distinct from others. Later when the Greek was separated from this group, there occurred another innovation, viz. the change of the Indo-European palatal *k'* to *s* in certain languages like Sanskrit, Avestan, Armenian, Albanian, and Balto-Slavic, but its continuation was a velar sound *k* in the rest. This distinction is widely known as satəm-centum devision based on the words for 'hundred' in Avestan on the one hand, and Latin centum on the other.

On the basis of the comparison made between the different languages comprising the Indo-European family, it has been possible to reconstruct the 'common origin' of these languages. The technique of such a study was first formulated by Franz Bopp in 1816 in his work: *Über das Conjugations-system der Sanskritsprache* and was further developed by August Scheleicher in 1852 in his work: *Formenlehre der Kirchenslawischen Sprache.* Now it is possible to assert that the 'similarities' between these languages are one-time 'identities' and demonstrate what that 'identity' could look like.

When one compares the sound systems of the different languages of the IE family with the sound system of the reconstructed original language, it is observed that Greek and Latin of the centum group have better preserved the vowel system of the original language (it has preserved the original *a*, *e*, *o* vowels while Sanskrit has merged them into a single vowel *a*) while Sanskrit of the satəm group has better preserved the original consonant system (Sanskrit has kept the distinction between voiced unaspirates and aspirates like *d* and *dh*, *b* and *bh*, while this distinction has been lost in other languages).

While[4] it is not likely that the community speaking the original IE language was a *racial* community, it must certainly have been an *economic* and a *cultural* community. The people of this community used a common language, Indo-European, for their intercourse. As far as the social organization of this community is concerned, it can be said that it was patriarchal in character. The people of this community had some definite ideas about the gods who ruled over the lives of human beings, and about death and the other world. They used some form of worship for these gods and knew the art of composing poetry in which they praised their gods.

[4] The information from here up to p. 59 of this article is based on Paul Thieme's *Die Heimat der indoger-manischen Gemeinsprache* (Wiesbaden, 1954).

The question about the original home of this community from where it spread to different parts of Europe and Asia has been discussed for a long time and many theories have been proposed. The two of these which gained some currency were those which placed them in Central Asia or in south Russia and the Kirghiz steppe. The latter theory is mainly based on the assumption that a part of the agricultural terminology which is common to other IE languages is lacking in Indo-Iranian. This means that one section of the community lived a more or less nomadic life which can be only in steppes. Therefore the home of the community must be found at a place where steppe and agricultural land come together. The land where boundaries of southern Russia and the Kirghiz steppes meet was considered as ideal to fulfil these requirements.

P. Thieme who has examined this theory in his *Heimat der indogermanischen Gemeinsprache* points out (p. 25) that P. Schrader himself who had advocated this theory had to admit in the first instance that not all, but only a few, IE items related to agriculture were missing in the Indo-Iranian and hence we have to admit that the Indo-Iranians too knew agriculture. It is of course likely that, as compared to the other IE communities, agriculture did not play at that time an important role in their life.

Among the items considered missing, it is mentioned that the Indo-Iranian group does not have a cognate for the IE root **se/sei* 'to sow'. But J. Bloch[5] has demonstrated that it, in fact, is to be seen in Sk. *sīra* (nt.) 'sowing, a plough for sowing', *sītā* (f.) 'furrow' (originally 'the bedecked'). From the explanations of J. Bloch, it also becomes clear why there is no correspondence in Sanskrit for Gk. *ārotron* 'a plough'. This is because the forefathers of the Indians in their wanderings came to know a new type of plough which was equipped with an arrangement for simultaneous sowing. This kind of plough was known in Mesopotamia already in the third millennium BC.

Schrader similarly missed the words in Indo-Iranian for IE words meaning 'to grind', 'domestic pig' (according to him Indo-Iranians knew only wild pig, cf. *sūkara*), and 'salt'. It is not necessary here to go into the details of the arguments. It is sufficient to note that these

[5] *BSOS*, 8 (1936), p. 411 ff.

objections have been successfully met and the knowledge of agriculture and pig-breeding can be definitely assumed for all branches of the IE family including the Indo-Iranian. Such people, unlike the nomads, could not have occupied a large territory as, for example, the one stretching from the Baltic Sea in the north to the Kirghiz steppe in the south.

It is, therefore, necessary to narrow down this region as far as possible. Thieme, with his now famous 'Lachs (salmon) theory' demonstrates how this narrowing down can be achieved. His argument can be briefly stated as follows: Old HG *lachs*, Anglo-Saxon *leax*, Old Norse *lax*, etc. point to a common origin IE *laks-/lakso- for 'salmon fish'. This kind of fish is to be found only in the rivers which flow into the northern oceans (the North Sea and the Baltic Sea) and their tributaries. There is no salmon in Greece and Italy. Hence we have no correspondences for IE **laks-/*lakso-* in Gk. and Latin, and also in south Slavic. The Celts had their own word which was later borrowed as 'salmo' in Latin. That the Old HG lachs and the related words are not an innovation in the Germanic and in the north Slavic is demonstrated by the fact that Tokharian, discovered in east Turkestan, has a correspondence in *lakṣi* meaning 'fish'. That the word in Tokharian does not mean 'salmon' is understandable, since there are no salmon in Central Asia. The Tokharian branch has thus preserved the old IE word but given it a more general meaning 'fish'. The presence of *lakṣi* in Tokharian clearly shows that the speakers of this branch came from the region where salmon was the fish par excellence.

If IE had a word like **laks-/ *lakso-*, its correspondence in Sanskrit would be *lakṣa*, but obviously it cannot have the meaning 'salmon' since that kind of fish is unknown to India.

Now Sanskrit does have a word *lakṣa* which means a very large number. In many languages there are words for things which appear in large number or in great mass and therefore are themselves expressive of large numbers. For example, in Avesta, the word *bāevar* meaning 'ten thousand' is derivable from a word which means 'a bee' (cf. Gmc. *im-pi-* 'swarm of bees'). In Sanskrit itself, the words *jaladhi* or *samudra* 'ocean' and *abja* 'lotus' signify large numbers. One of the characteristics of the salmon is that they appear in large numbers. Thus we can argue that Sanskrit has preserved the IE word **lakso-* in the form *lakṣa-*, not in the meaning 'salmon' but in the meaning 'one hundred thousand'.

A second characteristic of salmon is the red colour of its flesh. An adjective in IE from **laks/*lakso* would be **lākso* and would mean 'salmonish, red'. This corresponds exactly with Sanskrit *lākṣā* attested since the *Atharvaveda*, which means red lac tree which originally could have meant 'the red'.

In Ossetic, an Iranian dialect, we find a word läsäg which means 'trout', a variety of fish, similar to salmon, found in the Caucasian rivers.

All this evidence points to the north-central Europe as the probable home of the Indo-Europeans and not to the South Russia and the adjoining Kirghiz steppe.

On the basis of the evidence given by the IE word for the salmon, it is thus possible to narrow down the limits of the original home of the IE: in the east one does not have to go beyond the beach boundary (from Kalinigrad on the Baltic to Odessa on the Black Sea). In the west we need not go up to the river Rhine. This leaves the area of the salmon rivers Vistula, Order, and Elbe, roughly the area where the eastern IE languages like Baltic (Lithuanian) and Slavic (Polish) and western Indo-European (Germanic) meet, or the area corresponding to Poland and eastern part of Germany.

In this region we have trees and animals, words for which can be reconstructed for the IE on the basis of correspondences in the related languages. All these trees and animals are characteristic of this region and there is not a single item in the list which is not compatible with the region. These can be listed as follows:

A. Trees: birch, beech, aspen, oak, pine, fir
B. Animals (domestic): dog, ox, sheep, horse, pig, goat
C. Animals (non-domestic): wolf, bear, fox, stag, hare, mouse, serpent, turtle
D. Birds: eagle, heron, owl, crane
E. Aquatic birds: goose, duck, diver
F. Insects: fly, wasp, bee, louse

Thieme asserts that there is in the above list no animal, domestic or otherwise, that we cannot assume for the later Stone-, Bronze-, and Copper-periods in the German low level land.

It seems to me that Thieme has very cogently argued his case. Just as on the basis of the linguistic evidence which consists of finding out words which can be reconstructed for the Indo-European and which designate animals and trees which are characteristic of a given region—in this instance, particularly the words for salmon fish and for beech and fir trees—he has pointed to the north-central Europe as the home of the Indo-Europeans, he has excluded other countries whose most characteristic plants and animals have no parallels in other languages and hence cannot be considered for being the home of the Indo-European people. All these words must be looked upon as later borrowings in those respective languages which the speakers of these families came to know after they arrived in those lands. He thus excludes India as the home of the IE due to the impossibility of reconstructible words for elephant, tiger, monkey, fig-tree, etc.; Iran, because there are no IE words for camel, donkey, lion, etc.; the Mediterranean countries like Greece, Italy, Albania, France, and Spain for the absence of IE words for donkey, lion, olive, vine, cypress, etc.

The case for India can be excluded further on the basis of the available language situation in this country—the concentration of Indo-Aryan languages in the north and of Dravidian languages in the south with some pockets in the north—the geographical knowledge from the Ṛgveda downwards showing gradual expansion towards east and the south from the north-west, and ancient legends pointing to invasions of the people speaking Sanskritic languages towards south rather than the other way round.

The Ṛgvedic singers seem to be more or less settled down in the land of the river Sindhu and that of the seven rivers, that is the north-western part and Punjab of the undivided India. They knew the river Gaṅgā, but the river had not then assumed the importance which it did in later Sanskrit literature. They had yet no knowledge of the lotus, the *nyagrodha*, the tiger, and rice, which are all foreign to the north-west of India.

The authors of the *Atharvaveda* hymns show further advance towards east and the south. The tiger now appears as the most feared beast of prey and his skin becomes the sign of king's power.

When we come to the period of the *Brāhmaṇa*s we notice that the land known as *Brahmāvarta* or the land of Kurus (*Kurukṣetra*) lying between the rivers Sarasvatī and Dṛṣadvatī and of the Pāñcālas, the land between the Gaṅgā and the Yamunā (the Doab) assumes importance.

The story of Videgha Mādhava as narrated in the *Śat. Br.*[6] clearly points to the expansion of the Vedic Indians to the east. The fire which came out from the mouth of Videgha Mādhava started from the river Sarasvatī in the west towards the river Sadānirā (modern Gaṇḍak?) in the east. The Brāhmaṇas had never crossed the river Sadānīrā before this incident. But now they settled down[7] even to the east of the river Sadānīrā.

Similarly the legends of the sage Agastya who first burnt the Rākṣasas in the north and then destroyed those who had taken shelter in the southern direction,[8] and his crossing the Vindhya mountain and settling down in the south[9] point to the expansion of the Vedic Indians to the south.

This gradual expansion of the Vedic people taking them to the newer and newer lands and their getting to know new animals and grains show clearly that they came to India from outside. If the Vedic Indians were the indigenous people, there is no reason why they should not mention anything peculiar to the central, eastern, and southern parts of India in the hymns of the Ṛgveda.

[6] 1.4.1.10

[7] Ibid., 1.4.1.14–15.

[8] *Mbh.* 13.140.7–13.

[9] Ibid., 3.102.

6

Vedic Aryans, Non-Vedic Aryans, and Non-Aryans

Judging the Linguistic Evidence of the Veda

Madhav M. Deshpande

Madhav M. Deshpande's article examines the Vedic evidence for Aryans (including non-Vedic Aryans, that is, Aryans who were outside the Vedic religion) and non-Aryans. The argument hinges on the variability of the 'R' and 'L' sounds in early North Indian (Indo-Aryan) languages, and their geographical patterning as shown in Mehendale's survey of the inscriptions; for example, Ashoka calls himself *laja* rather than *raja* in some versions of his inscriptions. Deshpande has made major contributions to the study of retroflexion in the Veda and on the sociolinguistics of India. This article carries that work forward, trying to specify the social conditions that would account for the distribution of the evidence, that is, what kind of language contact and what kind of bilingualism among the general population and the religious specialists who compiled the Veda can account for the linguistic features of the text.

[From *The Indo-Aryans of Ancient South Asia: Language, Material Culture and Ethnicity*, ed. George Erdosy (Berlin and New York: Walter de Gruyter, 1995), pp. 67–84.]

Introduction

At the very outset of my paper, I would like to clarify my point of view. I an not an archaeologist. I do consult research in archaeology, but I claim no expertise in evaluating it. I will strictly represent the point of view of a Sanskritist and a linguist. In 1977–8, I published an article, 'Some aspects of Pre-Historic Indo-Aryan'. Arguments from this article were incorporated into a more extensive study 'Genesis of Ṛgvedic Retroflexion: A Historical and Sociolinguistic Investigation', which was published in 1979. While these two pieces dealt with primarily linguistic matters, I have also treated certain enthnographic issues relating to ethnic intermixture and identity retention in an article titled 'Aryans, Non-Aryans, and Brāhmaṇas: Processes of Indigenisation', which is to appear in the *Journal of Indo-European Studies*. In my presentation at this conference, I will try to pull together issues and arguments from my own previous and ongoing studies, as well as from more recent studies by other scholars, and add some of my latest thinking on these matters. I will restrict myself to the earliest period on Indo-Aryan languages, though references to later periods are obviously unavoidable.

Nature of Linguistic Evidence

Focusing our attention on the available material, we must keep in mind the following points. The oldest extensive linguistic data in the Indo-Iranian branch are represented by the Ṛgveda (dated since the days of Max Müller to somewhere between 1500 and 1000 BC). They are followed by the Mitanni treaties, dated much more securely to the fourteenth century BC. Afterwards, we have the Avestan and Old Persian materials. Finally, we may also list the Prakrits as seen in Aśokan inscriptions. These materials are not always available to us in their pristine, original form. While the Mitanni documents, the Old Persian documents, and the Aśokan edicts, coming from inscriptions as they do, are frozen in time, that is not the case either with the

Ṛgveda or with the Avestan texts. These have been subjected to a long oral tradition before they were codified, and the texts available to us represent a state of affairs at the end of this long oral transmission, rather than at the starting point of their creation. As we deal with possible contact languages or language-families in this area, we are dealing with equally uneven materials. It is not always clear what the linguistic form of the Austric languages was during the period of the Ṛgveda. With the Dravidian languages too, we do not have the actual linguistic material contemporary with the Ṛgveda, but we must deal with the reconstructed stages of Dravidian. Even if one accepts the identification of the Indus valley people with Dravidians, and the language of the Indus valley inscriptions as a form of Dravidian, we know precious little about the actual language to compare it with another. Thus, when we consider this ancient period, the period of the Ṛgveda and beyond, we are dealing with apples and oranges, actual language materials and reconstructed texts, and states of languages. Since this is the nature of the material we possess, we have to make the best of it. However, we must keep this complexity and uneveness of materials in mind.

Focusing on the Ṛgveda alone, we find that there were numerous stages in which this material was created, collected, collated, edited, and preserved. The oldest books of the Ṛgveda are the so-called family books, namely Books 2 through 8, and the organizational principles of the text (in the Śākalya version) are as follows:

Maṇḍala	RV divided into ten Maṇḍalas ('Chapters')
Anuvāka	Each Maṇḍala has several Anuvākas ('Sections')
Sūkta	Each Anuvāka contains several Sūktas ('hymns')
Ṛk	Eact Sūkta contains several Ṛks ('verses')

Maṇḍala	*Anuvākas*	*Family of Sages*	*Theme*
1	24	Miscellaneous	Miscellaneous hymns
2	4	Gṛtsamada	Hymns to a set of deities
3	5	Viśvāmitra	do
4	5	Vāmadeva	do
5	6	Atri	do

(Contd)

(Contd from previous page)

Maṇḍala	*Anuvākas*	*Family of Sages*	*Theme*
6	6	Bharadvāja	Hymns to a set of deities
7	6	Vasiṣṭha	do
8	10	Kaṇva + Miscellaneous	do
9	7	Miscellaneous	Hymns to Soma
10	12	Miscellaneous	Miscellaneous hymns

It is clear that the hymns included in the family books (Books 2–8) are composed by members of those specific priestly families. However, each family book represents a collection of hymns produced by several generations, both young (*nūtana*, *navya*) and old (*pūrva*). We would expect this language to change somewhat from generation to generation. Then the hymns in each family book are organized in terms of the deity to which they are addressed and the number of verses in the hymns. This organization reflects the activity of the editors of the entire collection of the Ṛgveda, rather than the activity of the particular priestly families, because the same principles are found in all the family books. Thus, it is clear that the editors homogenized the received hymns to a certain extent. Also consider, for instance, the following fact: it is clear that Vasiṣṭha and Viśvāmitra are bitter enemies, who curse and accuse each other in their hymns. Their descendants cannot marry each other even today in India. Thus, it is inconceivable that the hymns of these two families could be placed in a common collection. However, the fact that they are placed in the Ṛgveda as two family books indicates that the time gap between the composers of the hymns and the collectors, editors, and collators was quite large. This gap must have been long enough to lead to a kind of imposed homogenization. Whatever linguistic differences do survive in the Ṛgveda are a mere fraction of the real differences which must have existed in the original compositions.

The Ṛgveda thus represents a collection of hymns by priests of several different families, several different generations of those priests, and several families in bitter conflict with each other. As is clear from the hymns, the Ṛgvedic tribes are not united among themselves and against the non-Aryan *dāsas*. Some Aryans are allied with the *dāsas*, while others are not. All this would lead us to expect far greater linguistic diversity than what we actually find in the existing text. I do not mean to under-estimate the value of linguistic diversity detected in the Ṛgveda by scholars like Pinault[1] (1989), Pirart[2] (1989), and Elizarenkova[3] (1989), but would also like to assert that this diversity is only what has survived the homogenizing effects of the unifying editorial activity and does not reflect the total amount of diversity in the lost original texts. This complexity of the linguistic evidence gets further compounded when we realize that Śākalya was only one of the editors of the Ṛgveda, and that his recension represents only one of several. We know that Śākalya based his recension in part on the earlier recension of Māṇḍūkeya which was prevalent in the north-eastern region of Magadha, while the original Ṛgvedic hymns were composed in the north-western region. The Māṇḍūkeya recension, which is not available to us, reportedly had different rules for euphonic combinations, and differed in the amount of retroflexion from some other contemporary recensions. For later Vedic Saṃhitās, such as those of the Atharvaveda, Yajurveda, and Sāmaveda, we are in possession of several different recensions. However, only one recension of the Ṛgveda has survived. Thus, the linguistic conclusions based on the language of the received Śākalya recension need to be re-examined by keeping the above facts in mind.

A further dilemma is posed by Śākalya's recension itself. Unlike the contemporary version, that known to Pāṇini did not have the retroflex consonants *ḷ* and *ḷh* for intervocalic *ḍ* and *ḍh*. To me it seems most likely that Śākalya's recension itself underwent some

[1] Pinault, G.J., 'Reflets dialectaux en Védique ancien', in *Dialects dans les littératures indo-aryennes.* Publications de l'Institut de Civilisation Indienne, Série in-8°, Fascicule 55, edited by C. Caillat, 19–23. Paris, Diffusion de Boccard, 1989.

[2] Pirart, E., 'Avestique et dialectologie Ṛgvédique', in *Dialectes dans les littératures indo-aryennes.* Publications de l'Institut de Civilisation Indienne, Série in-8°, Fascicule 55, edited by C. Caillat, 35–96 Paris, Diffusion de Boccard, 1989.

[3] Elizarenkova, T.A., 'About traces of a Prakrit dialectal basis in the language of the Ṛgveda', in *Dialectes dans les littératures indo-aryennes.* Publications de l'Institut de Civilisation Indienne, Série in-8°, Fascicule 55, edited by C. Caillat, 1–17. Paris, Diffusion de Boccard, 1989.

gradual phonetic changes indifferent regions and periods. Thus, when we refer to linguistic evidence from the Ṛgveda, we need somehow to keep in mind all these problems. My own conclusion regarding retroflexes in the Ṛgveda is that the original compositions were either free from retroflexion of fricatives, liquids, and nasals or that those sounds had only marginal retroflexion. The retroflexion we see in the available recension of the Ṛgveda is a result of the changes, which crept into the text during centuries of oral transmission. I have argued my case in detail elsewhere (Deshpande 1979a)[4] and need not enter into a longer argumentation here.

Vedic Aryans, Non-Vedic Aryans, and Non-Aryans

Several problems concern us regarding the migration of Aryans, and about the identity of the non-Aryans they met in India and before reaching India proper. Theories abound and the following is a brief sample, based on linguistic evidence.

Hoernle (1880: xxx-xxxii)[5] postulated the existence of two early Aryan groups in North India, the Māgadhan and Śaurasenī, representing waves of Indo-European language speakers, of which the Māgadhans were the older. This idea was supported by Grierson (*Imperial Gazetteer of India*, 1: 353–9) and given an ethnological footing by Risley[6] (1915:55). Oldenberg also supported and elaborated this idea and pointed out that 'probably the first immigrants, and therefore, the farthest forward to the east ... are those tribes ... the Aṅga and the Magadha, the Videha, the Kośala,

[4] Deshpande, M.M., 'Genesis of Ṛgvedic retroflexion, a historical and sociolinguistic investigation', in *Aryan and Non-Aryan in India*, edited by M.M. Deshpande and P.E. Hook, 235–315. Ann Arbor: Karoma Publishers, Inc. and Center for South and Southeast Asian Studies, University of Michigan, 1979a.

[5] Hoernle, A., *A Grammar of the Eastern Hindi Compared with Other Gauḍian Languages*. London: Karl Trübner, 1880.

[6] Risley, H., *The People of India*. 2nd edition. London: W. Thacker and Co., 1915.

and Kāśī'.[7] He (1890:9) also claims that it was the second wave that produced the Vedas. This theme has been linguistically upheld by Meillet who shows that the Vedic dialect, like the Iranian, is an *r*-only dialect in which the Indo-European **l* merged into *r*, but the dialect of the redactors of the Vedas was an *r*-and-*l* dialect, where the original Indo-European **r* and **l* were retained; the redactors of the Vedic texts have put this *l* back into some of the Vedic words, where the original Vedic dialect had an *r* (Meillet[8] 1912–13; Bloch[9] 1970:2). In later Prakrits we clearly see the eastern Prakrit, Māgadhī, developing into a pure *l*-only dialect; whereas the western and particularly the north-western dialects, almost devoid of *l*, represent the early *r*-only dialect (Mehendale[10] 1948:297).

We should explore the difference between the *r*-only dialect, and the *r*-and-*l* dialect (and possibly an *l*-only dialect) further. Burrow[11] provides a perceptive analysis of this issue:

> ... the *r*-dialect prominent in the early Ṛgveda shares a common change (of *s* -> *ś*) with Iranian. It is unlikely to have undergone this change independently and consequently we must assume that it took place when a group of Indo-Aryan migrants was still in contact with Iranians. ... On the other hand, those Indo-Aryans who preserved the difference between *r* and *l* had already departed to India, and so they were unaffected by it. The speakers of the *r*-dialect were the latest comers on the Indian scene and there ensued a mixture of the two dialects.

This is an important proposal, as it suggests that there was a branch of Indo-Aryan which, like the parent Indo-European, had retained

[7] Oldenberg. *Buddha: His Life, His Doctrine, His Order*, tr. W. Hoey. London, Williams and Norgate, 1890; *Ancient India, Its Languages and Religions*, tr. W. Hoey, 1890, Reprint Calcutta, Punthi Pustak, 1942, p. 9. He also points out (ibid: 10–11) that the river Sadānīrā was the dividing line between the Vedic Aryans and the outlandic Aryans. The sacrificial fire had not crossed to the east of it.

[8] Meillet, A., 'Les consonnes intervocaliques en Védique', *Indogermanische Forschungen*, 31, 120–5, 1913.

[9] Bloch, J., *The Formation of the Marāthi Language*. Translated by Dev Raj Channa. Delhi: Motilal Banarsidass, 1970.

[10] Mehendale, M.A., *Historical Grammar of Inscriptional Prakrits* (Pune, Deccan College, 1948).

[11] Burrow, T., 'A reconsideration of Fortunatov's Law', *Bulletin of the School of Oriental and African Studies*, 35, 531–45, 1972.

the distinction between *r* and *l*, and that this branch came into the region of Iran, and later into India, before the migrations of the standard Indo-Aryan branch. Burrow's 1973 article, entitled 'The Proto-Indo-Aryans', displays a further refinement of his ideas. In this study, Burrow proposes that there was a common Indo-Iranian homeland of the Proto-Aryans in northern Iran. He suggests that ancestors of Iranians and Indo-Aryans lived together in this common homeland. Then, at first there was a southward migration of the ancestors of the Indo-Aryans, or Proto-Indo-Aryans. The Proto-Indo-Aryans spread both eastward to India and westward toward the Near East. Then came the second southward migration, that of the Proto-Iranians. The migration of the Proto-Iranians split the Proto-Indo-Aryans from their Western branch, those who are eventually represented in the Mittani documents. In this scenario, all three groups—the Proto-Iranians, the Western branch of the Proto-Indo-Aryans, and the Eastern branch of the Proto-Indo-Aryans—represent the *r*-only dialects of common Indo-Iranian heritage. The Eastern branch is represented by the Ṛgvedic Aryans. The Western branch of the Proto-Indo-Aryans represented in the Mittani documents is also an *r*-only dialect. This is clear from the following epithets of horses cited by Burrow[12] and Parpola:[13]

Mittani	*Vedic*	
papru-nnu or *babru-nnu*	*babhrú-*	'brown'
pinkara-nnu or *bindara-nnu*	*pingalá-*	'reddish brown'
paritta-nnu or *baritta-nnu*	*palitá-*	'grey'

In these examples, the Mittani-Aryan dialect has *r* even where the Vedic words have an *l*. How about the *r*-and-*l* branch of Indo-European which presumably reached India before the Ṛgvedic Aryans? Where did they come from? Did they reach India via Iran? If so, did they leave any trace of themselves in Iran? Were the speakers of the *r*-and-*l* dialect of Pre-Vedic Indo-Aryan a totally different branch

[12] Burrow, T., 'The Proto-Indo-Aryans', *Journal of the Royal Asiatic Society*, NS 2, 123–40, 1973.

[13] Parpola, A., 'The coming of the Aryans to Iran and India and the cultural and ethnic identity of the Dāsas', *Studia Orientalia*, 64, 195–302, 1988.

from the Indo-Iranian? These are difficult questions. Parpola (*op. cit.*) suggests that 'The change *l* -> *r*, which characterizes the common proto-language of Ṛgvedic and Avestan, seems to have taken place relatively late in Proto-North-Aryan, since it has not reached peripheral dialects, including Ossetic and a number of Pamir dialects within East Iranian. Several etyma suggest that Proto-Nuristani retained the original PIE *l*; others attesting to the change *l* -> *r* are probably early loanwords from Proto-Dardic (i.e., Proto-Ṛgvedic). The nearly 1900 Iranian proper names in the Persepolis tablets contain possible traces of an *l*-retaining dialect in western Iran in the early fifth century BC.' Anyway, one would still have to assume the entry of *r*-and-*l* dialects of Indo-Aryans into India before the arrival of the Ṛgvedic Aryans to account for the fact that *r*-and-*l* dialects in India were more easterly in relation to the Ṛgvedic dialect.[14]

The significance of the *r*-and-*l* dialect moving earlier into the interior of India and eventually on to eastern areas like Magadha (where dialectally *r* -> *l*) is further enhanced by its connection with the operation of Fortunatov's Law. The law states that in the group PIE **l* + dental, in Sanskrit the *l* is dropped and the dental is changed to a cerebal (cf. Skt. *paṭa*- 'cloth' Oslav. *platino*, Russ. *polotno*). Here an original Indo-European cluster yields a single retroflex, while *r* + dental in Middle Indo-Aryan always results in a cluster, dental as well as retroflex (cf. Skt. *vartate*, Pkt. *vaṭṭai* beside *vattai*—Burrow

[14] This is the general argument, unless of course one subscribes to a possible alternative that the first wave produced the Veda, and that a second wave of non-Vedic Aryans pushed through the north-western settlements of the Vedic Aryans and migrated further into north-eastern areas. See Chanda, R.P., *The Indo-Aryan Races*. Rajshahi: Varendra Research Society, 1916. Chanda argues that 'the Indo-Aryans of the outer countries originally came from an ethnic stock that was different from the stock from which the Vedic Aryans originated'. However, for him the second wave of post-Vedic Aryans bypassed the 'inner' Vedic Aryans and went into the outer regions. See Chakladar, H.C., 'Eastern India and Āryāvartta', *Indian Historical Quarterly* 4.1, 84–101, 1928 and Chakladar, H.C., 'Aryan occuption of eastern India', *Indian Studies, Past and Present*, 3, 103–28, 245–312, 1961–2. Chakladar argues that the second wave of post-Vedic Aryans pushed the Vedic Aryans into the outer lands and itself occupied the inner lands. However, these are minority views, and not supported by linguistic or archaeological evidence.

op. cit.). The particular connection of Fortunatov's Law with *l*-clusters means that it cannot apply in dialects such as Iranian and Ṛgvedic Sanskrit, where every PIE **l* -> *r.* Burrow (ibid.) has defended Fortunatov's Law and tried to date the beginning of its operation on the basis of the Ṛgvedic word *gáldā-* 'dripping, flow' beside the *r*-dialect form *gā́ldā-*. The fact that *gā́ldā-* is still found in the Ṛgveda, while later Sanskrit has the derived root *gaḍ*, implies, according to Burrow (*op. cit.*), that 'the change according to Fortunatov's Law took place during the period of the early Ṛgveda, so that it was possible for one form antedating that change to be preserved in that collection'.

Be that as it may, one can ask the following question: was Fortunatov's Law purely an internal development, or was it a result of Aryan–non-Aryan contact and/or convergence? In any case, it seems that the *r*-and-*l* dialect did not undergo Fortunatov's Law in Iran, as there are no traces of retroflexes in Iran. The effect of Fortunatov's Law is observed only in India. This raises a number of interesting linguistic questions. The arguments alluded to by Parpola (*op. cit.*) and others would suggest that the Aryans came into contact with non-Aryans, perhaps Dravidians, already in Iran. However, Fortunatov's Law seems to have gone into effect only in India. It could suggest several possibilities. It is possible that the non-Aryan communities in Iran did not speak a retroflexed form of language. Another possibility is that the contact with non-Aryans in Iran was not powerful enough to affect the phonology of the Aryan dialects. One may also speculate whether Dravidian itself acquired retroflexion after entering India through contact and convergence with pre-Dravidian populations. The theory which considers Dravidian to be a sub-branch of the Nostratic family also needs to account for the emergence to retroflexion in Proto-Dravidian. Thus, it would seem that while the Aryans did indeed come into contact with different sorts of non-Aryans in Iran before reaching India, the retroflexing influences seem to have begun only in India. Thus, we may need to make a distinction between retroflex-speaking non-Aryans versus non-retroflex-speaking non-Aryans, and to consider the possibility that Dravidians themselves may have acquired this habit in India through convergence with pre-Dravidians.

Then, consider the next problem. If Fortunatov's Law applied only to an *l*-retaining dialect of the pre-Vedic Indo-Aryans, and if at least a partial motivation for that law lies in contact and/or convergence with non-Aryans, then what happened to the *r*-only dialects of the Indo-Iranians? Did they come into contact with different non-Aryans? Was it not a retroflexing influence? From the absence of retroflexes in Iranian we can certainly infer that the linguistic influence the Aryans received in Iran from non-Aryans did not include retroflexion. This would apply equally to the *r*-only and to *r*-and-*l* dialects. The retroflexing influence begins as the Aryan dialects enter India. Even here, however, the *r*-and-*l* dialect seems to have undergone greater retroflexion, perhaps due to its longer stay in India as compared to the *r*-only dialect of the Ṛgveda.

Where in India was the brunt of the retroflexing influence?[15] Since the *r*-and-*l* dialects are generally attested from the eastern part of North India, and the *r*-only dialects from the north-western part, one can make an additional distinction. The strong retroflexing influence seems to come in as the Aryan dialects move into the eastern parts of northern India, but this retroflexing influence does not seem to make its presence felt as much in north-western India.

The fact that the *r*-only dialect of the north-west and the *r*-and-*l* dialect (and possibly the *l*-only dialect) of the north-east underwent different developments with respect to retroflexion can be demonstrated by referring to early inscriptional Prakrits. In particular, Mehendale's monumental *Historical Grammar of Inscriptional*

[15] Professor Peter Hook (pers. comm.) suggested that of all Indo-Aryan languages, retroflexion seems to be the strongest in the Shina language of Gilgit. However, we have no information for the ancient period comparable to the Ṛgveda or even Aśoka. It is often hazardous to extrapolate from modern language data any conclusions about ancient periods. For instance, Burusaski, as we know it, has retroflexes, but we do not know if it acquired those through contact with Indo-Aryan or Dravidian (see Morgenstierne's *Preface to Lorimer*, 1935, p. xxiii). Also contrast Southworth, who (1974: 211–12) concludes that the strength of retroflexion was greater in the north-west and in the south and that it was weaker in the north-eastern region. See Southworth, F.C., 'Linguistic stratigraphy of North India: Contact and Convergence in South Asian Languages', *International Journal of Dravidian Linguistics*, No. 3, 2, edited by F.C. Southworth and S. Apte, 201–23. Madras: 1974. However, this is based on counts from modern languages. For a discussion, see Deshpande 1979 'a' or 'b' (*op. cit.*).

Prakrits throws a flood of light on this problem. Mehendale (*op. cit.*) points out that cerebralization of dentals in the environment of *r* is predominant in the eastern inscriptions, but 'it will be observed that the western dialect is the least affected by cerebralisation.' Bloch (*op. cit.*) and Burrow also emphasize this point. Burrow[16] further points out that even within the north-western region, the Niya Prakrit in the further west preserved *r*+dental clusters better than the north-western Aśokan inscriptions. He concludes that, phonologically, the language of the former presents a pronouncedly more archaic aspect than that of Aśoka's edicts, namely by better preserving such consonant combinations as *rt* and *rdh*. Burrow's conclusion is extremely significant (*op. cit.*):

> Obviously we cannot derive the Niya Prakrit from the language of Aśoka, and the most natural conclusion to draw from the fact that phonetically it is better preserved is that its home is to be sought further to the west. Because it seems clearer (then as now) that the more remote a language was in the direction of the north-west the less liable it was to phonetic decay.

This also raises a serious dilemma for our understanding. If the *r* + dental clusters in the north-western dialects of Indo-Aryan are retained without change, could it be because they are somehow inherently immune to such a change? That seems unlikely because these same clusters are changed to retroflexes in the north-eastern dialects. Consider the Sanskrit forms *vartate* and *vardhate* corresponding to the Prakrit *vaṭṭati* and *vaḍḍhati* cited by Patañjali. Here we would expect the north-western dialects to retain the clusters *rt* and *rdh*, but they are changed to *ṭṭ* and *ḍḍh* in the Eastern Prakrits. This would suggest that the *r* + dental clusters were not in principle immune to the retroflexing influence, but that this influence was not strong in the north-western region. Assuming that the retroflexing influence implies some sort of strong contact and/or convergence with a population speaking retroflexed languages, such a contact was substantially weaker in the north-western region. This does raise a suspicion in my mind: could the non-Aryan languages the Aryans

[16] Burrow, T., 'The dialect position of the Niya Prakrit', in *Indian and Iranian Studies Presented to George A. Grierson*, 419–35. London: University of London, p. 42, 1936.

encountered in the north-western region have had retroflexed sounds? Can we think of Dravidians of the north-western region without retroflexion in their language? I do not have a clear answer to this dilemma at this time.

This poses many complicated problems in our understanding of the contact and/or convergence of Aryans with non-Aryans in different parts of India, and outside India. One thing seems to be clear. The contacts with non-Aryans outside India did not lead to retroflexion either in the Indo-Iranian dialects, or in the pre-Indo-Iranian (*r*-and-*l*) dialects. The retroflexing influence was manifest in India. Even here it is manifest more in the eastern parts of North India than in the north-western parts. Is it because there was less intense contact and/or convergence in the north-west? Or, is it because the non-Aryans in the north-west did not have retroflexion in their speech?

We may also refer to the problem of the origin of the retroflex sounds *ḷ* and *ḷh* for intervocalic *ḍ* and *ḍh* in Śākalya's recension of the Ṛgveda. Most scholars take for granted the existence of these sounds in the Ṛgveda. I disagree with this view. I think that, like other eastern retroflexes, *ḷ* developed when the Ṛgvedic recitational traditions moved eastward into North India. Evidence to support this possibility comes from inscriptional Prakrits where, as Mehendale (*op. cit.*) points out, the 'change *ḍ* -> *ḷ* occurs in the non-Western groups'. This shows that the change of -*ḍ*- to -*ḷ*- did not occur in the north-western regions of India at the time of Aśoka. Pāṇini, who comes from the north-west and precedes Aśoka by about two centuries, does not have the sound *ḷ* in his Sanskrit. His rules concerning the Vedic language give no indication of the existence of the sound *ḷ* in the Vedic texts known to him. In fact, in rules like P.6.3.113 (*sāḍhye sāḍhvā sāḍheti nigame*) and P.8.3.54 (*iḍāyā vā*), he refers to Vedic usages such as *sāḍha* and *iḍā* without *ḷh* and *ḷ* for the intervocalic *ḍh* and *ḍ*. Pāṇini obviously knew Śākalya's Ṛgveda, and hence it is surprising to find him not recording the existence of *ḷ* in that text. Thus, even though we reconstruct these retroflex *ḷ* sounds in Proto-Dravidian, this sound does not manifest first in north-western Indo-Aryan. This indicates that even if we assume the inhabitants of the Indus valley to be speakers of some sort of Dravidian and that contact and/or convergence with them occurred in the north-west, it does not seem to have led to massive retroflexion in the region. The massive retroflexion appears in the central and eastern parts of North India, and then in the south.

Intensive and Extensive Bilingualism

We cannot deny that the incoming Aryan-speakers came in contact with certain non-Aryan people in India. There is ample evidence for such contacts. Emeneau[17] not only proposes that there was 'extensive bilingualism', but that 'Sanskrit was handed down at some early period by a majority of speakers who learned it as a second language, their first language being Dravidian'. However, it is impossible to believe that the majority of the composers of the Ṛgveda had Sanskrit as their second language and had some Dravidian language as their first language. The existence of Prakriticisms in the language of the Ṛgveda suggests that the colloquial language of the Ṛgvedic masses may have been some early form of Prakrit, rather than Dravidian.

This does not contradict the existence of several words in the Ṛgveda which can only be explained as loanwords from Dravidian and Munda languages. The loanwords do indicate contact with non-Aryan peoples. However, even if one accepts the entire list of Ṛgvedic loanwords provided by Kuiper, Burrow, and Southworth,[18] the total

[17] Emeneau, M.B., 'The Indian linguistic area revisited: Contact and Convergence in South Asian Languages', *International Journal of Dravidian Linguistics*, No. 3, 2, edited by F.C. Southworth and S. Apte, 92–134. Madras, 1974.

[18] See Burrow, T., *Collected Papers on Dravidian Linguistics*. Annamalainagar, Annamalai University, Department of Linguistic Publications no. 13, 1968. Burrow refers to twenty-five Dravidian loanwords in the Ṛgveda and says that 'it is not many, compared with the number in later Sanskrit,' See Kuiper, F.B.J., 'Ṛgvedic loanwords', in *Studia Indologica: Festschrift für W. Kirfel zur vollendung seines 70 Lebensjahres*. Studia Indologica, Bonner Orientalische Studien, Neue Serie, Band 3, edited by O. Spiess, 137–85. Bonn, Selbstverlag der Orientalischen Seminars der Universität Bonn, 1955. Kuiper lists numerous additional non-Aryan loanwords in the Ṛgveda, but many of these are debatable. Also see Southworth 1979. Deshpande (1979: 301) shows that the Dravidian loan words pointed out by Southworh (1979) were de-retroflexed in the language of the Ṛgveda.

number of these words in the Rgveda is still not as great as the number of Indo-Aryan loanwords in Tamil or South-east Asian languages. Neither the South-east Asian languages nor British English pick up retroflexion, in spite of borrowing a very large number of words from retroflexed languages.

Ananthanarayana[19] basically accepts the concept of bilingualism as proposed by Emeneau and Kuiper, but derives a slightly different conclusion: 'It is suggested that in the first period of this contact bilinguals were recruited chiefly from the native population. Support for such an assumption is provided in the greater number of Sanskrit loans (in Dravidian languages) as opposed to an insignificantly small number of Dravidian words in Sanskrit.' This would mean that more Dravidians accepted Aryan words than Aryans accepted Dravidian words. This also suggests that the initiative for adoption was more prominent on the part of the native non-Aryan than on the part of the incoming Aryan. Thus, to account for retroflexion in Indo-Aryan, it is necessary to assume that a large number of speakers of Indo-Aryan were native Dravidians, rather than Aryans influenced by Dravidians as assumed by Kuiper.[20] Kuiper himself[21] says that foreign words were 'Sanskritized' in the process of being incorporated into Sanskrit: 'Sanskritisation of foreign words by substitution of *tr*, *dra* (or *rt*, *rd*) for *ṭ*, *ḍ* is well attested in the classical language.' He carries this tendency farther back in the Ṛgveda. 'The explanation of *kartá-* as a Sanskritisation of *kāṭá-* would seem to be rather the only one that is phonetically admissible according to our present knowledge.' If one accepts Kuiper's explanation of *kartá-* <- *kāṭá-*, which is by no means certain, it would appear that the Ṛgvedic Aryans did think of *rt* as being more native to the Aryan tongue, and of *ṭ* as being somewhat foreign.[22]

[19] Ananthanarayana, H.S., 'Prakrits and Dravidian languages', in *Proceedings of the Seminar in Prakrit Studies*, edited by R.N. Dandekar and A.M. Ghatage, 65–75. Pune: University of Poona, 1970.

[20] Kuiper, F.B.J., 'The genesis of a linguistic area', *Indo-Iranian Journal*, 10, 81–102, 1967.

[21] Kuiper, F.B.J., 'Ṛgvedic Kīrín- and KrīḶí-', *Indian Linguistics*, 1, 349–62, 1958.

[22] See Bloch, J., *Indo-Aryan, From the Vedas to Modern Times.* Revised French edition translated by A. Master. Paris, Libraire d'Amérique et d'Orient,

Emeneau did recognize this problem. Instead of saying that the Aryans interpreted allophones of Proto-Indo-Aryan in terms of the foreign, Dravidian phonemic system, he considered it more logical to assume that Dravidians interpreted allophones of Proto-Indo-Aryan in terms of their own native phonemic system in the process of adopting the foreign, Aryan language. In his excellent paper 'Bilingualism and Structural Borrowing', Emeneau points out, as early as 1962,[23] that 'the evident Dravidianisation of Sanskrit in some of its structural features must lead to the partial conclusion that a sufficient number or proportion of certain generations of Sanskrit speakers learned their Sanskrit from persons whose Dravidian linguistic traits were translated into Indo-Aryan and who provided the model for succeeding generations'.

In his 1962 article, Emeneau proposed an essentially correct sociolinguistic process for the development of retroflexion in Sanskrit, but he was not sure of the exact chronology or of the intensity of this process with reference to early Vedic texts. Were Dravidians participating in a significant proportion in the use of Sanskrit in pre-Vedic times? At that time, he was not sure. In 1974, making essentially the same sociolinguistic argument, Emeneau (*op. cit.*) claims more confidently that such a process must have taken place before the composition of the Ṛgveda, and agrees with Kuiper that retroflexion in the existing Ṛgveda is an indication of pre-Ṛgvedic Dravidianization of the Aryan language.

In order to be able to evaluate the arguments put forward by Emeneau and Kuiper to establish bilingualism between the Vedic Aryans and Dravidians, we must take into account a recent analysis of bilinigualism by Nadkarni,[24] who points out that:

Adrien Maisonneuve, 1965. Bloch thinks that *kāṭá-* is derived from *kartá-*. Referring to Bartholomae's attempt to connect *kāṭá-* and *kartá-*, Burrow (*op. cit.*) comments: 'The connection of *kāṣá* with *kartá-* is anything but certain; it could have been spontaneous cerebral and be connected to *kā́tu-* "hole" along with which it is listed in Nighantu 3, 23.'

[23] Emeneau, M.B., 'Bilingualism and structural borrowing', *Proceedings of the American Philosophical Society*, 106.4, 430–42, 1962.

[24] Nadkarni, M.V., 'Bilingualism and syntactic change in Konkani', *Language* 51, 672–83, 1975.

structural borrowing at all levels of language, including syntax (the so-called 'deepest' level), can take place irrespective of the factor of social prestige, but solely as a consequence of 'intensive and extensive' bilingualism with a certain time depth. ... By 'extensive' bilingualism, I mean a situation in which bilibgualism is co-extensive with the entire community, as in the case of K [annad] S[arasvat] K[onkani] speakers. By 'intensive' bilingualism, I mean a situation in which a community whose mother tongue is language A is not merely conversant with language B, but actually uses it for a wide range of purposes in the course of normal, everyday living. Extensive bilingualism, in particular, seems necessary for structural borrowing to be stabilised, since it renders all the members of the community more or less equally receptive to influences and traits of the non-native language—which, first randomly, and gradually more and more regularly, find their way into the mother tongue. A linguistic innovation has a strong chance of stabilising itself in a language if it attracts no notice, and therefore no resistance from speakers, particularly in the early stages. This is possible only in situations of extensive bilingualism.

Kuiper's data, as well as the information on loanwords supplied by Southworth, indicate 'sporadic' bilingualism but are insufficient to demonstrate extensive or intensive bilingualism as defined by Nadkarni. I am pleased to report that Emeneau[25] now agrees with my suggestion that retroflexion in the existing recension of the Ṛgveda needs to be explained more in terms of an increasingly Dravidianized oral transmission of the text, rather than in terms of this trait being part of the language of the original composers.

Linguistic, Cultural, and Biological Identities

Since the terms 'Aryan' and 'Dravidian' have acquired a variety of different meanings, it may be helpful to sort out the terminological problem. We may formally state the following:

1. A person who speaks an Aryan language as his first language is—linguistically speaking—an Aryan person.
2. A person who considers himself to be a member of an Aryan (cultural) community and is accepted to be so by the other members is—culturally speaking—an Aryan person.

[25] Emeneau, M.B., 'Review of *Aryan and Non-Aryan in India*', edited by M.M. Deshpande and P.E. Hook, *Language*, 57.2, 468–70, 1981.

3. A person who is biologically speaking a member of a group defined to be Aryan on the basis of some physiological characteristics is—biologically speaking—an Aryan person.

A person could be Aryan in all those respects, or he could be Aryan only in some respect. For instance, from a purely linguistic standpoint, one can say that it is necessary to have a Dravidian speaker of Indo-Aryan in order to explain the emergence of retroflexion. This simply amounts to saying that a person who is linguistically Aryan, a speaker of a non-retroflexed form of language, is less likely to pick up retroflexion through contact with speakers of retroflexed languages, that is, Dravidians. On the other hand, a speaker of a retroflexed language, a Dravidian speaker, is more likely to use retroflexes in adapting to an Aryan language. Here, we are using the words Aryan and Dravidian in purely linguistic terms. However, consider the case of Kavaṣa Ailūṣa or a Vasiṣṭha in the Ṛgveda. Several modern scholars such as Kosambi[26] and Kuiper (*op. cit.*) have argued that these persons are non-Aryans recruited into the Brāhmaṇa communities. If that is the case, then we could perhaps say that these linguistically and ethnically Dravidian individuals culturally Aryanized themselves. Thus, it is possible to combine these various types of identities. This kind of distinction between cultural and linguistic Aryanhood is made even by Manu:

Those communities in the world, which are not included among the communities born from the mouth, arms, thighs, and feet [of the creator, i.e., the four *varṇas*], are all considered to be non-Aryan, irrespective of whether they speak an Aryan or a non-Aryan language.[27]

A person born to a non-Aryan female from an Aryan man may become an Aryan through his virtues. However, it is determined that a person born to an Aryan female from a non-Aryan man is indeed a non-Aryan.[28]

[26] Kosambi, D.D., *Ancient India.* New York: Meridian, 1965.

[27] *mukha-bāhūru-paj-jānāṃ yā loke jātayo bahiḥ* | *mlecchavācaś cārya-vācas te sarve dasyavo matāḥ* | Manusmṛti 10.45.

[28] *jāto nāryām anaryāyām āryād āryo bhaved gunaih* | *jāto py anāryād anārya iti niścayah* | Manusmṛti 10.67. Manu (10.68) shows that while he considers that child of an Aryan man born from a non-Aryan female as Aryan in some sense, he does not regard that child to be fully eligible for Aryan sacraments (*saṃskārya*).

Manu does not consider it sufficient to be a speaker of the Aryan language for a person to be recognized as ethnically Aryan. Ancient Indian culture, in line with the inherited Indo-European idea of patrilineality, recognized a son of an ethnically Aryan man to be Aryan, without any regard to the identity of the mother. However, a son of a non-Aryan father was not acceptable as an ethnic Aryan. Such conceptions allowed racial intermixtures without the loss of ethnic identities. I have studied this phenomenon extensively in my forthcoming article 'Aryans, non-Aryans and Brāhmaṇas: Processes of indigenisation'. This explains to a certain extent how there could emerge a large population which regarded itself as culturally Aryan, and yet had significant linguistically and ethnically non-Aryan elements in it. Consider the following charts showing the genealogy of Kṛṣṇadvaipāyana Vyāsa:

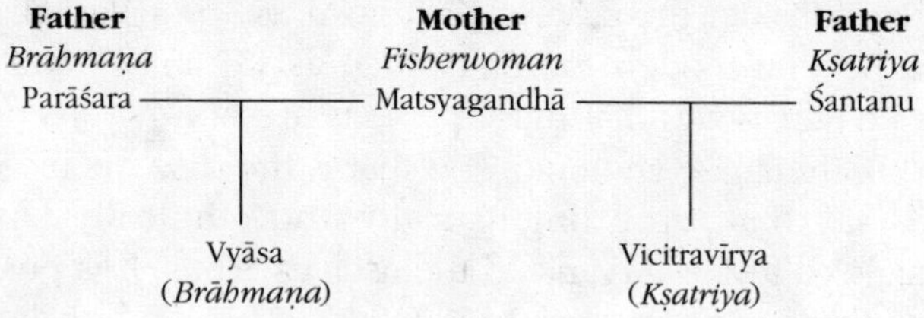

Detailed Genealogy of Vyāsa

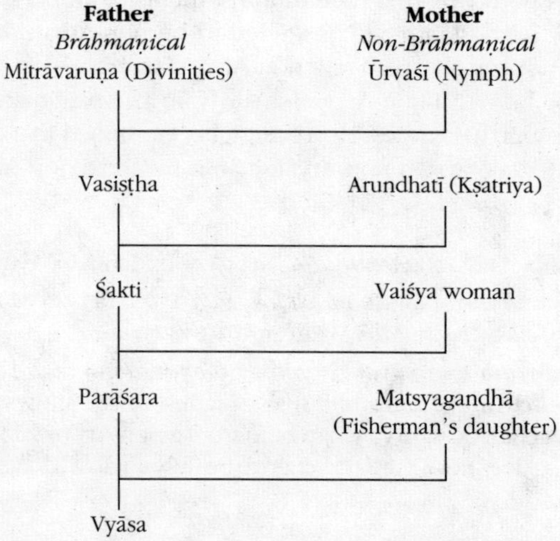

It is my contention that the authors, at least of the Ṛgveda, are largely Aryan in linguistic, ethnic, and cultural terms, mixed perhaps with a small number of 'Aryanized' non-Aryans.[29] This is what is indicated by the fact that the few Dravidian loanwords one finds in the Ṛgveda are phonetically Aryanized (Deshpande, *op. cit.*). By the time of the Late Vedic, Epic, and Classical periods, this 'Aryanized' element was probably the largest segment among the users of Indo-Aryan languages. It is during this later epoch that one finds evidence for large-scale structural Dravidianization of Indo-Aryan structures.

Disciplinary Limitations and the Need for Caution

In the recent works of Parpola (*op. cit.*), Fairservis and Southworth[30] and others (listed exhaustively in Sjoberg, *op. cit.*), there is a laudable effort to interface research in archaeology and linguistics. One can add studies of physical anthropology to this as well. Such conjoined reconstructions are indeed fascinating and necessary. At the same time, one needs to proceed with a great deal of caution. William Bright[31] has sounded all the necessary notes of caution regarding linguistic inferences from archaeological evidence, and I need not repeat those. While these different disciplines do contribute to solving each other's problems up to a point, there remains a large residue of linguistic problems that are not soluble by archaeology and vice versa.

[29] See Sjoberg, A., 'The Dravidian contribution to the development of Indian civilisation: A call for a reassessment', *Comparative Civilisations Review*, 23, 40–74, 1990. Sjoberg argues, 'The earliest of these, the Ṛgveda, stands somewhat apart from the others in terms of its mainly Aryan (i.e., Indo-European) content. Some non-Aryan (mainly linguistic) influence in the Ṛgveda can be discerned, but a non-Aryan component seems more apparent in the later Saṃhitās.'

[30] Fairservis, W.A. and Southworth, F., 'Linguistic archaeology and the Indus Valley culture', in *Old Problems and New Perspective in the Archaeology of South Asia*, edited by J.M. Kenoyer, 133–41. Madison, Wisconsin Archaeological Reports 2, 1986.

[31] Bright, W., 'Archaeology, linguistic and ancient Dravidian', in *South Asian Languages: Structure, Convergence, and Diglossia*, edited by B. Krishnamurti, 108–12. Delhi: Motilal Banarsidass, 1986.

The limitations of these disciplines need to be consciously recognized. Consider for instance the following narrative from Parpola (*op. cit.*):

> The arrival of Namazga V people seems to have disrupted the political and cultural unity of the Indus Valley soon after 2000 BC. ... The newcomers did not stop in the Harappan area, however, but pushed on further both into the Deccan and towards the Gangetic Valley.

I have no reason to doubt the veracity of this description. However, the point I would like to make is that such a description remains opaque at best to a linguist. Were the Namazga V people speakers of an Aryan language? Which variety of Aryan did they speak? Indo-Iranian, Proto-Iranian, Proto-Indo-Aryan, the *r*-only dialect or the *r*-and-*l* dialect? Was their language already influenced by their contact with non-Aryans? Did these non-Aryans speak a retroflexed language? There are numerous such linguistic questions which will perhaps always remain unanswered. One can make a leap from archaeology to linguistics, but, with the best expertise at hand, it is not always easy to judge if one has landed on the right target. I should also hasten to say that we may encounter the same problem when going from linguistics to archaeology.

Finally, I would just like to list issues which are of concern to a linguist such as myself. These need to be addressed as fully as possible to reach a satisfactory resolution of linguistic problems:

1. The Vedic texts as we have them are the end-products of a long oral transmission. Any conclusions based on their linguistic features need to take into account the possible linguistic changes that may have crept into the text during this process.
2. We need to distinguish language and social contact from language and social convergence. Evidence for the first does not necessarily imply the second. We cannot have convergence without contact, but we can have contact without convergence.
3. When we speak of bilingualism we need to make a distinction between sporadic, intensive, and extensive bilingualism. These different types may possibly lead to different linguistic consequences.

4. Whose linguistic output is available to us as evidence in the Ṛgveda? Do we have Aryans influenced by Dravidians, or Dravidians influenced by Aryans? Is there any place for the polarity between Aryanized Dravidian versus Dravidianized Aryan, or is there a homogenized result due to convergence with the resultant loss of polarities?
5. Linguistic, biological, and cultural identities must be kept separate for our analytical purposes. There is also a difference between identity as defined or assumed by a person for himself as against that person's identity in the eyes of others. In classical India, the orthodox Brāhmaṇas, Jains, and Buddhists created parallel, but conflicting, notions of 'Aryan'.[32]

Keeping these notes of caution in mind, we can indeed proceed with our interdisciplinary adventures. While we are not assured of indubitable success, we can indeed be assured of the thrill and excitement of conceiving new possibilities and probabilities.

[32] Deshpande, M.M., *Sociolinguistic Attitudes in India: A Historical Reconstruction* (Ann Arbor, Karoma Publishers, Inc., 1979b).

7

Constructing the Racial Theory of Indian Civilization

Thomas R. Trautmann

The following article, by historian Thomas R. Trautmann, shows that, during the colonial period, the Aryan/Dravidian linguistic difference was interpreted in a highly racialized way by British and other Western scholars, prior to the discovery of the Indus Civilization. Evidence from the Ṛgveda was over-interpreted in a racializing direction, especially apparent in the treatment of the single passage on the supposed 'noseless' character of the Dasas or Dasyus whom the Vedic Aryans considered their enemies. Linguistic and religious markers of difference between them are much mentioned in the Ṛgveda but are minimized in the racial interpretation. This racializing tendency in the interpretation of evidence in the colonial period was conditioned by the formation of a racial division of labour in the aftermath of the ending of slavery in the West, including the indenture system to which Indians were subjected. It is not only a question of whether there was a difference of complexion between Aryans and indigenous people—there may have been—but of the way in which the idea of race was understood. The strong tendency of Western scholars of the period was to assume that contemporary attitudes of whites toward dark-skinned people were unchanging through history and to interpret the evidence in the light of that belief.

[From *Aryan and Non-Aryan in South Asia*, ed. Johannes Bronkhorst and Madhav M. Deshpande, pp. 277–93. Harvard Oriental series, opera minora. Cambridge, Mass.: Department of Sanskrit and Indian Studies, Harvard University.]

At the first conference on 'Aryans and Non-Aryans in South Asia', organized by Madhav Deshpande and Peter Hook nearly twenty years ago, it seemed sufficient to illuminate the evidence of India's past in the light of dispassionate reason, and to pay no attention to the political misuses of the Aryan name. Things have changed a lot since then.

In the first place, the Aryan Nations and other white identity groups in the country as well as in Europe have seen to it that our students, who arrive in the elementary Indian civilization course with little knowledge of the Indo-European language family, are nevertheless perfectly aware of the association of the Aryan name with the politics of racial hatred. The vividness of such associations these days obliges us to address the political meanings of the Aryan idea in the twentieth century, if only 'by the way', as we try to convey a sound knowledge of ancient India.

In the second place, the ideal of a disinterested, non-partisan knowledge has melted away under the attacks of its critics, most notably (as it affects the second 'Aryan and non-Aryan' conference), the book of Edward Said,[1] which appeared the same year as the first conference. This polemic work, however one may feel about its hostility toward Orientalism (of the substance of which, moreover, it knows little and refuses to examine), has been immensely successful in changing the direction of debate, and opens the way to surprising new understandings of Orientalism, if it is taken as an encouragement to look more closely and not (as it too often is) as a settled conclusion about Orientalism. Speaking for myself, having been awakened from my dogmatic slumbers and having gone back to the British pioneers of Indology for a closer look, doing so has been a revelation to me, filled with unexpected discovery. At the outset, it became apparent that every one of the British Sanskritists, without exception, were Empire loyalists and scholars who took it for granted that there was a close connection between their

[1] Said, E.W., *Orientalism* (New York: Pantheon Books, 1978).

scholarship and the British colonial adventure in India. After the conquest of Bengal, British scholar-administrators quickly came to a knowledge of Sanskrit, and created at Calcutta, the seat of the new colonial government, a new Orientalism centred upon India and the Sanskrit language.[2] The connection between knowledge formation and colonialism lies so visibly on the surface of the new Orientalism formed at Calcutta that it is in no need of unmasking; the problem is not to show that knowledge has lost its innocence, but to explain when and how after the eighteenth century it acquired it. The kind of attitude that now seems puzzling is expressed very well in the preface to a classic study of the East India Company I happened to come across the other day, in which the (Euro-American) author says that the ideal historian of modern India would be someone who is neither European nor Asian—but in the absence of such he will do his best to be impartial.[3] The aspiration to write history from no point of view now appears for what it is—an impossibility. The notion that the ideal scholar is someone who has no personal connection with the subject seems bizarre, at a time when it is becoming all too familiar to hear the opposite argument, that only scholars who are ethnically qualified may speak for a given people.

The drift toward ethnic credentialism is not the only reason we cannot regard the loss of innocence as an unmitigated good. Scholarly

[2] The phrase in mine, but the argument for the newness and India-centredness of the new Orientalism was made by Raymond Schwab in his admirable book. See Schwab, R., *The Oriental renaissance, Europe's Rediscovery of India and the East 1680–1880.* English tr. of *La rennaissance orientale* (1950) by Gene Patterson-Black and Victor Reinking, Foreword by Edward W. Said (New York: Columbia University Press, 1984). Kejariwal, O.P., *The Asiatic Society of Bengal and the Discovery of India's Past 1784–1838* (New Delhi: Oxford University Press, 1988). Kejariwal has put together an excellent survey of the scholarship of the Calcutta Orientalists, and also see Kopf, D., *British Orientalism and the Bengal Renaissance: The Dynamics of Indian Modernization 1773–1835* (Berkeley and Los Angeles: University of California Press, 1969). David Kopf shows the interconnections between the Asiatic Society, the College of Fort William, the government, and Bengali society.

[3] Furber, H., *John Company at Work: A Study of European Expansion in India in the Late Eighteenth Century* (Cambridge: Harvard University Press, 1951).

knowledge of ancient India, which is of small account in the West, has become a political football in India itself as well as other countries of South Asia. Just when the ideal of disinterested, expert knowledge is most needed in South Asia to defend scholarship against political manipulations of the crudest kind, it is being rapidly dismantled in the West.

How to find a viable way forward is by no means clear. This paper gives the gist of my attempt to grapple with these problems in the concrete, and in ways that would be intelligible to my students. It draws upon a book (just completed) on the Indo-European idea among the British Sanskritists, called *Aryans and British India*, and research I have just begun toward another book, on the Dravidian idea.[4] It assumes that knowledge is not reducible to political interests in a simple way, and that there is a real world independent of our will, that is worth attempting to know, but that the facts are generally ambiguous and insufficiently resistant to have the power to decide among competing interpretations.

Let us take it as our problem to account for the formation of what I call 'the racial theory of Indian civilization'; the theory, that is, that Indian civilization was formed by the clash of invading, civilized, Sanskrit-speaking Aryans and dark, indigenous savages, identified with the Dāsas or Dasyus. This version of Indian history was utterly new and different from views that anyone, Indian or European, had entertained before the nineteenth century; and it has been so successful that it remains the metanarrative of Indian history, resistant to new facts such as the discovery of a pre-Aryan civilization in the Indus valley, which undermines the nineteenth century consensus on two capital points, showing that pre-Aryan India was not sunken in savagery, nor was India first civilized by the Aryans.

Aryans

Accepting it as our starting point that knowledge free of point of view is an impossible dream, it by no means follows that an idea

[4] Trautmann, T.R., *Aryans and British India* (Berkeley and Los Angeles: University of California Press, 1997).

such as the concept of the Aryan has a stable meaning that inheres in it, or a unitary politics attaching to it. The Aryan or Indo-European idea has at least three different readings belonging to different political contexts: (1) The exclusionary sense is the one associated with Nazism and other modern racial hate doctrines, while (2) for the Orientalists of British India, the Aryan idea had always an inclusionary sense, as a sign of the kinship of Britons and Indians, related to Orientalist policy positions; and (3) for Indians, the Aryan idea tends to be equated with the celebration of Hinduism. This multiplicity of political tendencies is a capital fact, showing the historically contingent character of the conjuncture.

When we focus upon the British Sanskritists who created the new Orientalism at Calcutta in the latter half of the eighteenth century, it becomes apparent that the Aryan or Indo-European idea always had an inclusive sense for the British, and served them as a sign of British-Indian kinship, within the empire, quite unlike the exclusionary sense made more familiar for us by twentieth-century fascisms. This came to me as an epiphany in Oxford where, in the entryway of the old Indian Institute building, one can read on the foundation stone Sanskrit ślokas, composed by Monier-Williams, the Boden Professor of Sanskrit. I quote the first and fourth verses, and the official English translation given on a brass plaque beneath:

śāleyam prācyaśāstrānām jñānottejanatatparaiḥ /
paropakāribhiḥ sadbhiḥ sthāpitāryopayoginī // 1 //
...
īśānukampayā nityam āryavidyā mahīyatām /
āryāvartāṅglabhūmyoś ca mitho maittrī vivardhatām // 4 //

This building, dedicated to Eastern sciences, was founded for the use of Aryans (Indians and Englishmen) by excellent and benevolent men desirous of encouraging knowledge
.... By the favour of God may the learning and literature of India be ever held in honour; and may the mutual friendship of India and England constantly increase!

In other places and times, a sign saying that the building was for the use of Aryas would be taken to mean that Jews, blacks, Asians, and others should keep out; or again, if it had been written by a pandit we might suppose that it was for Indians only, and that Englishmen must keep out—which is not so far-fetched; Monier-Williams says that the name of the Indian Institute tended to be taken in that sense.[5] But the appended translation tells us, to the contrary, that the word here has the meaning comparative philology gives it and we are to take it in an inclusive sense to mean English *and* Indians, even though elsewhere in the inscription *ārya* signifies Indians, as in āryavidyā = the literature of India, and the opposition of Āryāvarta (India) to Aṅglabhūmi (England). Finally, we note the underlying issue of mutual friendship between Indians and Britons, within, of course, the colonial relation. This is the Aryan brethren theme, of which Max Müller (Monier-Williams' contemporary and rival for the Boden chair) was the greatest champion.

Let us separate two features of the Aryan brethren theme for closer inspection: the aspect of the kinship between Britons and Indians, as attested by comparative philology of the Indo-European languages; and the aspect of friendship or love.

As we all know, the Indo-European or Aryan idea was adumbrated by Sir William Jones in a famous passage of his Third Anniversary address to the Asiatic Society, delivered early in 1786.[6] When

[5] Indian Institute. *Record of the Establishment of the Indian Institute in the University of Oxford* (Oxford: Horace Hart, 1897).

[6] In the most accessible edition of Jones' works (1807), the Anniversary Discourses are found together in volume 3, and they were reprinted as a separate volume in 1824. The famous passage is a single sentence: 'The Sanscrit language, whatever be its antiquity, is of a wonderful structure; more perfect than the Greek, more copious than the *Latin*, and more exquisitely refined than either, yet bearing to both of them a stronger affinity, both in the roots of verbs and in the forms of grammar, than could possibly have been produced by accident; so strong indeed, that no philologer could examine them all three, without believing them to have sprung from some common source, which, perhaps, no longer exists: there is a similar reason, though not quite so forcible, for supposing that both the *Gothick* and the *Celtick*, though blended with a very different idiom, had the same origin with the Sanscrit; and the old Persian might be added to the same family, if this were the place for discussing any question concerning the antiquities of Persia'. See Jones, W., *The Works of Sir William Jones*, 13 vols, ed. Anna Maria Jones (London: John Stockdale and John Walker, 1807); Aarsleff, H. *The Study of Language in England, 1780–1860* (Princeton: Princeton University Press, 1967). Aarsleff rightly notes the essentially ethnological (rather than narrowly linguistic) character of the Anniversary Discourses.

we examine the anniversary addresses as a set, we see that they are a survey of the ethnology of Asia, of which the underlying logic is the Genesis narrative of the three sons of Noah, from which the various nations of the world descend. This logic, which is the logic of what anthropologists call the segmentary lineage, groups all nations in a single scheme of classification in which everyone is kin to everyone else, but in varying degrees of nearness. Jones accounted for the strong similarities he found among Sanskrit, Latin, Greek, Gothic, Celtic, and Old Persian by assuming a lost ancestral language from which they were descended, and by assuming that the people speaking these languages descended from Ham, son of Noah.[7] The Biblical tree of nations as an ethnological grid is of course very old and is shared by the religions of the Bible, so that in India, Jones and his compatriots encountered among Muslims the idea, which had become standard, that Indians were sons of Hind, son of Ham, son of Noah. What is new is the emphasis upon language as a privileged means of laying bare the ethnological relations of history. As comparative philology takes shape, it develops an official history for itself, which serves as its charter as a true science by ignoring or denying the Biblical element in its ancestry. But in truth the tree diagram continues to be the central metaphor of historical linguistics, and it has its roots deep in the Bible and the segmentary lineage ideologies of the Middle East and Africa.

The second aspect has to do with the politics of love. The new Orientalism was conscious of its newness, and developed a propaganda of its own based on the idea that knowledge of Indian languages leads to understanding of Indians, and that understanding necessarily leads to sympathy. Thus, in the 1760s, Holwell, one of the pioneers, formulates the argument that all previous accounts of India, whether by the ancient Greeks or the modern Christian

[7] Jones' Hamian theory was a continuation by other means of the now-forgotten comparative mythology of Bryant (Bryant, J., [1807, First published 1744–6], *A New System; or an Analysis of Antient Mythology* [London: J. Walker]), according to which the Hamians were the inventors of civilization, but also the first to fall from the primitive monotheism of Noah into paganism. The Bryant/Jones theory of descent from Ham did not take; most Europeans put the Indo-Europeans in the line of the other son of Noah, Japhet, and the speakers of Semitic, of course, in the descent of Shem, after whom they are named.

missions, have misrepresented Indians as idolators; but, he argues, these are based only upon knowledge of the exterior person, the external testimony of the eye, whereas the new Orientalism, through knowledge of Indian languages, sees into the minds of the Indians and finds a belief in one God behind the welter of images of the gods.[8] Again and again we find the new Orientalism, in its self-representations, making this linkage between knowledge of Indian languages and sympathetic understanding of Indians, as well as the reciprocal, the love of Indians for Orientalists. This latter is exemplified by the tears of the pandits at the death of Jones, which his Orientalist biographer, John Shore,[9] finds it important to depict.

These claims are of moment because of course the Orientalists in British India were all of them involved in the government of India in some capacity, and were scholars on the side. Orientalism was not just a scholarly activity, however, it was a political policy and a faction of government from the time of Warren Hastings; and it affected not just the well-known question of education, but the fundamental issues of policy. And it had a coherent point of view, an ideology. With the formation at the seat of the new government of British India of the Asiatic Society (1784) and the College of Fort William (1800) for the teaching of Indian languages and other subjects to new civil servants sent out from England, there was an easy circulation of ideas and persons connecting the government, the courts, and the new Orientalism.

Orientalist policy was to conform the government of India to the culture of the people so far as possible. This chiefly meant the protection of Indian religions, and the enforcement of Indian laws in the courts, as they affected the private sphere of marriage and inheritance. In carrying this policy forward, some combination of the following ideas tended to make up the outlook of Orientalists in government: The indigenous people of India are the Hindus, conquered long ago by the Muslims. The Indians were one of the

[8] Holwell, J.Z., *Interesting Historical Events, Relative to the Provinces of Bengal, and the Empire of Indostan.* 3 vols (London: T. Becket and P.J. De Hondt, 1765–71 [vol. 1: 1765; vol. 2: 1767; vol. 3: 1771].

[9] Shore, J. (Lord Teignmouth), *Memoirs of the Life, Writings, and Correspondence of Sir William Jones* (Philadelphia: Wm. Poyntell, 1805).

earliest civilizations, connected somehow to the civilization of ancient Egypt. Prior to Muslim conquest, India was prosperous due to the mildness of the climate, the fertility of the soil, the benevolence of its laws, and the enlightened government of the ancient kings. The present miseries of India are due to Muslim oppression, and the dislocations caused by the recent warfare on the subcontinent. British rule, by drawing back the overburden of rule by Muslims and bringing peace, will allow Hindu society to spring back to its former happy state, and will set in strain the gradual assimilation to Hindu learning of modern scientific knowledge.

Connected with this vision was the scholarly project of recovering the specifics of the 'ancient constitution' of India so that it could be restored. Among other things this involved questions of land tenure. Orientalists were notable among those who denied the theory of Oriental Despotism, devised by Aristotle, revived in European descriptions of the Ottomans and transported to India—the theory that the king is owner of all the land and the people hold land of him as tenants paying tribute. They tended to regard this theory, where it could be found in India, as a Muslim imposition, and to hold that ancient India knew true private ownership of land.[10]

Dravidians

While the Calcutta Sanskritists put Sanskrit into relation to the languages of Europe by means of the Tree of Nations scheme they

[10] Outstanding examples are Mark Wilks' fifth chapter on land tenures in his *Historical Sketches of South India*, vol. 1. See Wilks, M., *Historical sketches of South India, in an attempt to trace the History of Mysoor: From the origin of the Hindoo government of that state, to the extinction of the Mohammedan dynasty in 1799. Founded chiefly on Indian authorities collected by the Author while officiating for several years as political resident at the court of Mysoor*, 3 vols (London: Longman, Hurst, Rees and Orme, 1810–17). F.W. Ellis' *Treatise on Mirasi Right*. See also Ellis, F., *Replies to Seventeen Questions Proposed by the Government of Fort St. George Relative to Mirasi Right with Two Appendices Elucidatory of the Subject* (Madras: Government Gazette Office, 1818). Reprinted in C.P. Brown, ed., *Three Treatises on Mirasi Right ... with Remarks Made by the Hon'ble the Court of Directors* (Madras: D.P.L.C. Connor, 1852).

had brought with them to India, their ideas of the languages of India were strongly influenced by the ideas of their teachers, the pandits, from the science of linguistics or Vyākaraṇa, in which of course the Indians were more highly advanced than any other of the ancient civilizations. Accordingly, they read the doctrine of eternal Sanskrit and the derivation of all languages from it by a process of corruption as true, but true only within India; that is, they believed in the linguistic unity of India and the derivation of its modern languages from Sanskrit. This was the prevailing view of the Calcutta Sanskritists, in 1801, and as then expounded by their great leader, H.T. Colebrooke, in his important essay on the Prakrit languages.

To be sure, that linguistic unity was not quite absolute; Colebrooke asserted the Sanskrit ancestry not of *all* languages spoken in India, but of all *polished* languages, that is, the ones with writing systems. Even in Jones we meet the idea, which became general, that the people and languages of the hilly regions may be pre-Aryan, a kind of altitudinal ethnology according to which savages rise to the top, and civilization floods the agricultural lowlands. Jones had said that nine-tenths of Hindi vocabulary is Sanskrit-derived but the remaining one-tenth is foreign, and may be Tartar, which in his ethnology means that of a nomadic and unlettered people—the first enunciation of a linguistic substratum in India. Still and all, the doctrine of linguistic unity of India covered the vast majority of its people. It derived the lettered Dravidian languages from Sanskrit, so that the discovery of the Dravidian language family had to make its way against the prevailing view put out by the Calcutta Orientalist establishment.

How this came about is a story I am in process of working out. Originally I thought I knew that answer: the discoverer of the Dravidian language family was of course Robert Caldwell, author of the classic work, *A Comparative Grammar of the Dravidian or South-Indian Family of Languages* (1856).[11] But the date is far too late, a good seventy years after Jones' famous pronouncement on Indo-European. When one examines the scholarship of the intervening

[11] Caldwell, Robert. *A Comparative Grammar of the Dravidian or South-Indian Family of Languages* (London: Harrison, 1856).

interval, one finds that the real discoverer of the Dravidian family is Francis Whyte Ellis, civil servant at Madras, and his proof was published as early as 1816, the year of Bopp's famous pamphlet on the comparative grammar of Indo-European and the early writings of Rasmus Rask, often taken to be the starting point of comparative philology.

The proof is developed by Campbell[12] and Ellis[13] jointly. It consists of showing that once the words the pandits identify as Sanskrit derivatives are removed from the vocabularies of the southern languages (that is, those identified *tatsama* and *tadbhava*), as well as the Persian and Arabic additions (*antardeśya*), the remaining words are the indigenous ones (*deśya*). The deśya words form the core of the vocabulary, including as they do words for parts of the body, kinship relations, and numbers, which, because they are necessary for any language, are highly likely to be original rather than borrowed. Furthermore, they are similar between Telugu, Tamil, and Kannada, as Ellis shows with parallel lists of words. The two parts of the proof, that the Sanskritic component of the south Indian languages is borrowed and not part of the central core, and that the core vocabulary of the three southern languages is filled with mutual cognates, is simply and beautifully done.

Ellis' proof is presented modestly as part of a team effort. It is printed as an introductory note in A.D. Campbell's *A Grammar of the Teloogoo Languages*, published by the College of Fort St. George for whose students it was intended. Woodiagherry Vencatanarrain, Patabhirama Sastri, and an unnamed Tamil master, all involved in teaching languages in the College, are named as contributors to the book.

Ellis did not publish much and he died, prematurely, at the age of forty-one years, three years after the publication of the proof. I

[12] Campbell, A.D., *A Grammar of the Teloogoo Language, Commonly Termed the Gentoo, peculiar to the Hindoos Inhabiting the North Eastern Provinces of the Indian Peninsula* (Madras: College Press of Fort St. George, 1816)

[13] Ellis F., 'Note to the introduction', in A.D. Campbell, *A Grammar of the Teloogoo Language*, 1–20 (Madras: College Press of Fort St. George, 1816).

have found unpublished letters and papers of Ellis that throw a good deal of light on his programme and the Dravidian issue.[14] I had initially thought that the College and the team he formed there had the effect of marshalling together the knowledges, European and Indian, and the pedagogic purpose that would have made the relationships of the Dravidian languages inter se and to Sanskrit transparent. But what I found was that the reverse was true; that Ellis had come to the Dravidian concept earlier, and worked it into the design of the curriculum of the College, which he brought into existence and presided over: for students were obliged to study Tamil first, and then to learn Telugu or Kannada as a variation of it.[15] In fact, the Dravidian doctrine is traceable a decade before its publication.

What was the politics of this knowledge? It was quite different from the Aryan brethren theme, and quite specific to Madras. The constant theme of Ellis' Orientalism is, 'But the south is different'. For example, the Calcutta Orientalist establishment had tried to form a code of Hindu law, directed by Jones, executed by Tarkapañcānana, and translated by Colebrooke. This Ellis vigorously attacked in his many writings on Hindu law, showing that quite different authorities prevailed in the south; above all, Vijñāneśvara's *Mitākṣarā*, and that in particular the treatise on partition by Jimūtavāhana, authoritative in Bengal, was not recognized in the south.[16] In short, Ellis was out to show that the Orientalism of the Calcutta establishment constructed a homogenized picture of the ancient constitution of India that

[14] Some had been rescued from waste papers at the College of Fort St. George by Walter Elliott and deposited in the Bodleian Library by Pope. But the greater part of the Ellis paper that have survived were letters and articles sent to Walter Erskine, which ended up in the India Office Library, the British Library, and the National Library of Scotland.

[15] 'Rules for the College of Fort St. George', IOL, Erskine Collection. From the Ellis papers in the Bodleian we find him trying to find a relationship of Dravidan with Semitic, through comparisons of Tamil words with Arabic, Chaldean (presumably Aramic), and Hebrew. Thus Ellis had the same Biblical tree-of-nations ethnological fame the Jones did, and looked for the Dravidians in a branch different from the one—Hamitic or Japhetic—containing the Aryans.

[16] Ellis (1827) and 'Memorandum respecting the proposed translation of the Rju Mitácsharà', IOL MSS. Eur. D. 30.

generalized from Bengal to all of India, but was in fact wrong for Madras, and that accordingly Madras needed an Orientalism of its own that mastered the peculiarities of the south as a region. The case of language was similar, and it had become urgent, since Carey, at Calcutta, had published a grammar of Telugu just two years previous to Campbell's, in which he had asserted that Telugu derived from Sanskrit;[17] Campbell's (and Ellis') reply in his grammar is part of the project of clearing a space for the authority of the Madras Orientalists and their team. In Ellis' short lifetime, he created the College of Fort St. George as Madras' answer to the College of Fort William, and participated in the creation of the Madras Literary Society which, with the earlier formation of the Literary Society of Bombay, ended the monopoly of Calcutta in the production of the new Orientalism. Thus the institutions of Calcutta were replicated at Madras, in order to assert the authority of Madras as against that of Calcutta.

Sanskrit and Race Science

Much of the British discussion subsequent to Ellis, both in British India and in the metropole, was occupied with the attempt to show that the pre-Aryan aborigines of India were a single people; the unity, as we would say, of the Dravidian and the Munda language families. This was the thesis of the Rev. John Stevenson, missionary of Bombay, and Brian Hodgson who was among other things British resident in Nepal.[18] The real achievement of Robert Caldwell in his 1856 book was not the discovery of the Dravidian family but the *consolidation* of the Dravidian thesis of Ellis in great detail and in its full extent;

[17] Carey, W., *A Grammar of the Telingana Language* (Serampore: Mission Press, 1814).

[18] The critical papers are Stevenson and Hodgson; see Stevenson, J., 'An essay on the language of the aboriginal Hindus', *Journal of the Bombay Branch of the Royal Asiatic Society*, 1:103–26, (1841–4); see also Hodgson, B.H., 'The aborigines of Central India', *Journal of the Asiatic Society of Bengal*, 17, pp. 550–8, (1848). but there are many more. The whole is discussed in Trautmann (*op. cit.*), Ch. 5.

and also the rejection of the aboriginal unity thesis, that is, the rejection of any connection between Munda and Dravidian. He established in short the modern linguistic consensus, that the three main language families of South Asia are not related to one another.

We need to think of these British discussions as being essentially concerned with ethnology, and not just language. Viewing the issue in this way, we can say that there are several striking things about British ethnology before Darwin. It was largely led by language, and its preferred method was the comparison of word lists. This was especially true in British India where the Orientalists, specifically the Sanskritists, and their findings governed the ethnological enterprise, and not the scholar-administrator in the field as such. But it is also true in Britain, where J.C. Prichard was the leading ethnologist. The case of Prichard is especially interesting in that he was a medical man and his writings made lots of reference to physical features; but the dominating frame for his classifications of races was supplied by languages, and physical features were subordinated to them (see especially Prichard, 1813,[19] and the fine study contained in George Stocking's introduction to the reprint). It is worth remembering just how many quite unexpected, even counter-intuitive ethnological relationships were discovered by these means, and the role of the British Orientalists in these discoveries. A short list would include the Indo-European languages (Jones), the Indo-European character of the language of the Gypsies (William Marsden, in part) and Sanskrit cognates of the same (Jones), the relation uniting Malayo-Polynesian languages from Madagascar to Oceania (Marsden), affiliations of the languages of Indo-China (John Leyden) and the non-Sanskritic character of Dravidian (Ellis).

In the eighteenth and early nineteenth centuries, British ethnological discussions freely exchanged the words 'nation' and 'race', using them in senses that are not yet the ones we are familiar with; the nation was still not charged with political content by the nation-state ideal, as that of which the state is the destined

[19] Prichard, J.C., *Researches into the Physical History of Man*, ed. and with an introductory essay by George W. Stocking, Jr. (Chicago and London: The University of Chicago Press, 1973 [1813]).

end; nor was race then biologized and scientized in quite the way we are familiar with now. What is striking is precisely that language and physical form are presumed to run together, and their association was simply not imagined to be problematic. Max Müller was not really saying something new when he insisted on the blood kinship of the British and the Indians on the evidence of language, he was simply putting it more strikingly and with greater rhetorical skill and daring than others: language proves, he argued, that the same blood flows in the veins of the English soldiers as flows in the veins of the dark Bengalese.[20] This is the Aryan brethren theme at its strongest, pitting the evidence of language against the evidence of complexion.

It provoked a storm of criticism.[21] By mid-century in Britain there was a considerable body of new thinking about what Nancy Stepan[22] had denominated 'race science', and it was impelled by a new sense that race affords the key to history, hitherto hidden. According to this view, it is race that explains why the Irish are unimprovable, why the northern countries of Europe became Protestant, and so forth. This race science pits itself against what it calls 'the tyranny of Sanskrit' as exemplified for its votaries by Max Müller, and refuses the association of blood and language, replacing it with the connection of blood and complexion. The inner, unseen truth of race ('blood') is revealed by its bodily signs, not by language; and at this time, one finds an abundance of statements propounding what

[20] Max Müller, F., *The Languages of the Seat of War in the East, with a Survey of the Three Families of Language, Semitic, Arian, and Turanian*, 2nd ed. (First ed.: *Suggestions for the Assistance of Officers in Learning the Languages of the Seat of War in the East*, 1854) (London: Williams and Norgate, 1855).

[21] Max Müller's critics were, above all, the second generation of ethnologists, Prichard's renegade children, John Crawfurd and R.G. Latham, asserting the logic of complexion against that of language. See Crawfurd, J. 'On the Aryan or Indo-Germanic theory' *Transactions of the Ethnological Society of London*, 1861, n.s., vol. 1: 268–86; 'On the commixture of the races of man as affecting the process of civilization', *Transactions of the Ethnological Society of London*, 1865 n.s., vol. 3: 98–122. See also Latham, R.G., *Descriptive Ethnology*, 2 vols (London: John and Voorst, 1859).

[22] Stepan, N., *The Idea of Race in Science: Great Britain 1800–1960* (London: Macmillan, 1982).

to us is the most obvious commonplace, but then was a newly-discovered and disconcerting truth—that language and race have no necessary connection.

It is instructive to see the logic of the new science unfold in the writing of Issac Taylor,[23] who was reader of the latest authorities from the Continent and who synthesized them for the British reading public. The new primacy of the body as the sign of race affected the Indo-European idea profoundly, for the speakers of its languages are not all of them of the same race by this new standard, as proved, for example, by the fact that blacks in America speak English. That being so, the Aryan idea was detatched from its necessary connection with language and was now available as an expression of the idea of racial whiteness in the narrowest sense. Accordingly, Taylor reports the arguments of those for whom the original Aryans are a small, localized, white population by whom the Indo-European languages were spread to a larger, racially hetergeneous population. The only thing left to argue over was whether the homeland of those original pure white Aryans was to be located by reference to archaeological finds in Scandinavia, Germany, or France; they certainly weren't Indians. Race science had refashioned the Aryan idea into a form readily usable for a racially exclusionary politics of hate. It is part of the irony of this story that the politics to which the Aryan idea gets itself attached comes to be very bad news at different times for various branches of the Indo-European family tree: the Gypsies, the Indians, and the Slavs. Racial whiteness, not language, now governs the new idea of the Aryan.

The Racial Theory of Indian Civilization

Though the new idea of the Aryan made its way in the world by attacking the Sanskritists, that is not to say that the Sanskritists were the good guys against the race science bad guys. Indeed, British Sanskritists were the architects of a new and lasting consensus, that

[23] Taylor, I., *The Origin of the Aryans; An Account of the Prehistoric Ethnology and Civilisation of Europe* (London: Walter Scott, c. 1889).

reconciled the competing evidence of language and of complexion in what I call the racial theory of Indian civilization. This is the theory that Indian civilization was formed by a big bang, caused by the conquest of light-skinned, Aryan, civilized invaders over dark-skinned savage aboriginal Indians, and the formation of the caste system which bound the two in a single society, at once mixed and segregated.

If this theory were true, there ought to be evidence in the earliest Vedic text. Max Müller, engaged as he was in editing the Rgveda for publication, was the first to interrogate the text by means of this theory. Subsequently, the proof texts were published *in extenso* by John Muir,[24] in an important collection that was intended not only to solidify the new view of Indian history in the West but to propagate it among Indians as well. By the time of the *Vedic Index* (1912), in which A.A. Macdonell and A.B. Keith summarized the results of a century of Orientalist research on the Veda, it was firmly established.

When we follow the building of the racial reading of the Ṛgveda stick by stick, we see several instances in which the will to find a foundation for the racial theory goes beyond its means. Let me mention the leading points:

1. Max Müller, in his earliest pronouncement on the matter, finds 'no allusion to any distinct physical features' of the aborigines in the Vedic hymns, but he offers tentatively the evidence of noses: the Aryan gods have beautiful noses (*suśipra*), the Dāsas are called *vṛṣaśipra*, perhaps goat or bull-nosed.[25] But later he finds the *śipra* has to do with the jaw (or cheek) and not the nose,[26] and we hear no more of this foundation of the racial interpretation of Indian civilization.

[24] Muir, J., *Original Sanskrit Texts on the Origin and History of the People of India, Their Religions and Institutions.* 5 vols (London: Trubner & Co., 1874–84).

[25] Max Müller, F., 'The last results of the researches respecting the non-Iranian and non-Semitic languages of Asia and Europe, or the Turanian family of languages', in *Bunsen* 1854, vol. 1, pp. 263–472.

[26] Ṛgveda, *Vedic Hymns*, tr. F. Max Müller. Part I. Sacred Books of the East, vol. 32 (Reprint Delhi: Motilal Banarsidass, 1891 [1964]).

2. We hear a lot, however, of the other item Max Müller introduced, tentatively, in the same text: a single passage (ṚV 5.29.10) in which the enemies are called *anās*, which Max Müller interprets to mean *a* + *nās*, 'noseless', that is, flat-nosed in comparison to the Aryans (Max Müller, 1854, op. cit.).[27] H.H. Wilson ably points out that in the meaning Sāyaṇa gives the word, *an* + *ās*, mouthless or faceless, the mouth or face stands by metonymy for *śabda*, speech. The Dasyus are 'without speech', coordinate with *mṛdhravāc*, which Sāyaṇa has glossed as *hiṃsitavāgiṃdriyān*, 'having defective organs of speech'.[28] Thus, the traditional explanation is cogent and consistent with the great emphasis upon difference of language (as well as religion) as the marker of the Dāsa or Dasyu; whereas the 'noseless' interpretation makes this a unique passage without other support. Nevertheless the interpretation stuck; and although there is only one such passage, H.H. Risley, the anthropometrist proponent of noses as ethnic markers, multiplies it: 'No one can have glanced at the literature of the subject and in particular at the Vedic accounts of the Aryan advance, without being stuck by the frequent references to the noses of the people whom the Aryans found in possession of the plains of India. So impressed were the Aryans with the shortcomings of their enemies' noses that they *often* spoke of them as 'the noseless ones', and their keen perception of the importance of this feature seems almost to anticipate the opinion of Dr Collignon that the nasal index ranks higher as a distinctive character than the stature or even than the cephalic index itself'[29] (emphasis added). The interpretation of Max Müller was clearly strengthened by the current trend in anthropometry to go for the nose.

[27] Max Müller, 1854, *op. cit.*

[28] Ṛgveda, *Rig-Veda-Sanhita: A Collection of Ancient Hindu Hymns.* 4 vols, tr. H.H. Wilson (London: H. Allen and Co. 1854–57).

[29] Risley, H.H., 'The study of ethnology in India', *Journal of the Antrhopological Institute of Great Britain and Ireland*, 20, 253–63, 1891.

3. Thus the first attempt to find physical markers of ethnic differences separating Arya from an-Arya in the Ṛgveda comes down to a single passage of arguable meaning. It was only later that two passages speaking of hostile persons of black skin (*kṛṣṇa tvac*: ṚV 1.130.8 and 6.40.1) enter the discourse (Macdonell and Keith,[30] s.v. Dāsa). Here, as elsewhere in the Ṛgveda, it is unmistakable that the verses in question are describing enemies of the Aryans and of their gods in the most unflattering terms, but we cannot always tell whether the persons being described are human or supernatural. Sāyaṇa takes the first of the passages to refer to a legend according to which a demon (*asura*) named Kṛṣṇa (The Black), having advanced with followers to the banks of the Aṃśumatī river where he caused great devastation, was defeated and stripped of his skin by Indra, who had been sent with his Maruts by Bṛhaspati. Thus, accepting that the Dasyus/Dāsas are human enemies of the Aryans—which seems probable—some uncertainty attaches to the substance of the racial interpretation. Beyond that, even if the racial interpretation is right on this point substantively, it is wrong adjectivally, since the two passages on skin colour are very few on which to base a theory of a systematic colour prejudice, and are far outweighed by references to the shortcomings of the Dasyus/Dāsas in respect of religion and language.
4. Much is made of the fact that the four varṇas, that is, the central institution of caste which under the racial theory of Indian civilization configures the intermixture and segregation of the foundational ethnic groups, employs a Sanskrit word having the ordinary meaning of 'colour'; and furthermore that the Vedic texts speak of an Ārya-varṇa in contrast to the Dāsa-varṇa (discussed at Max Müller, 1854, op. cit.,[31] but without mention of skin colour; but see

[30] Macdonell, A.A. and A.B. Keith, *Vedic Index of Names and Subjects*, 2 vols (London: John Murray, 1912).

[31] Max Müller, 1854, *op. cit.*

> Macdonell and Keith,1912, op. cit.,[32] s.v. varṇa). This second point is crucial, for the doctrine of the *four* varṇas makes no mention of skin colour as such, and it would go against the theory in question if it were taken to refer to a racial difference between all four. But the argument is of no effect by itself and without the crucial reference to physical features. On the evidence of use, it appears that varṇa here simply means, 'category, social group'.

Taking the evidence together, if we wish to cast the Dāsas or Dasyus in the role of the dark-skinned savages, we have very little help from the Vedic text as to physical features, while on every hand, the authorities agree that religion and language are mentioned again and again. What about the other side of the binary? What about the savagery of the Dāsa or Dasyu? Here, if anything, the evidence of the Ṛgveda is directly unhelpful, depicting the Dāsa or Dasyu chief Śambara, for example, as possessed of ninety, ninety-nine, or 100 forts, which Indra destroys to aid the Aryans, who are evidently weaker and poorer than their enemies. This gets minimized by Macdonell and Keith, 1912, op. cit.,[33] who suggest, 'Śambara was quite possibly an aboriginal enemy in India, living in the mountains'. They assimilate him to the old idea of pre-Aryan mountain-dwellers. This downplays Śambara's power where the text plainly means to magnify it.

In conducting this analysis—of which I can only give a brief indication here—I have argued that if one adopts a moderate degree of scepticism to the rereading of the evidence for the racial interpretation, one discovers that it rests on very little, and that a considerable amount of evident over-reading is necessary to reach the desired result.

[32] Macdonell and Keith, 1912, *op. cit.*

[33] Macdonell and Keith, 1912, *op. cit.*

Discussion

But is not the minimizing interpretation guilty of the opposite fault, of under-reading the evidence for colour prejudice in the Ṛgveda? Evidence that Indians of all periods took a great interest in complexion is abundant, as one can read in Madhav Deshpande's *Sanskrit and Prakrit: Sociolinguistic Issues*, in which for example he cites a passage from Pantañjali's *Mahābhāṣya* to the effect that a Brahmin is *gaura*, 'fair' and that no dark person can normally be identified as a Brahmin.[34] Deshpande opens a window on the complexion geography of India in Rājaśekhara's *Kāvya-mīmāṃsā*, according to which the people of northern India are *gaura*, 'fair', those of eastern India are *śyāma*, 'dusky', of the south are *kṛṣṇa*, 'dark', and of the west are *paṇḍu*, 'pale, yellowish-white', while the Middle Country is a mixture of *gaura*, *śyāma*, and *kṛṣṇa*. Indian preference for a bride of fair complexion is attested in texts as ancient as *Vāsiṣṭha Dharma Sūtra* 18.18 and as recent as the matrimonial advertisements in the Sunday newspaper. How can one argue against the racial theory in the face of such facts?

It is important to be clear what is at issue, and not be distracted by facts of this order. Complexion is not race, but at most it is a supposed sign of race, and to collapse the two so that race—which has to do with the conception of a fixed, inner essence that is unseeable and known only through external signs—is to confuse the sign with the signifier. Such narrowing of the discussion will miss the main point, which is that the racial theory is a double binary of skin colour *and* civilization; so that even if a difference of complexion between Aryan and Dāsa/Dasyu existed (it may have) and even if we take it to have been socially salient (which is at best very weakly attested by the ṚV), archaeology has shown that the inhabitants of India at the time at which the Sanskrit language makes its appearance were already greatly advanced, in many respects more so than the people of the Veda.

[34] Deshpande, M.M., *Sanskrit and Prakrit: Sociolinguistic Issues* (Delhi: Motilal Banarsidass, 1993).

The second half of the nineteenth century when the racial theory of Indian civilization took shape was a period in which there was an unprecedented juxtaposition of peoples brought about by the European conquest, settlement, and empire. Because of this, new rules had to be devised for the relations among peoples that would produce the desired cocktail of (largely economic) mixture and (especially sexual) segregation, new rules justified by reference to racial attitudes which were attributed to a fixed and immutable human nature. It is not surprising that the British Sanskritists were affected by the prevailing racial thinking of the high Victorian period, or that they explained the system of castes by analogy to the Jim Crow system of the American South after the Civil War or the racial apartheid of South Africa, and derived all of them from inborn, permanent attitudes of whites toward blacks. From these beginnings, a large literature on the relation of caste and race has grown up, asking whether, as systems of mixture and segregation, they are the same.

What has changed since then is that race, like caste, has come to be viewed as socially constructed and historically contingent. The problem with the racial theory of Indian civilization is that it is stuck in the racial essentialism of its first formulation, founded on attitudes believed to be inborn and unchanged by history. Indian civilization as we know it is certainly a product of conjuncture: the conjuncture of the people of the Indus Civilization and the Sanskrit-speakers; of Indo-Aryan, Dravidian, and Munda; but not of the logic, supposed immutable, of white and black races. That the racial theory of the Indian civilization has survived so long and so well is a miracle of faith. It is high time to get rid of it.

8

Some Appropriations of the Theory of Aryan Race Relating to the Beginnings of Indian History

Romila Thapar

Romila Thapar carries the story forward, by considering ways in which, within India, the Aryan/Dravidian linguistic difference was interpreted under the shaping influences of colonialism and nationalism. The article concerns two main opposing interpretations, the Dalit one pioneered by Jyotiba Phule, and the Hindutva one pioneered by Veer Savarkar. The Dalit interpretation, with its anti-Brahmin tendency, embraces the Aryan invasion theory in its highly racialized form, positing a two-race theory of Indian history, a pre-Aryan golden age—subsequently identified with the Indus Civilization—followed by Aryan invasion of India and oppression of its indigenous inhabitants. The Hindutva interpretation follows a strong imperative to stress the racial unity of the Indian people prior to the coming of Islam and the solidarity of Brahmins and non-Brahmins within Hinduism as well as the difference of Hindus from Muslims and Christians. It tends to reject an Aryan homeland outside of India, and to identify Vedic civilization with the Indus Civilization. This is achieved at the cost of ignoring much of the linguistic evidence, implicitly or explicitly, including the Aryan/Dravidian language distinction.

[From *Invoking the Past: The Uses of History in South Asia*, ed. Daud Ali (New Delhi: Oxford University Press, 1999), pp. 15–35.]

The theory of Aryan race, which seeks to explain the beginnings of Indian history, has been used in a variety of ways not only to structure knowledge about the past, but perhaps more directly to give legitimacy to the conflicts of the present. The theory has a genesis in colonial attempts to 'discover' the Indian past, a discovery which was rooted in the colonial present. Indian concerns with trying to define an identity had to do with the colonial-nationalist relationship, as well as the relationship among Indians insisting on particular definitions. But the latter are also facets of the former since they would not have taken the form which they did outside of a colonial context. The two dichotomous interpretations discussed here—that of Phule and the Dalits and that of the propagators of Hindutva—are bot in dialogue with the colonial interpretations and with mainstream nationalism. The theory of Aryan race was not limited to historical reconstruction and is an example of how historical perceptions of the past can be related to conflictual situations of the present. Interpretations of the past have a bearing on how the conflict is conducted and the conflict in turn fashions the shape of what is viewed as the historical past.

Purāṇic chronology and list of descent groups were the initial source material for the reconstruction of Indian history in the work of the early Orientalists. But the narrative changed with access to the Vedic corpus although the change was not immediate. William Jones' discussion of Sanskrit as a cognate of Greek and Latin led to his concern with the monogenesis of these languages, although his work preceded the adoption of the term 'Aryan'. This idea was further built upon in the studies of comparative philology at various European universities in the nineteenth century, drawing on the Vedic corpus which had recently become available. Increasingly, monogenesis came to be applied to the speakers of these languages as well. These studies contributed to the notion of an Indo-European family of languages, descended from a single ancestral language. This in turn required tracing the homeland of this ancestral language. By the latter half of the nineteenth century, European scholarship was enthused with notions of Aryan origins and the search for the Aryan homeland, a search partly encouraged by German Romanticism and the view that India could be the cradle of the human race.

Further studies in comparative philology coincided with the theories of the Comte de Gobineau for Aryan identities in Europe and warning against interbreeding. The classification of race, borrowed from biological studies, became influential as did the idea of the evolution of the survival of the fittest as applied to human societies. The demonstrable impact of European colonialism also acted as a factor in changing the European view of itself and its origins. European origins were thus liberated from being tied down to Biblical history, and the latter was substituted with the theory of Aryan race. What has been described as race-science was viewed as an accurate identification of human groups.[1] With the increasing success of imperialism and the view that Europe was the most advanced among the nations, it was inevitable that the original Aryan would be relocated. By the end of the nineteenth century it was held that the Asian Aryans had their homeland in Central Asia but that the European Aryan originated from the Nordic blondes of northern Europe.[2]

The theory of Aryan race came to be viewed as foundational to Indian history largely through what has been called the twinning of the theories of British Sanskritists and ethnographers,[3] and the influential role of Max Müller. The texts which initially encouraged the idea were those constituting the Vedic corpus and in particular the Ṛgveda. Viewed as the most ancient literature and the key to Sanskrit and to Hindu civilization, its references to the *ārya*s (Aryans) and to their hostility to the *dāsa*s were eagerly fitted into the theory that a clan of Aryans migrated from Central Asia, invaded northern India enslaving the indigenous people, the dāsas, and settled in India. The reference to varṇa/colour in the earliest text was easily read as skin pigmentation and seen as a graphic description of the fair-skinned Aryans conquering the dark-skinned aborigines.

[1] Stepan, N., *The Idea of Race in Science: Great Britain 1800–1960* (London, 1982).

[2] Taylor, I., *The Origin of the Aryans* (2nd ed.) (London, 1892).

[3] Trautmann, T., *Aryans and British India* (New Delhi, 1997).

The equation of language and race was instrumental in the formulating of the theory. Conquest introduced both the language Indo-Aryan and what has come to be called the distinctive Aryan civilization. This was the opening narrative of Indian history. Racial separateness required a demarcation and the conquest became the mechanism by which caste came to be viewed as a form of racial segregation and central to Indian social institutions. Having given rise to the Aryan race, deriving from the Indo-Aryan language, the parallel to this theory was soon established in the notion of the Dravidian race based on the Dravidian languages, formulated in the early grammars of Dravidian languages,[4] and in the idea that Dravidian speakers are racially native to India. In later years, Max Müller stated that language and race were distinct categories but by then the equation had become an axiom and he himself frequently confused the two.

The equation has not only affected the understanding of the earliest past, in that the theory of Aryan race and the Aryan conquest of northern India became foundational to the beginnings of Indian history, but it has also been crucial to the conflicting views over Indian identity sought to be established in more recent times. A range of social and political groups in India over the last century and a half have interpreted the theory variously in order to support their own political and social aspirations. Aryanism as a fact of the historical past is not contested, but what creates divergent views is the question of whether it was alien or indigenous.

The debate over how it was to be interpreted provides an insight into the political agendas of the groups who used it. These groups were involved in seeking identities from the past and in countering each other's claims to these identities as well as choosing a homeland and working out a national culture. The interpretation therefore hinged on specific ideological needs. Modifications in the interpretations suggest changes in the status and role of the groups identifying with it. The primary concern in establishing an Indian identity was the need to define the rightful inheritors of the land, all within the context of a gradually growing nationalism where the

[4] Caldwell, R., *A Comparative Grammar of the Dravidian or South Indian Family of Languages* (London, 1856).

question of origins and affirmation of common descent were central to nation-building. Such a concern required legitimation from history, therefore the theory was of prime importance to the beginnings of Indian history. To this extent, the theory played the same role in India as it did in Europe, servicing various European nationalisms. But in India it was extended to discussions on a wider range such as the origins of caste and the constituents of culture. The revival of interest in the theory is linked to the political assertions of caste identities as well. My attempt here is to focus on two important but contradictory views of the theory, both of which have resurfaced in post-colonial political developments in India.

The application of the theory of Vedic India was picked up in Christian missionary circles in India through the writings particularly of John Muir and J. Wilson. They maintained that the lower castes were the indigenous inhabitants who had been conquered and oppressed by Brahmins who represented the Aryan conquest. This provided one perspective for what was eventually to be labelled the Dalit view of the theory as expounded initially by Jyotiba Phule. Writing in the latter half of the nineteenth century, Phule argued that the original inhabitants of India were the *ādivāsi*s, among whom he includes the Sudras, the ati-Sudras and the untouchables, who were descendants of the heroic peoples led by the *daitya* king, Bali. Various such categories were included under the generic label of *kṣatriya*. The indigenous peoples under the leadership of Bali, fought the arrival of the Brahmins who for Phule represented the Aryan invasion, but the ādivāsis were conquered and subordinated. Phule's 'golden age' was the period prior to the Aryan invasion when Sudras were cultivators, landowners, and warriors, and had their own culture. The Brahmins are said to have deliberately invented caste so that the Sudras would be kept permanently servile and divided among themselves. The Brahmin–Sudra dichotomy reflected the demarcation as it existed in nineteenth-century Maharashtra where Brahmins were projected as ex-Peshwas and non-Brahmins such as Marathas and Kunbis as the less powerful, but nevertheless aspiring to power in the new colonial administration.[5]

[5] O'Hanlon, R., *Caste Conflict and Ideology* (Cambridge, 1995); Omvedt, G., *Jyotiba Phule: An Incomplete Renaissance* (Surat, 1991).

Phule drew on well-known myths to emphasize his point. Thus Bali was deprived of his territory by the deceit of Viṣṇu when he took the three steps as agreed upon but so expanded himself as to cover earth and heaven in the three. The loss of territory is also a loss of status. Repeated reference is made to the Brahmin Paraśurāma who annihilated the kṣatriyas twenty-one times. These legends are not found in the *Veda*s but in the *Mahābhārata* and the *Purāṇa*s.[6] Nevertheless Phule treats them as early history. The stories of the ten avatāras were also woven in. The earliest Aryans came by sea in ships which were referred to as *matsya* and *kurma*; the later Aryans came by land and were associated with the *varāha*, *narasiṃha*, and *vāmana* avatāras conquering and killing the kṣatriyas.

Phule was not merely concerned with the indigenous origins of the lower castes but was also a 'social reformer' working towards educating Sudras and women with the intention of providing them with a sense of relative independence. The founding of the Satyashodhak Samaj was intended to encourage an awareness among the lower castes of their rights. In the colonial-nationalist divide, his views were not entirely supportive of either. British administration was seen as less severe than the previous Peshwa regime which had oppressed the tax-paying lower castes and supported the upper-caste moneylender.

In this version, the Aryan invasion was a necessary event and has now become an essential part of the Dalit version of Indian history. It was to influence a variety of non-Brahmin movements particularly in different parts of the peninsula, but more generally elsewhere as well. The dichotomy between Brahmin and non-Brahmin was seen to provide a rational explanation for the pattern of history and the suppression of the non-Brahmin by the Brahmin. This dichotomy was easily slotted into the linguistic division of the Aryan and Dravidian languages where the Brahmins were seen as Sanskrit-educated Aryans and the other castes using Dravidian languages were the non-Aryans. The input of language demarcation was perhaps one reason for the non-Brahmin movement being more influential in peninsular India than elsewhere. The self-perception

[6] Mahābhārata, *Adi-parvan*, 98.1 ff.; *Bhāgavatapurāṇa*, 9.15.13.ff.

of Dravidian speakers was tied to the anti-Brahmin movement symbolizing the rejection of Aryan dominance. The political importance of this interpretation lay in the idea that true nationalism required giving power to the original inhabitants of the land. Phule used the theory to oppose Brahmin domination, arguing that they were alien Aryans and therefore not the rightful inheritors of the land, the latter being the lower castes. Phule radicalized the theory in order to use it in his campaign against Brahmin domination.

Interestingly, the confrontation from the Brahmanical side arose from, among others, the views of a group of Brahmins, some Chitpavan and some others, based in Maharashtra. The Chitpavan Brahmins had been privileged as Peshwas but were no longer so, leading to both discontent ad attempts to negotiate concessions from the colonial administration. These groups did not debate the issue of caste status with the followers of Phule but preferred to work out their own interpretation of the Aryan theory, contradicting that of Phule. This became central to the notion of Hindutva.

A move in this direction can be seen earlier in the writings of the Theosophists and particularly those of Colonel Olcott in the late nineteenth century.[7] Olcott maintained that *āryavarta* was the cradle of civilization and the Aryans were a race indigenous to northern India, their literature being the source of all philosophy and religion. Many Theosophists felt that Hinduism came closest to being a universal religion, which was much sought after at the time, and that Hindu practice and the Aryan heritage should be conserved even though it meant retaining caste hierarchies. Above all, the Aryan was identified with the Hindu. The views of Olcott and Annie Besant in particular in this regard, were eagerly endorsed by many Hindus who believed in their veracity as coming from British sympathizers with what was now regarded as a Hindu 'renaissance'. They could well have infiuenced Hindutva thinking.

The Hindutva version, formulated in the 1920s, glossed over the question of an invasion, and referred to the Aryans as having settled in northern India, emphasizing their racial distinctiveness and their

[7] Leopold J., 'The Aryan theory of race in India 1870–1920, nationalist and internationalist visions', *Indian Economic and Social History Review*, 7, 2, (1970).

role as the progenitors of the Hindus. This facilitated the endorsing of the indigenous origins of the Aryans, which followed closely as a theory as did the insistence that Indo-Aryan equated with Sanskrit was an indigenous language and ancestral to the other Indo-European languages. Living in the Sindhu/Indus plain welded the Aryans into a nation and gave them the name of Hindu, derived from Sindhu. There was an insistence on a homeland within the Indias subcontinent. Since India was the homeland of the Aryans, Aryan civilization travelled from India to the West. All Hindus are members of the Aryan race, and therefore are not aliens. Hindus are united by the bonds of common blood, the blood of the mighty race, incorporated with and descended from the Vedic forefathers.[8] The race-spirit of the Hindus did not die out and enabled the Hindus to defend themselves against 'the murdering hordes of mussalman freebooters'.[9] Equally clear is the listing of common cultural characteristics. The constituents of a nation are hereditarily occupied territory, race, religion, and culture, which create the race-spirit, and language.[10] Those who do not belong to the Hindu nation cannot live in India except as foreigners unless they agree to be 'naturalized', namely discard their religion, culture, and language.

This view is clear about what constitutes the Indian/Hindu identity. Savarkar maintained that an Indian/Hindu is one for whom India is *pitṛ bhūmi* and his *puṇya bhūmi*, the land of his ancestors and the land of his religion. This definition of the Indian/Hindu and the Hindu Aryan effectively cut out the Muslims and the Christians which was intentional according to the text, and to this was also added the Communists! There is therefore a confusion of categories—race, religion, and ideology. The link between these views and the beginnings of Indian history is that they have become influential in popular versions of early history, and the demands of political ideology led to attempts by the first Bharatiya Janata Party government in Uttar Pradesh to give the Hindutva interpretation in school textbooks.

[8] Savarkar, V.D., *Hindutva: Who is a Hindu?*, p. 68, (Poona, 1969)

[9] M.S. Golwalkar, *We or Our Nationhood Defined*, p. 10, (Bombay, 1938).

[10] Ibid., p. 18 ff.; p. 28 ff.

The concept of the Hindu Aryan created problems in relation to what were by then called scheduled castes. The debate among caste Hindus was whether the scheduled castes constituted Hindu Aryans or not. The more orthodox supporters of Hindutva were for excluding them, but when the game of numbers was seen as supporting the argument about majoritarianism in democratic institutions, there was a move to incorporate the scheduled castes as Hindus and thus swell the numbers of the Hindus. Reference was made by some to the common blood of all Hindus from the Brahmin to the Caṇḍāla.[11] But the issue remained somewhat confused in the Hindutva version because Golwalkar returns to the concept of the race-spirit inspired by Nazi Germany,[12] although his actual intention was the separating of Hindus and Muslims. Common blood and the purity of race allowed for a separate Hindu identity. But if the Aryans incorporated the non-Aryans then it could be argued that this had interfered with racial purity.

The theory had to be changed from that of Phule in order to claim the antiquity and continuity of the Hindu *Rāṣṭra* (territory) and to provide a different identity to the Hindu, distinct from Indians following other religions. Phule saw the theory of Aryan race as an attempt by the upper castes to consolidate power and hierarchy through insisting on inequality in relation to supposed origins. For him, the Aryan was 'the Other'. In the Hindutva version it is not the Aryan who is 'the Other', but the non-Hindu. This is a significant shift. But neither of these two versions was initially hegemonic.

There was a mainstream version which, deriving from Müller, was acceptable to upper-caste middle-class Hindus. Müller was seen as sympathetic to Indian civilization, which for him was essentially Hindu. This is the version with which we are all familiar from histories of India: Aryans, speaking Indo-Aryan or Vedic Sanskrit, entered north-western India, conquered the indigenous, largely primitive population, racially distinct from the Aryan, and established Aryanism as the civilizing current of Indian history. The endorsing of the theory took some rather emphatic forms. Müller and Muir had maintained

[11] Savarkar, *Hindutva*, p. 89.

[12] Ibid., pp. 39–40.

that upper-caste Hindus were the biological, lineal descendants of the Aryans. The claim to kinship ties with the British based on the Aryan connection became an attempt at self-promotion by upper-caste Hindus.[13]

Colonial historians found the theory attractive because it provided a parallel to the British conquest of India and the introduction of Western civilization through this process. This view was partially responsible for the rejection of the Aryans being other than indigenous in some extreme nationalist opinion. The colonial view would endorse the idea that the progress of India was dependent on the return of the Aryan in the guise of the British. The explanation of caste as racial segregation made it more comprehensible and easier to manage than the more complex theories of kinship, occupation, and rules of purity and pollution. Indian history was also brought into the current European discourse on race.

Some nationalist opinion had a different reading. Dayanand Sarasavati propagated a return to the Vedas, the source of Indian civilization, and Sanskrit, the mother tongue of all languages, thus emphasizing the status of the Brahmins. The purity of Sanskrit was insisted upon and contributed to a suspicion of modern linguistics since it did not endorse this purity. B.G. Tilak visualized a long march from the Arctic lands which he placed at the time of the receding Ice Ages. Tilak had little time for the views of Phule. For him, the coming of the Aryans was a positive development in Indian history. He took the date of the Ṛgveda back to 4500 BC largely on the basis of what he computed and presented as evidence from the position of the constellations. He placed the homeland in the Arctic and posited two groups of Aryans who migrated away from the homeland: the European Aryans who had settled in northern Europe but had soon relapsed into barbarism and those who finally arrived in India and came to be seen as the Indian Aryans who retained their cultural superiority, and conquered the non-Aryans. Indian civilization continued as a timeless civilization going back to the original Aryans. Tilak's views created some problem for the supporters of the Hindutva theory since he was arguing for an Arctic homeland and

[13] Sen, K.C., *Keshab Chander Sen's Lectures in India*, p. 323, (Calcutta, 1892).

the Aryans as alien conquerors. This was too great a parallel to what the Hindutva ideology was battling against—the Muslims as alien conquerors pouring in from the north-west. The only way around it was a reformulation stating that the Aryans did inhabit the area of the north pole but in those early days, the north pole was located in present-day Bihar and Orissa.[14]

In these cases, the theory was closely tied to nationalism and was used to strengthen the status of the upper castes from which there came the new middle class professionals. There is now an inching towards a class utilization of the theory to explain the superiority of those belonging to the emergent middle class. The caste/class agenda of these readings seems to be so essential that there is little or no attempt to even dismiss Phule's reading. Implicit in much of the wider discussion was the notion that caste was a form of racial segregation[15] and a scientific way of organizing society.

Whereas Phule is less interested in race and concentrates on caste, in the Hindutva version, racial identity and nationalism are collapsed. There is a swing therefore between concerns of caste to the purity of blood, the two not being identical. The concept of race was alien, hence the translation of the word as jāti. The choice was probably determined by the circular argument that caste was racial segregation. To assume that this was a correct translation because jāti can be seen as 'species', is problematic. Although the word jāti is linked to birth, the identification of jātis is also drawn from a variety of social and religious activities and these continually change the boundaries of jāti identity. The recognition of interbreeding among jātis would also militate against its being defined as race, as does the fact that jātis are constantly incorporating and creating new jātis. Caste had been frequently contested in history but with other markers such as language, occupation, or sect, and had been continually redefined. But when race was introduced into this contestation, it was projected as the most 'scientific' of the markers.

The history of social change within a caste-based society was given little attention by earlier historians, many of whom were content

[14] Golwalkar, *Our Nationhood*, p. 8.

[15] Risley, H., *The People of India* (London, 1908).

to argue that caste was frozen and unchanging social form. With language and caste both being identified as racial identities, cultural history was frequently explained in terms of the spread of the Aryan race and its culture, monitored by the presence of Brahmanical belief and practice. A gradual departure from this general assessment of the impact of the Aryans was the realization by historians, sociologists, and anthropologists and some studying Indian religion, that there was more than upper-caste Aryanism in the making of Indian history and civilization.[16] This was also an attempt to broaden the base of nationalist inclusive history.

The varied interpretations of the Aryan theory illustrate its role in the political agendas of various social groups and the nature of the contestation between these groups. It reflects therefore what has been called the organizing capacity of intellectual rationalizations in the form of theories of fictive ethnicity.[17] Appeal to a seemingly scientific explanation of biological heredity is made to coincide with racial categories. It provides nationalist myths of selective linear history in which the genetic descent of a 'nation' is sought to be traced and authority comes naturally to those of the upper castes or of the dominant religion; or alternatively a demand is made for the restitution of the rights of those who see themselves as having been denied their claims to being the inheritors of the land. Racism presupposes a fear of bastardization and underlines separateness. It is at the same time intelligible to large numbers and touches on commonly felt insecurities. It has also endorsed sub-nationalist identity myths, again based on the equation of language with race.

For a few decades, the theory received less attention, perhaps because the earlier linear historical narrative had been shaken up by the newly discovered archaeological evidence of the Indus Civilization and this evidence had to be incorporated into the theory, and accommodated to the evidence of the Vedic corpus, creating a new problem since the two sources were not compatible. Indo-European language studies more generally were also having to

[16] Karve, I., *Kinship Organisation in India* (Bombay, 1961); Ghurye, G.S., *Vedic India* (Delhi, 1979); Bose, N.K., 'Caste in India', *Man in India*, 31, 3–4, (1951), pp. 107–203.

[17] Balibar E., and I. Wallerstein, *Race, Nation, Class* (London, 1991).

consider archaeological evidence in the reconstruction of societies said to be using Indo-European languages. The discovery of the Indus Civilization raised pertinent questions regarding the Aryan beginnings of Indian history. There was of course the inevitable search for the Aryans in archaeological evidence and for a while every new archaeological culture dating to a period between 3000 and 1000 BC tended to be labelled as 'Aryan'. In a sense, the fashion had been set by Gordon Childe, but without his caveats it became a wild goose chase. Cautioning against equating archaeological cultures with languages in the absence of a deciphered script, was generally dismissed.

The foremost of the obstacles posed by the archaeological data was the existence of the urban, Harappan civilization which was prior to the Vedic sources and very different in culture from the Vedic; and, equally important, what appeared to be the absence of evidence of any large scale invasion during this period. Such a change in evidence was problematic for all the accepted theories.

The development of Harappan urban centres in northern and western India observed a similarity of cultural form which is distinctively different from the diversity of pre-Harappan cultures each limited to a particular region.[18] The Harappan cities used these as a base although the process of urbanization seems to have had its genesis in the Indus valley itself in about 2600 BC The Indus Civilization had widespread trading contacts with the Gulf, Mesopotamia, and Elam, apart from sites extending from Badakshan in the Pamirs to Gujarat and northern Maharashtra in the subcontinent.[19] These places, with the possible exception of Afghanistan, were not familiar to the Ṛgveda. The urban commercial culture of the Indus cities is again not reflected in the Vedas where there is little evidence of sophisticated exchange or concern with the organization of resources and production or descriptions of granaries or craft workshops. Nor is there a familiarity with the complex layout of the cities and the

[18] Allchin, F.R., (ed.), *The Archaeology of Early Historic South Asia* (Cambridge, 1995); Chakrabarti, D.K., *The Archaeology of Ancient Indian Cities* (Delhi, 1995).

[19] Ratnagar, S., *Encounters: The Westerly Trade of the Harappan Civilisation* (Delhi, 1981).

structures constructed on brick platforms, or even something as basic as a script. The Harappan was a bronze using culture whereas the Vedic moved to iron technology. The introduction of the horse, the chariot, and the spoked wheel, often associated with the speakers of Indo-European languages cannot be dated in the Indian subcontinent to earlier than the second millennium BC.

Late Harappan cities declined by the mid-second millennium BC, but some of the smaller settlements continued and then petered out or else were mutated through contact with other logically evolved cultures which sometimes provided periods of overlap between the Late Harappan and the subsequent culture, such as that of the Painted Grey Ware in the Punjab. Some continuities, albeit limited, can therefore be posited between the Harappan and post-Harappan cultures. New archaeological cultures emerged at various places by the end of the second millennium as in the Swat valley, Baluchistan, Gujarat, Punjab, Rajasthan, and the Ganges valley, but had their own individual and recognizably different characteristics. There is more than a hint of continuing contacts across the Indo-Iranian borderlands. The question then is whether the new items which surfaced as a result of these contacts can be linked to the presence of Indo-Aryan speakers.

The questioning of the theory of an Aryan invasion arose from the paucity of archaeological evidence suggesting such an invasion. There is occasional evidence of what appears to be the destruction of a site, sometimes by burning, as at Kot Diji. Skirmishes and local conflicts can be expected. But there was no replacement on a large scale of local cultures by an intruding culture or the destruction of sites systematically over a sizeable area.

The questioning of the theory of Aryan invasion has been received differently by the supporters of the Dalit and the Hindutva versions of the beginnings of Indian history. The invasion hypothesis was foundational to the Dalit version, therefore there continues to be an insistence on a large-scale Aryan invasion irrespective of the evidence for it. The Indus Civilization is now associated with Phule's pre-Aryan 'golden age' and the archaeology of the cities is used to emphasize the superiority of the earlier culture over the Vedic upper caste culture. The more recent label of Dalit Bahujana has been introduced into the narrative to make it more appropriate to the historical reconstruction, which would endorse the claims of the Dalits and the lower castes to political status. Indra is said to have led the Aryans who exterminated the Adi-Dravidians who were also the Adi-Dalit Bahujanas, then living in the Indus plain.[20] Viṣṇu was especially incarnated to kill Bali, the Dalit Bahujana *cakravarti*, because Bali did not believe in Hindu Brahminism and worked to establish a casteless society.

The Hindutva version claims to have been vindicated if the evidence for an invasion is slight or absent, for now it can be more emphatically argued that the Hindu Aryan and Brahminism were indigenous to India.[21] Such an argument has also pushed back the date of the Aryans, since there is archaeological evidence of societies of an earlier period. Therefore the large amount of archaeological data prior to the generally accepted date of the Vedas are sought to be incorporated into the story by insisting that Harappan culture is the archaeological counterpart to the Ṛgveda, the date of which would go back to the fourth millennium BC. The Vedas therefore remain foundational to the beginnings of Indian history. Archaeological cultures are sought to be explained in terms of Vedic texts and the historicity of the texts is established by equating them with archaeological cultures. Inevitably, it is claimed that the Harappa script has been deciphered and is in fact an early form of Sanskrit. Thus, the Aryans remain distinctive, superior, indigenous, and the progenitors of an Indian/Hindu civilization. The Hindu Aryans can now be easily differentiated from non-Hindu foreigners and have an even longer and stronger lineal descent than before.[22]

[20] Ilaiah, K., *Why I am not a Hindu*, p. 73 ff, (Calcutta, 1996).

[21] Deo, S.B., and S. Kamath (eds), *The Aryan Problem* (Pune, 1993); D. Frawley, *The Myth of the Aryan Invasion of India* (New Delhi, 1994).

[22] It is perhaps not surprising that this view is also endorsed by some Indian scientists working in the US or retired from the US, who maintain that their explanation of the Aryan problem is value-free because they are scientists familiar with the scientific method and are using computers! That they are virtually unfamiliar with archaeology, linguistics, and history does not seem to prevent them from making wish-fulfilling statements about the Aryans, see Rajaram, N.S., *The Politics of History: Aryan Invasion Theory and the Subversion of Scholarship* (New Delhi, 1995). In a strange confusion of intention, they describe

Archaeologists supporting this view maintain that the Indus Civilization should be renamed the Indus-Sarasavatī civilization on the basis of a large number of pre-Harappan sites clustered on what was in the third millennium BC the Hakra river, identified with the later Sarasavatī river, and the importance of this connection is enhanced by the prominence of the river in the Ṛgveda.[23] The argument derives from a mechanical counting of sites irrespective of their size or significance along the now dry river-bed of the Sarasavatī, and from the location in the same area of a large Harappan mound of an urban centre as yet unexcavated. This can be seen as an attempt to capture the Indus Civilization for Hindu India. It also reflects the priority given to territory as the basis of the Hindu Aryan identity, as the home of the Aryans is said to be located in the subcontinent but to the north-west. The original homeland—Sindhusthan, or the Indus plain—being now in Pakistan, is an irritant to this view and encourages an insistence on a Hindu Indian identity for the foundational civilization.

Not surprisingly, these various Hindutva versions either deny the validity of the linguistic analyses or else ignore them. Linguistic analyses of Vedic Sanskrit, establishing it as part of the wider Indo-European family with cognates in Old Iranian, grew out of studies in comparative philology. Subsequent to this, Grierson's *Linguistic Survey of India*, dominated the study of Indian languages. The history of language in India tended to be seen largely in terms of the spread of Indo-Aryan. More recently, non-Aryan components in Indo-Aryan

themselves as 'Indo-Americans', to demarcate themselves from the scholars who have accepted the theory of Indo-European languages. Clearly the problem here is not the reconstruction of the beginnings of Indian history but the assertion of a Hindu/Indian identity in the US, where the Hindu/Indian professional middle class has the monetary wherewithal but lacks an adequate social and political recognition. Once again, the Hindu Arya claims to be the descendant of the oldest and purest civilization, a sufficiently telling gesture in the recently nascent society of the US.

23 Gupta, S.P., 'Longer chronology of the Indus Sarasvati Civilisation', *Puratattva,* 23, (1992–93), pp. 21–9; Misra, V.N., 'Indus Civilisation and the Ṛgvedic Sarasvatī, in A. Parpola *et al.* (eds), *South Asian Archaeology 1993*, pt. II, pp. 511–26, (Helsinki, 1994).

even as early as the Ṛgveda have been established.[24] The identity of the non-Aryan languages is controversial but non-Aryan elements in Vedic Sanskrit are conceded, and one view describes some elements as linguistic convergence.[25] This research has obvious implications for the claim to the purity of language of the Vedic Aryans. And a mixing of languages also implies a mixing of societies and people, pointing to a different set of historical assumptions from those supporting the exclusiveness and superiority of the Aryans.

Apart from the close links between the language of the *Gāthās* and the older section of the *Avesta* and that of the Ṛgveda, there has also been the discovery of occasional words close to Indo-Aryan in documents from northern Mesopotamia. These are not texts but what seem to be loanwords as they are confined to names and to a few technical terms used in the training of horses. This collection of words has been labelled Proto-Indo-Aryan to distinguish it from Indo-Aryan and although the two are very close they are not identical. These occurrences date to between the seventeenth and the fourteenth centuries with some possible names in texts of the nineteenth century. This is an Indo-European linguistic intrusion, probably brought by horse-riding adventurers who, however, failed to retain their identity, for the language disappears after 1300 BC.[26] A similar phenomenon occurs briefly with the Kassites and their horses in Babylon in about the sixteenth century. This also accords with the fact that there is no evidence of Indo-European in West Asia or Iran prior to the second millennium BC, a fact which has a bearing on the date of the Ṛgveda as well.

The isolated occurrence of Proto-Indo-Aryan with no intervening evidence from places located between northern Mesopotamia and

[24] Kuiper, F.B.J., *Aryans in the Ṛgveda* (Amsterdam, 1991); Emeneau, B.M., 'Indian linguistic area revisited', *International Journal of Dravidian Linguistics*, 3, 1, (1974), p. 93 ff.; Burrow, T., *The Sanskrit Language* (London, 1965); Burrow, T., 'The Proto-Indo-Aryans', *Journal of the Royal Asiatic Society*, vol. 2, (1973), pp. 123–40.

[25] Hock, H.H., 'Subversion or convergence? The issue of Pre-Vedic retroflexion re-examined', *Studies in the Linguistic Sciences*, 23, 2, (1993), pp. 74–109.

[26] Mallory, J.P., *In Search of the Indo-European* (London, 1989).

northern India, remains unexplained. Attempts to circumvent this problem result in having to maintain that Proto-Indo-Aryan is later than Vedic Sanskrit and therefore derived from the latter and has to be seen as pure Sanskrit, and is an example of the spread of Indo-Aryan from an Indian homeland: a view which specialists in linguistics would find unacceptable. Even archaeology does not provide any similarities in the material cultures of northern Mesopotamia in the second millennium BC and those of India, nor for that matter any comparable changes in the northern Mesopotamian cultures at that time. That Vedic Sanskrit preceded Proto-Indo-Aryan would be necessary if the Ṛgveda is dated to 4500 BC rather than 1500 BC which is the date preferred by most Indologists. But since Proto-Indo-Aryan is firmly dated to the mid-second millennium BC, Vedic Sanskrit cannot be much earlier. A more plausible explanation suggests that Proto-Indo-Aryan speakers from northern Iran branched off, with some migrating to northern Mesopotamia and others to Iran and finally to northern India.[27] There may well have been a period of an original Indo-Iranian language, which would explain the closeness in the language of the *Gāthās* and the Ṛgveda subsequent to which the Indo-Aryan speakers migrated to India.

The monitoring of non-Aryan in Vedic Sanskrit provides an interesting pattern. Non-Aryan is present in the Ṛgveda but makes a stronger presence with the shift in geographical location from the Punjab to the Ganges valley, a shift which is evident from the distribution of the dialects of Indo-Aryan in the Vedic corpus[28] and the occasional reference in the Vedas to migrations eastwards. The archaeological picture of the Ganges valley indicates that it was peopled with earlier settlements with whom those coming from the Indo-Gangetic watershed would have had to make adjustments. A case in point is the spread of the Painted Grey Ware culture into the *doāb* where it occupied sites close to those of the earlier Ochre Colour Pottery culture and those of the Black-and-Red Ware cultures.[29] Any

[27] Burrow, 'The Proto-Indo-Aryans', *op. cit.*

[28] Witzel, M., 'Tracing the Vedic dialects', in C. Caillat (ed.), *Dialectes dans les Litteratures Indo-Aryennes,* Paris, 1989, p. 97 ff.

[29] Roy, T.N., *The Ganges Civilisation* (New Delhi, 1983).

single one of these cultures need not be identified with 'the Aryans', but there was an interaction between these cultures which may have been reflected in the languages of the Indo-Aryan speakers as recorded in the later Vedic corpus. Not only was there a borrowing of some vocabulary, as for example words relating to agricultural processes, but also the currency of morphological and phonetic forms and syntax from Proto-Dravidian and Austro-Asiatic. This was a mixing of at least two distinctive language systems, the agglutinative Proto-Dravidian and the inflectional Indo-Aryan. This has reinforced the theory that the speakers of Indo-Aryan migrated into northern India from north-eastern Iran and Afghanistan and settled among non-Aryan speakers, with possibly a long period of bilingualism which accounts for the presence of non-Aryan in Vedic Sanskrit.[30] Differences in Vedic dialects and the emergence of a variety of Prakrits by the middle of the first millennium would also suggest a mingling of the speakers of various languages, quite apart from the changes resulting from the natural evolution of the language.

From the Hindutva perspective, archaeology is now viewed as important to the identity of the Aryans, but not so linguistics. The past is thought to be out there, waiting to be discovered. Archaeology provides tangible data and greater chronological precision than literary sources, but it poses other problems. In stating that the Harappans were Vedic Aryans, the earlier priority given to the Vedic corpus is tied into archaeological data even if it means some distortion of statements from the Ṛgveda or of the interpretations of archaeological artefacts. The evidence from linguistic data supports the early form of Indo-Aryan having migrated from across the borderlands, therefore those favouring the indigenous origins of Indo-Aryan prefer to ignore the linguistic evidence. Denying or under-emphasizing this evidence relates not only to the controversy over whether Indo-Aryan was indigenous but to the far more significant questions of the processes of historical change in the first millennium BC.

The replacing of the terminology of invasion by that of migration raises another set of questions. These would require a change in

[30] Emeneau, B.M., 'Indian linguistic area revisited'.

perspective among mainstream historians as well as among those using the theory as political ideology. Did the Aryans decimate the dāsas and was the differentiation one of skin colour? A detailed analysis of the description of the *dāsa*s and the *dasyu*s in the Ṛgveda indicates that references to dark skin are rare and even at that, are ambiguous. Sāyana's commentary on the Ṛgveda written in the fourteenth century AD explains the terms *tvacam kṛṣṇām* on which the racial theory is largely based, as a reference to the name of an *asura* and there is no mention of skin pigmentation.[31] Similarly the word *anās* is not *a-nās* meaning 'noseless' and therefore broad-nosed, but as *an-ās* meaning without a mouth, that is, not knowing the speech of the authors of the hymns.[32] The negative prefix used for the dāsas was generally in association with rites, deities, speech, and resort to magic, the difference being essentially cultural and linguistic. They were wealthy in cattle and therefore the Aryan speakers raided them for this wealth.

The questioning of the racial presuppositions of the Aryan invasion, requires a reorientation in interpreting the history of these times. If Aryan is a language label and has no racial connotation, then the historian has to explain how the language entered India and came to be established as the language of the elite. Languages come with people but those that speak the same languages need not be racially the same. The spread of a language does not have to be linked to overwhelming numbers of people. The process of language change can be achieved if other factors relating to the historical context encourage it.

Archaeology, in the absence of inscriptions, cannot provide the evidence for linguistic change. But it can provide the evidence for the functioning of various societies, contacts between societies, and a broad delineation of the social and economic system. It can be suggested on the basis of what seems to have been much coming and going across the Indo-Iranian borderlands, judging by the presence of artefacts in different areas, that there may have been small-scale migrations motivated by pastoralism and incipient trade,

[31] Ṛgveda 1.130.8.

[32] Ṛgveda 5.29.10.

both of which were well-established activities from earlier Harappan times. Migrations and the interchange of language in these areas has been a constant feature of its history over the millennia. In the course of such movements, it is possible that pastoral clans with a mobile segment using horses, began to negotiate alliances with the settlements, which had survived the economic collapse of the Harappan system. In a period of predators, protectors would have the advantage. This advantage did not depend solely on conquest or coercive dominance. It would have involved skirmishes and raids of the kind which are referred to in the Ṛgveda as also negotiations and alliances and a slow process of interaction with the existing populations. The latter may have resulted in groups which fissioned off and their culture would be far more mixed and distanced from the original migrants. Such processes take their own time and it is not surprising that the change in geographical location and the linguistic changes from the Ṛgveda to the later Vedic corpus took more than half a millennium and probably longer. The conflicts referred to in the Vedic corpus can better be viewed from a historical perspective as between a variety of social groups—among pastoralists, between pastoralists and peasants, and the territorial claims of chiefships. But even these were not clearly demarcated and there were many overlapping forms.

Language reflects vertical and horizontal relationships between groups. Particular groups come to be associated with particular languages. Historically this requires a study of incorporation and negotiation where oppression and intolerance are identified within the society rather than as racial outsiders. Such an approach would do way with the simplistic explanation of caste being the result of conquest and racial separateness, or, conversely, the denial of oppression through insisting that the population had an unchanging identity. The *āryas* emerge not as a distinctive people, physically different from others and known as 'the Aryans' but as persons of status in many of the societies of that time.[33] Nor were the differentiations between āryas and dāsas—based on perceptions

[33] Burrow, T., 'Iranian *Arya* and *Daha*', in *Transactions of the Philological Society* (1959), p. 71 ff.

of ways of living, economies, custom, ritual, languages—static definitions, for identities kept changing over time and the connotations of these labels also changed. Socio-economic differences reflected in the Ṛgveda and the *Brāhmaṇas* require historical explanation. Both the Dalit and the Hindutva perspectives would have problems with such an approach and in maintaining their original explanations, force the new evidence into earlier theories.

It is paradoxical that the early Indian texts which claim to narrate the Indian past do not situate the beginning in anything which resembles the conquest of the area nor do they refer to the Aryans as being the founders of Indian culture. Thus the *vaṃśānucarita* section of the *Viṣṇu Purāṇa* starts the narrative with the reign of the seven Manus which is followed by a deluge after which the two main descent groups—the *sūryavaṃśa* and the *candravaṃśa*—are established, with lengthy lists of kṣatriya *rājās*. The Mahābhārata war virtually marks the termination of this list and the history of the subsequent period is narrated in the form of dynasties, which continue until the time of the Guptas. As in many traditional perceptions of the past, an unbroken, lineal narrative is sought. But there is no reflection of these various scenarios in the debate on the Aryan theory.

The question of Aryanism and the beginnings of Indian history remains a complex problem because it still carries, at the popular level, the baggage of nineteenth-century European preconceptions, even if in the European context it has now been rejected as a nineteenth-century myth.[34] It has overwhelmed Indian history; but in fact is not so central. It is now less important to a nationalist reconstruction of the past, although the Hindutva version claims to derive from a nationalist cause and accuses those who disagree of being anti-national. Its real function in their hands is political in that it is used to separate the supposedly indigenous Hindu Aryan from the alien, the Muslim and the Christian; or the indigenous lower

[34] Leach, E., 'Aryan invasions over four millennia', in E. Ohunki-Tierney (ed.), *Culture Through Time* (Standford, 1990); Poliakov, L., *The Aryan Myth* (New York, 1947).

castes from the alien upper castes. It is thus a mechanism used by various social groups in contemporary confrontations over identity and rights. The crux of the debate is the crisis of identity and status in the claims to political and social power and a contestation over what is viewed as alternative forms of national culture and ethnic homogeneity.

PART 3

The Veda and the Indus Civilization

The readings in the final section (articles 9–18) address the main questions: Are the Vedic and Indus Civilizations the same or different? Are the Aryans indigenous or did they come into India from without?

The first subgroup consists of four articles on the archaeology of the Indus Civilization and after. The first two articles, by Shereen Ratnagar and B.B. Lal, form a pair of opposing interpretations, carefully stated arguments for what we have called in this volume the standard view and the alternative view, respectively. They are followed by a long extract from an even longer article on the proposed concept of an Indus-Sarasvati Civilization by S.D. Gupta, which lays out the evidence favouring the continuity or identity of the Indus Civilization and the Vedic Aryans. This new name is meant to replace that of the Indus Civilization, and implies a commitment to the alternative view. It is controversial, and it remains to be seen whether it will be widely accepted within the community of scholars. The final selection in this group is from a book by Colin Renfrew, which proposes that the spread of Indo-European languages is linked to the first spread of agriculture. The passage given here examines the implications of that hypothesis for the early history of India.

The second subgroup is a sampling of important articles on the horse and whether horses are attested in the sites of the Indus Civilization, as we should expect if its peoples were Aryans. B.B. Lal provides evidence that horses were known in the Indus Civilization; Asko Parpola, reviewing the evidence, argues the reverse. The remaining three articles of this subgroup are from a series of articles published as a set on the horse question, by Sándor Bökönyi, on bones from the Indus Civilization site of Surkotada, with comments by Richard H. Meadow and Ajita Patel, and an overview of the archaeology of the domestication of horses in Asia by David Anthony. A related question, not addressed in these readings, has to do with the chariot and the spoked wheel, not yet shown to exist in the sites of the Indus Civilization.

Finally, a single article, by Kamil Zvelebil, serves as an overview of the nearly one hundred decipherments of the Indus script that have been proposed so far. This is the central enigma of the Indus Civilization finds, and resolving it would go a long way to settling the Aryan debate. Unfortunately, as the article confirms, none of the decipherments proposed so far has won the approval of the community of scholars.

ARCHAEOLOGY

9

The End of the Harappan Civilization

Shereen Ratnagar

The most contentious aspect of the Aryan debate concerns the relation of the Aryans of the Veda to the inhabitants of the Indus Civilization, and whether they are different or the same. This article and the next illustrate the two broad interpretations of the Indus Civilization in its relation to the Veda and Indian Civilization of later times. Both are by eminent archaeologists, Shereen Ratnagar and B.B. Lal. Both are from books on the Indus Civilization aimed at a general readership, and are therefore works of synthesis and interpretation rather than reports of new research findings. And although the two articles develop sharply different interpretations, each is given with due caution and respect for the limitations of the evidence. In the first article, Ratnagar discusses the end of the Harappan or Indus Civilization, causes of systemic civilizational collapse and the archaeology of successor societies which include the Aryans of the Veda.

[From *Understanding Harappa: Civilization in the Greater Indus Valley* (New Delhi: Tulika, 2001), ch. 10, pp. 139–53.]

We cannot suppose that the authors of the Harappan civilization, meaning its rulers, shamans, craftsmen, shepherds, tillers of the soil, shipbuilders, and seafarers, actually disappeared or became extinct. What disappeared was the coherence of the civilization as an overarching system, with its regional crafts, modes of elite control, and systems of long-distance procurement of materials. The erroneous idea that the population ceased to reproduce is largely due to the nature of the archaeological evidence, namely the large-scale abandonment of Harappan cities, craft towns, garrisons, and villages. Mohenjo-daro was abandoned, and Harappa saw squatters living in abandoned houses or removing bricks from structures to construct crude shelters, and using the cemetery for their own burials. Ganweriwala, Dholavira, and Rakhi Garhi, the other large settlements, were deserted. On the Hakra stretch, of more than eighty habitation sites, only one small village has continued occupation into the next, 'Cemetery H', culture period. The culture is attested at about twenty-eight (new) settlements in the Hakra plains. The total settled area in this region fell to less than half the Harappan settled area. Did the inhabitants switch to pastoralism, or did the villagers migrate upstream to lands with more reliable groundwater resources?

Because of the large-scale desertions, scholars have been led to infer that some kind of holocaust or natural calamity, or a catastrophic event like a supposed Aryan invasion, brought about the end of the Harappan Civilization. This kind of interpretation is somewhat simplistic, but before dismissing it, let us consider the arguments for floods and for climatic change.

Sindh has suffered serious floods throughout history, as we have seen. Fifteen exceptionally destructive floods in the course of one century are not uncommon. But the 'flood theory' argues for exceptional floods, caused by earthquakes. This region is prone to earthquakes and in 1818, for example, there was a major upthrust of the ground at Sehwan downstream of Mohenjo-daro and upstream of Amri and Chanhu-daro. This pushed the Indus river water back and a gigantic lake was created for about two years. It is this kind of phenomenon that is envisaged as being responsible for the end of Mohenjo-daro, although it is also known that rural life resumed its rhythm a few years after 1818. Another problem with this theory is the absence of definitive evidence for third-millennium floods. What some archaeologists took to be deposits laid by still water on the southern edge of Mohenjo-daro, is now believed to be the remains of mud platforms. (The two are not always easy to differentiate.)

We have seen earlier that the evidence for climatic change comes mainly from pollen in the Rajasthan lake deposits. This evidence prompted an inference that there was more winter rainfall in Harappan times than later, and that the summer rainfall was appreciably higher. But when did the rainfall begin to decrease? We cannot assert that desiccation—if any—began in precisely the last decades or centuries of the Harappan period. Climatic changes are not dated with calendrical precision. Indeed, it was initially stated that around 1800 BC, which is the approximate terminal date of the civilization, rainfall was exceptionally good. Many also doubt whether the pollen evidence can indicate the magnitude of change in rainfall. The palynologists' conclusions were that agriculture began in western Rajasthan around 7000 BC, but no Neolithic or Chalcolithic sites of such early times have been found by the exploratory expeditions conducted in that region.

An important additional point that needs to be remembered is that climatic change in the strict sense is a global phenomenon, and that several Bronze Age civilizations weathered the environmental crises, if any, without collapse in the early second millennium BC. The Mesopotamian civilization, in spite of westward shifts of the channels of the Euphrates, soil salinity brought about by canal irrigation, and repeated invasions and immigrations of pastoralists from the desert, retained its language, writing methods, literary forms and texts, pantheon and temple architecture, well into the late first millennium BC, while there were changes in the social and economic structure.

Not all environmental change is a matter of rise or fall in annual rainfall. Local changes in the flora and fauna of particular areas can be brought about by overgrazing and steady consumption of large amounts of charcoal for brick-firing or metallurgy. The only systematically argued hypothesis about environment was formulated decades ago by Walter Fairservis. It remains a model study, even if we do not agree with the details. It takes into account the natural resources around Mohenjo-daro (soil, forest, pasture) and calculates the food requirements of the estimated population of the city. The estimated food requirement is used to calculate the acreage under crops in any year in the region around Mohenjo-daro. This in turn enabled Fairservis to estimate the number of cattle required for tillage and hence the total cattle population. He found that the cattle could not have been stall-fed, so that free-ranging would have been necessary. The scale of free-grazing by cattle, he concludes, entailed a 'formidable assault' on the natural vegetation of the locality. Even if the population and cattle estimates need to be revised, Fairservis laid down a valuable principle of ecological history that points our search to paths other than sudden and natural calamities. Let us take note in this connection that the population of Larkana town near Mohenjo-daro, as late as the nineteenth century, was less than 11,000. This figure is lower than the most conservative population estimate for Mohenjo-daro. Perhaps certain nodes on the landscape were 'overpopulated' and, over the centuries, depleted of their natural vegetation. This kind of reasoning sees people and their actions as responsible for their fate, though it cannot be an adequate explanation for total civilizational collapse.

In this last context, the later history of Mohenjo-daro is relevant. It is marked by signs of trouble. The structure of the finely-paved pillared hall was altered; the granary went out of use; shell-cutting was done in the northern citadel areas; and kilns encroached into the northern residential area. Here, two sizes of brick were now used haphazardly for the same wall and were laid without precision. Scored goblets, roughly made on the wheel and shaped so that they could be tied with string, are found by the dozen in the late levels.[1] Occasionally seal-impressed, their contents could possibly have been standard amounts of handouts (flour?) to the populace. Several massive limestone column bases were gathered together in one room of a house in the lower city; the excavator suggested they were gathered there 'after the final desertion of the city', with the intention of removal.

[1] G.F. Dales found that this kind of pottery is late in the history of Mohenjo-daro. It occurs also at Harappa, but not at many other Harappan sites. Because such pots occasionally carried a written message, they may not have been made for simple drinking purposes; instead, their content required some kind of official stamp or guarantee. The question then arises, why did the authorities need to utilize mass-produced pots of standard capacity?

That times were uncertain and strife/warfare/invasion was feared, is also indicated by jewellery hoards cached away under house floors in the last phase of Mohenjo-daro's existence. Not all hoards are indicators of uncertainty; for example, in the northern area of the city we find a hoard that could have been a metallurgist's working material. But caches with gold, strings of etched carnelian beads, silver foil, a silver lump and bracelet, jade and long carnelian beads do appear to be family treasures that were secreted away under the floors, and for some reason never recovered by the owners. We do not know if it was hill people from the Kirthars, or enemies in the plains, or local rebel factions, whom the rich had feared. The head of the 'priest king' seems to have been broken and to have fallen, together with a wall, into a passage. We had referred to other desecrated sculptures earlier. The archaeological contexts of such pieces speak for internal domestic feuds or ideological confrontation in the last days of Mohenjo-daro.

It needs to be emphasized that desertions of sites are not easy to 'read'. The archaeologist can tell that there is no post-Harappan culture at a particular site, but is rarely able to differentiate a quick total abandonment from gradual, house-by-house depopulation of a village over, say, a generation or two. And the two are very different kinds of abandonment, with different causes. Some abandonments may have occurred during the Harappan period, others after. We can only predict that if abandonment is quick and caused by calamity, the fleeing population will leave behind jewellery, wooden doors, or heavy grindstones.

It also has been observed that when social coherence is weak or absent, villages are abandoned more rapidly. Abandonment can be caused by a rise in the death rate of a residential community due to epidemic, famine for several years, or floods, or else because the inhabitants find better soils or better social conditions elsewhere. In this case, all that we know is that few Harappan places remained settled in later periods, that new villages were founded in adjacent areas, and that some jewellery caches and heavy items like stone column bases and mortars were left behind, together with vandalized stone statuary.

There is also the matter of about thirty-five skeletons found in the last levels of Mohenjo-daro, some though not all belonging to the last occupation phase of the city. Some of them were hastily buried, as if the times were so bad that the dead could not be taken out to the cemetery. In the northern part of the lower city, two skeletons lay on some steps of a well room. They lay where they had died, as did a group of five people in the south-western part of the city. Other unburied skeletons seem to indicate that marauders from outside, or city gangs themselves, fought over the last spoils. If the nerve centre of the political system suffered a serious blow, the repercussions could have spread far and wide.

Whereas land routes across Afghanistan and Baluchistan had changed at the onset of the Harappan period, there were reversals again at the end of the period. We had said that states establish frontiers and that pastoralists from Baluchistan may not have had easy access to annual grazing in the Indus plains in the Harappan period. But it appears that routes had opened up again after 2000 BC, when there were widespread disruptions over the world. In Turkmenia, for example, at the end of the Bronze Age, the Kopet Dag piedmont settlements shrank in size and eleven new settlements were founded along one arm of the inland delta of the Murghab, in Margiana. The pottery, terracottas, and metalwork here are akin to those of late Altyn-depe. Gradually, six oases were also settled in this region. Meanwhile, roughly contemporary abandonments occurred of flourishing villages like Tepe Hissar and Yarim Tepe (the latter in the Gorgan valley) in north-eastern Iran.

Near Mehrgarh and Nausharo there lies a very small (one hectare) settlement, briefly occupied, called Sibri. Some of the pottery, figurines, seals, and bronze artefacts here have clear parallels in Margiana and Bactria, where walled settlements and metal industries flourished after 2000 BC. There are very characteristic 'violin-shaped' figurines, the profiles curved in an exaggerated manner, schematic representations of the female torso with scant attention to the limbs, in Bactria and at Sibri. Seals in both places are strikingly similar, with compartmented forms. Also, a shaft-hole adze-axe at Sibri appears to derive from Central Asia. This evidence speaks for the resumption of movement down the Bolan Pass after the urban period.

Another site in the Kacchi, settled around 1700 BC, is Pirak. It is much larger (about eleven hectares). Here too seals and violin figurines of Central Asian type were found. In addition, there were bones and figurines of the camel and the horse, both Central Asiatic animals. Pirak-type pottery occurs at sites in Loralai, the Quetta valley and near Kalat, and we can also infer that hill village re-emerged in Baluchistan after an interregnum, at the same time as the resumption of traffic across Baluchistan into the Kacchi. Meanwhile, in the northernmost mountainous corner of the subcontinent, in Swat, there is also a sequence of culture change. Swat alternated between periods of contact with the greater Indus valley and periods of contact with Central Asia or north-eastern Iran, especially in the matter of some very distinctive pottery.

Around 1800 BC, the sea trade between Mesopotamia, Bahrain-Kuwait, and India came to an end. In southern Mesopotamia, there had been an agricultural decline due to shifts of the Euphrates and soil salinity. As a consequence, individual settlements as well as total settled area shrank appreciably in the south and the political gravity moved northward. The newly important regions of central and northern Iraq developed links with the Levant and Anatolia for their wood and metal requirements, the routes moving along the Euphrates. The culture of Bahrain saw an eclipse in the second millennium. An important trade circuit, a source of wealth for the Harappan elite, had thus dwindled.

The end of its external trade can have serious consequences for an economy if that economy has been structured around trade. We could suggest that an economic structure was dependent on foreign trade if there was expansion of settlement to, or colonization of, mineral resource areas, the establishment of seaports, the institution of ancillary activities like forestry and shipbuilding, the deployment of labour for the manufacture of craft items for export, and so on. The end of trade could mean the disintegration of such institutions, so that the population would relocate over the land, with changed economic imperatives/goals. Reversion to individual households engaged in subsistence agriculture and/or pastoralism is a likely consequence.

Material culture resumed its local distinctions and regional differences after 1800 BC. A quick survey of the other successor cultures in the relevant zone now follows. Sibri and Pirak have been mentioned above. There was the Jhukar culture in Sind, with buff, Amrian-like pottery, often painted in two colours. It was a materially impoverished culture without a distinct architectural or craft tradition, utilizing stone, bone, and some metal tools. The Cemetery H sites on the Hakra plains and in the Cemetery H of Harappa, represent the culture of southern Punjab. No habitation site has been excavated. The pottery is superb, of finer paste, and better fired than the Harappan, a glossy red with black painted atars, peacocks, leaves, and other naturalistic elements. Large urns so painted, some on display at the National Museum, Delhi, took fragmentary remains of the dead, or entire skeletons in the case of infants. In the Gomal valley and north up to Sarai Khola, a peculiar system of disposal of the dead became established, the 'grave-cum-funeral pyre'. It consisted of a pile of wood on the floor of a large pit, overlaid with a sacrificed animal, more wood, earth, clay, and wood again, and then the corpse with grave offerings. The whole was sealed with clay and set afire. The grave was never opened thereafter.

Upstream in the Sutlej-Jumna divide, there was an increase in the number of settlements, probably caused by migration from the Hakra. This in turn was probably because the Hakra was gradually drying. M.R. Mughal suggests that the late Harappan or Cemetery H sites of the Hakra plain lie between Yazman and Fort Derawar because this area received water from an offshoot of the Sutlej, which joined the Hakra near Yazman. This stream also eventually dried up, and sites of the following period lie further upstream, in the dry bed of the Hakra. The drying of the Hakra is mentioned here as a likely cause of abandonment of some sites, but not as a 'cause' of the end of Harappan civilization. Village abandonments are not the same as civilizational collapse.

The Shivalik's streams that had once fed the Ghaggar and Sarasvati appear to have shifted, to be 'captured' by the Jumna and/or the Sutlej. (The land between the upper Jumna and Sutlej has no high ridges or hills to provide a clear drainage divide.) In the divide, we have seen, a regional culture had been encapsulated within the Harappan. But when the latter came to an end, the old lines of regional distinctions seem to reappear. The subsequent material culture (the Late Siswal) on the upper Ghaggar-Sarasvati shows some remnants of Harappan traditions, plus those of local traditions, in a new combination. The settlements were now rural, with wood and thatch huts and the occasional brick structure. Perforated jars and a few other Harappan ceramic forms survived, but not so the writing, or range of bronze craft tools, or cubical chart weights, or long carnelian beads. Terracotta cakes took new forms, and the locally popular biconical terracotta bead was transformed. Long chert blades were no longer in use. Ropar on the upper Sutlej continued to be an important centre through the ancient period because of its locational importance, but only after a centuries-long interregnum.

In contrast to the settlement shifts and de-urbanization in the Divide, in Kathiawad there was another kind of transformation, and this has received better scholarly attention. There had been only a few Mature Harappan sites like Rangpur and Lothal here, but for the early second millennium (Rangpur IIB-C and Rangpur III related phases) we can count more than a hundred sites. There are small settlements in all parts of Kathiawad; developments in Kutch are relatively unknown. *Ragi* and *jowar* were to become the mainstay of Kathiawadi agriculture, being better suited to the soil and climatic conditions of the peninsula as a whole than wheat or barley. Thus changes in agriculture may be connected with the proliferation of villages. Meanwhile, in this period the dockyard of Lothal had gone out of use; no Rohri chert was available; and small blades of local jasper came into use. Weights, shell, faience, gold, and carnelian became scarce. At most of the newly-founded villages of this period, the houses were made of mud, poles, and mats/thatch. Thus there was here, not just a sort of 'devolution' but also development of the subsistence economy in new and sustainable directions.

Mainland Gujarat, along the 'neck' of the Kathiawad peninsula and the eastern edge of the Little Rann, is also a dry, millet-growing region. Post-urban villages in this zone appear to have taken advantage of depressions scattered amongst the sand-dunes that help rainwater for some months in the year. There were Nagwada, Ratanpura, and other sites. Millet agriculture is possible, although these locations could also have attracted sheep- and goat-herders during the wet months. In fact, the shallow deposits of one or two of these sites make it probable that they saw seasonal occupation of hunters and gatherers. The small village of Nagwada (1.6 hectares) had wood post and thatch houses, and also stone rubble and mud-brick ones. Material equipment included flaked stone tools in the Harappan tradition and an insufficiently fired pottery. At

Ratanpura, round huts and many rubbish pits yielded flaked stone tools, animal bones, and some pottery that included a ware related to Rangpur III pottery. Except for bead production at Nagwada, crafts are not in abundance.[2]

In summary, the majority of towns and villages of the Harappan culture failed to see sustained occupation after about 1800 BC, and people seem to have emigrated. Routes of movement across the Afghan and Baluch uplands changed; in north-western Afghanistan, Turkmenia, and north-eastern Iran also there were settlement abandonments at roughly this time. In settlement form, metallurgy, writing system, house construction, crafts using ivory or carnelian, or in the use of seals, as also in major aspects like city life and maritime orientations, there was very little continuity of the Bronze Age way of life. There was, instead, a reversion to rural, tribal cultures of what we call the Chalcolithic stage, in which metal may have been in use but was not an essential or frequently-utilized material for tools of production.

We have surveyed the evidence for abandonments, natural calamities, and environmental degradation. We have also touched on internal factors such as political strife, and on the eclipse of the overseas trade. Sibri and Pirak testify to the renewal of movements between

[2] Mention needs to be made of the site of Daimabad, south of Nasik and on the left bank of the Pravara river, a tributary of the Godavari. Four huge bronze sculptures, obviously executed in the lost wax technique, were found here. There is a man driving a two-oxen chariot, an elephant, a rhinoceros and a buffalo—all animals known on the Harappan seals. The animals are on two-wheeled stands, the wheels being sold like the Harappan wheels. The four pieces together weigh 65 kilograms. Considering the above features and the scarcity of metal in the post-Harappan Chalcolithic cultures, some scholars are inclined to interpret the Daimabad bronzes as Harappan. Others ask if they could be much later, say, tribal work, of the eighteenth century. What needs to be said is that these did not show up in controlled excavation but were unearthed by Bhil farmers when they were digging out the roots of a tree. In excavations of the mound of Daimabad, material from the second period of occupation is, according to B.B. Lal, 'suggestive of a Late Harappan occupation'. But the 'sturdy red ware', button-shaped terracotta seals, seals inscribed and painted on pottery, and one mud-brick-lined grave are not totally convincing as Harappan.

Central Asia and South Asia. Hopefully a perspective has thus been provided for the problem of the 'Aryan invasion'.

The grassland or steppe of southern Europe, which extends into Central Asia, is accepted as the original home of the Indo-Europeans for two major reasons. First, early Indo-European and early Finno-Ugric (or Uralic) languages form two contrasting families but did have contacts and mutual influence, as can be made out by linguists from the large number of words they acquired from each other. This could only have been possible if the two languages had been spoken in neighbouring regions. The home of the Finno-Ugric languages (Finnish, Hungarian, Estonian, Volgaic, etc.) is undisputed: it is the southern forest belt of Europe west of the Urals. Therefore the steppe land of Eurasia immediately south of that forest belt would be the home of the Indo-Europeans.

Second, there is no disputing the fact that the horse was known to the earliest (or 'Proto') Indo-Europeans. Ample archaeological evidence attests to horse domestication, horse-herding, and even horse-riding (bit-marks on horse teeth) at early sites on the Eurasian steppe. The wild horse was indigenous to this region and was domesticated here. Moreover, in all Indo-European languages (Latin, Mitannian, Sanskrit, etc.) the word for horse is derived from the same Proto-Indo-European root, *ekwos*. The social and military importance of the horse to the early Indo-Europeans in Syria and Anatolia, in north-western South Asia, and in Iran, is well established. Archaeologists have discovered several third- and second-millennium sites and cultures in the Eurasian steppe, but these can only generally be linked with the Indo-Europeans, that too not with certainty.

There is evidence for movements out of Central Asia, the homeland of the Indo-Europeans and their Indo-Iranian branch, after about 2000 BC. We had seen that settlements like Yarim Tepe and Hissar were abandoned, so too settlements in southern Turkmenia. In southern Baluchistan we find new kinds of pottery, seals, and burial practices, which also point to newcomers. At Sibri and Pirak, we had seen the influx of Central Asian elements. In the Gardan Reg of Afghanistan lie extensive ruins of copper-smelting activity that date to this period (roughly 2000 BC), and may also be evidence for the movements of metallurgist groups in search of sources of copper/tin. None of these, however, is proof of the movement of people speaking a particular kind of language. There is no necessary link between a particular kind of material culture and its geographic boundaries on one hand, and specific language and its boundaries on the other. In other words, there is no obvious archaeological identification of a linguistic entity such as Indo-Iranian, Iranian, or Indo-Aryan. We can only confirm that the movements and migrations reconstructed by historical linguistics are not contradicted by archaeological evidence for migrations, in terms of period and direction of movement.

Indo-Aryan is the name of a group of Indian languages that were, around 2000 BC, part of the family of Indo-Iranian languages,[3] a group that had branched out from the Indo-European homeland. On the southern and eastern frontiers of the Indo-European homeland lay the Turkmenian settlements, and also a number of villages of the Gurgan valley, with Tepe Hissar a little further south. Any tribal schism or pastoral or military emigration out of the steppe could have repercussions on communities along these frontier zones. Therefore, the widespread abandonment of sites in Turkmenia and the Gurgan valley, and of Tepe Hissar, to which we have referred, does suggest outmigration from the steppe. But we cannot identify the emigrants as speakers of Indo-Iranian except at the level of reasonable probability.

It is also relevant that a language does not have to move into an area on the crest of an invasion. There is little evidence that those who spoke Vedic Sanskrit were destroyers or marauders, or that they left a trail of burned settlements in their wake. Language replacement has occurred repeatedly in history. For example, around

[3] Old Avestan is the earliest known Iranian language. It is the language of the *Gatha*s or the hymns of Zarathushtra, which are set in Central Asia-north-eastern Iran, in a rural, cattle-keeping culture. It is argued that Zarathushtra dates much before the period of Zoroastrian Achaemenid kings (sixth century BC) because of close linguistic similarities between Old Avestan and the language of the Ṛgveda. For example, in Avestan the words for camel, charioteer, cow, and horse are *ushtra, rathi, gau*, and *aspa*, respectively easily recognizable to those who know Sanskrit. Old Persian, the language of the Achaemenid kings (for example, the inscriptions of Darius), is a separate, south-western Iranian language, and probably much younger than eastern Iranian Avestan.

2000 BC, the Semitic language Akkadian replaced Sumerian, which had been the spoken and written language for almost a millennium in Mesopotamia. Sumerian and Akkadian are unrelated languages, yet Akkadian adopted the Sumerian script, with modifications. But there was no accompanying break in material culture nor a demographic hiatus of any sort. Often languages with high political or social status are adopted by speakers of other languages, initially as a second language. After such an onset of bilingualism, the high-status language may gain currency in an increasing number of social situations and thus become the dominant language. So language replacements are not necessarily caused by massive migrations of the speakers of a new language.

Next, even though there are hints of movements of people with Central Asian connections into South Asia, these traces are more marked in the fringes of Harappan territory—in Sibri-Pirak, Baluchistan, and the remote Swat valley in northernmost Pakistan—than in the Harappan heartland. When we referred to the scatter of unburied skeletons in the uppermost strata of Mohenjo-daro, it was to infer the existence of strife, or the collapse of social order, rather than to detect the 'hand' of 'the Aryans'. The movement of Indo-Aryans and the end of Harappan Civilization cannot therefore be seen as causally connected.

Whatever the weightage we may choose to give to various internal and external processes in the eclipse of the Indus Civilization, another question arises. Are we dealing with a social and economic system that carried the seeds of its own destruction? If the economy was, as we suspect, dependent on bronze tools that could be procured by elite-organized external trade, then a series of mishaps or dislocations in the world around (tribal movements, new settlements, decline in the power of certain elite groups, shifts in pastoral routes) could bring an end to that procurement. Local deforestation in the copper-smelting regions is also a factor we may consider. Copper technology is hugely wasteful of wood (charcoal).

The critical role of the elite in trade, crafts, and the founding of new settlements could also have meant that the economy was denied a secure foundation. Perhaps only those innovations and systems endure that are firmly rooted in the control of the individual family or village community and serve the interests of ordinary people (rather than rulers ensconced in citadels), and in which the knowledge of techniques is internalized into a people's heritage. Faience, bronze, seal-carving, or ivory-inlaid furniture could have relied on elite taste/ sponsorship or demand; but experience with different soils and rainfall regimes, knowledge of different varieties of crop, observation of animal breeding behaviour, and the fuel properties of different trees, these would be a part of popular science and would endure. So the house forms and construction techniques of Mohenjo-daro did not endure. Production of carnelian beads reappeared very much later, at Iron Age sites like Kodumanal, but the output was small beads, and the technique of making long and slender ones appears to have been lost. Lost wax casting is next attested only at Taxila in the early first millennium AD. It appears that soon after 3000 BC, society leaped, as it were, into a new technological frontier that could not be sustained over the long term. Perhaps the new social institutions did not develop sufficiently, or take adequately firm roots, to prevent the resurgence of tribalism.

This said, the 'moral' of our story enunciated, it still remains that the Harappan was a remarkably cosmopolitan and outward-looking phase of South Asian history. The Harappan world was an open one with foreign trade, external influences, and migrations. The urban centres had interactions with the hunters of Rajasthan, tribesmen in Makran, and settlers in Kashmir. The people had developed a taste for exotic stones and forest produce such as ivory. Meluhha entered the literary tradition of Mesopotamia as a source of exotic wares and fine boats, and those Harappans who returned from ventures abroad must have had fascinating experiences to narrate. We could say that cultural dynamism lies in openness, interaction, intermarriage and bilingualism, not in cultural closure or ethnic purity. And, in some ways, a spectacular failure of the past can be of as much interest as the lineages of steady continuity that we call tradition.

10

It is Time to Rethink

B.B. Lal

B.B. Lal, in the second article of this pair of big-picture examinations of the Indus Civilization and its relation to the Veda, gives careful consideration to the difficulties of the Aryan interpretation of the Indus Civilization. The issues he addresses include the existence of Dravidian loanwords in early Sanskrit texts, the problems of assuming Sanskrit or a close relative to be the language of the Indus people and their writing system, the lack of reference to cities in the Veda, the Vedic use of domesticated horses and spoke-wheeled chariots, and problems of chronology. He concludes, with commendable caution, that the disparity said to exist between the Vedic and Indus cultures is not as pronounced as it has been made out to be, and that considerations of geography and chronology do not rule out an early Aryan presence in the Indian subcontinent.

[From *The Earliest Civilization of South Asia (Rise, Maturity and Decline)* (New Delhi: Aryan Books International, 1997), pp. 281–7.]

Some colleagues who happened to have a look at the draft of this book at one stage or another suggested that I must express my views on the much-debated issue regarding the Harappan Civilization vis-à-vis the Indo-Aryans. I told them that I was planning to write a separate book on that topic and it would not be possible to do justice to such vast problem in the short space available in the present book. [In spite of my pleadings they insisted and hence this brief Appendix.]

The question which, I believe, has been agitating the minds of all of us is: who were the authors of this highly advanced civilization of the third millennium BC? The Dravidians? The Indo-Aryans?[1] Or still some others? There can be several lines of enquiry—for example linguistic, archaeological, literary, inscriptional, astronomical, and geographical. However, I shall take up only the more noteworthy of these. And even in doing so, I am afraid, I will have to recall, at the cost of repetition, some of the evidence already dealt with earlier in this book.

A very fascinating line of inquiry is that provided by linguistics. On the basis of the fact that many of the European languages, such as Greek and Latin, on the one hand and Asian languages, like Persian and Sanskrit, on the other have a large number of words akin to one another, it has been postulated that at some point of time the speakers of these languages formed a group, which has been designated as the Indo-European group. It has also been assumed that the original home of these Indo-European-language-speaking people was somewhere in Central Asia from where one group went westwards, spreading all over Europe, while another travelled south-eastwards, reaching India *via* Iran. The languages concerned have such common vocabulary as words for parts of the body, close family relationships, etc. and show such similar syntactical behaviour that it would be unjustified to deny this commonality.

With this as the starting point, and finding that certain words in the Ṛigveda and other Vedic texts do not fit into the postulated Indo-European language family, scholars have opined that these new words must have found their way into Sanskrit from a pre-existing language. Some of the words concerned are like *nīra* (water), and *mīna* (fish), etc., and since these words occur in the Dravidian languages, it has been argued that on arrival in India, the Indo-Aryans must have encountered the Dravidians. This nineteenth-century theory of the Indo-Aryans overrunning the Dravidians found a readymade archaeological prop when in the 1920s, the remains of an altogether unknown civilization—the Harappan Civilization—were brought to light. It was thus made out that the Harappans were

[1] The terms Dravidian and Indo-Aryan were once used in a racial sense, but are now mostly used in the linguistic.

the Dravidians and the 'barbaric' Indo-Aryans not only destroyed them but in the process also borrowed some of their words. Here it may be of interest to note that even amongst Dravidianists there is no agreement on the number of words borrowed. While some put the figure at a little over a thousand, others accept hardly 25 per cent of these words as having been derived from a Dravidian source.

In a similar manner, a case has been made out to explain certain other words occurring in the Vedic texts as coming from an Austro-Asiatic source and the Munda language has been thought to be the most likely creditor. Not finding the source of some of the words in either the Dravidian group or in the Austro-Asiatic family, the existence of some yet unknown sources has also been postulated.

To my mind, the exact number of the borrowed words is irrelevant to the issue. If even half-a-dozen words are definitely identifiable as coming from Dravidian/Munda sources, that should be good enough to accept a borrowing. But the whole issue hinges on the question: how exactly did this borrowing take place? Did the Sanskrit-speaking people borrow the words concerned from some people whom they overran, as has been made out by assuming that incoming hordes of the Indo-Aryans overran the Harappans? Or did the Sanskrit-speaking people borrow the Dravidian and Munda words from their neighbours with whom they had occasion to come in contact? This second hypothesis has a lot to recommend itself. If, for argument's sake, it turns out that the Harappans themselves were speaking Sanskrit, they could have easily borrowed the Dravidian and Munda words from their neighbours respectively on the south and east, who are not unlikely to have spoken these languages. It has been shown that there did exist Neolithic cultures in the south as well as in the east, called respectively the Southern Neolithic Culture and Eastern Neolithic Culture. Both these were contemporary with the Harappan Civilization at one point of time or another. There is also evidence of the Harappans having come into contact with these Neolithic people. For example, the Kolar mines, located in a Dravidian-speaking area, are thought to have been the source of gold for the Harappans. Likewise, we know that the Harappans population included a marginal number of proto-Australoids. In fact, even the Mongoloids are represented, howsoever scantily, in the Harappan population. Thus, one need not be surprised that if the

Harappans did speak Sanskrit, one day someone may come up with the identification of some words from that source as well.

The main question then is this. Did the Harappans speak Sanskrit? Were they themselves the Indo-Europeans?

Mortimer Wheeler,[2] on discovering in 1946 a fortification-wall around a part of the settlement at Harappa and on being apprised by a Sanskrit scholar of the occurrence of the word *puraṁdara* as meaning 'the destroyer of forts', declared:[3] 'On circumstantial evidence Indra [symbolic of the Vedic Aryans] stands accused [of destroying the supposedly non- and pre-Aryan Harappan Culture]'. This fitted very well into two pre-existing theories, viz. a nineteenth-century theory enunciated by Max Müller and tenaciously adhered to by others that the Ṛigveda is to be dated to c. 1200 BC, and another advanced by mid-twentieth century archaeologists that the Harappan Civilization came to a sudden end around 1500 BC. Both these theories are now obsolete. It is no longer accepted by scholars of Sanskrit literature that the Ṛigveda is as late as 1200 BC nor do archaeologists uphold the view of Mortimer Wheeler that the Harappan Civilization met a sudden end, much less at the hands of the Aryans. Wheeler's reference to the skeletons found at Mohenjo-daro as evidence of a massacre by the invaders has been proved to be wrong. The skeletons belong to different strata of the site and not to the uppermost level, which would have been the case had it been a massacre resulting in the abandonment of the site. Further, some of the skeletons bore cut-marks which had been healed, suggesting that the death did not take place immediately as a result of these injuries. Dales[4] has rightly dubbed this as a 'mythical massacre'.

While there may have been different causes for the abandonment of different sites—for example, Mohenjo-daro may have suffered heavily on account of Indus floods or Kalibangan may have been given up because of the drying up of the Ghaggar—the evidence

[2] ...

[3] Wheeler, R.E.M., 'Harappa 1946: The Defences and Cemetary R37', *Ancient India*, 3: 58–130, 1947.

[4] Dales, G.F., 'The Mythical Massacre at Mohenjo-daro'. *Expedition* 6(3): 36–43, 1964.

from most of the other sites indicates that there was a gradual devolution of the cultural constituents from about the beginning of the second millennium BC. To recall just one example, in the upper levels at Lothal, both the dockyard and the warehouse had gone out of commission and so also the fortifications. The well laid-out streets had been encroached upon by houses, which were now built with brickbats robbed from the earlier structures. The devolution noted at Lothal was further continued at Rangpur, resulting finally in a cultural milieu, which can no longer be recognized as Harappan. Likewise, the shift of the scenario from the middle Ghaggar to its upper reaches and thence to the upper Gangā–Yamunā *doāb* tells the same story. The cases of this decline were manifold: climatic aberrations and the wearing out of the landscape, both resulting in a fall of agricultural production, and not the least a sharp decline in trade, both internal as well external. Certainly no invaders can be invoked for an assumed sudden end. Indeed, the supporters of the Aryan-invasion theory have not been able to cite even a single example where there is evidence of 'invaders', represented either by weapons of warfare or even of cultural remains left by them. Even the supposedly alien cultures like those labelled as Jhukar and Cemetery H are regional transformations, respectively in Sind and the Panjab, from the Harappan Civilization itself, as was the case with the Rangpur phase in Gujarat.

Now whereas a refutation of Wheeler's theory is welcome inasmuch as it absolves the Indo-Aryans of the responsibility of destroying the Harappans, this refutation by itself does not in any way establish that they themselves were the authors of this civilization. We thus come back to square one where the authorship question is concerned.

Right from the time of the discovery of the Harappan Civilization in the early 1920s, attempts have been made to identify the language spoken by the Harappans, since that would have helped in tracking down the authors. More than two dozen serious attempts have been made to decipher the inscriptions on the Harappan seals and other allied material. Two major theses have been advanced. According to one, the language involved was proto-Dravidian, while according to the other, it was Sanskrit or a kind of proto-Sanskrit. In my various papers published since the 1950s, I have reviewed the claims of

Dravidianists such as Asko Parpola and I. Mahadevan and of Sanskritists like S.R. Rao and M.V.N. Krishna Rao and have shown that none of them has been able to hit the mark. I have also demonstrated as to where they have faulted in their methodology, which has led to unacceptable results. Any valid decipherment of the script should pass at least two tests: one, that the value one assigned to any given sign is not altered according to exigencies and two, that the language arrived at conforms to the principles of the language concerned. Thus, while no aspersions are cast on any of the scholars, let it be clearly restated that all attempts to identify the language of the Harappans have not helped us so far in identifying the authors of that civilization.

It has been stated by the supporters of the Dravidian theory that the Aryan invaders chased away the Dravidian-speaking Harappans to the southern part of India where they are now located and only a handful of them were left behind, who now dwell in a small pocket in Baluchistan, speaking the Brahui dialect. Let those who hold this view squarely answer this. If the Aryans pushed the Harappans all the way down to South India, how come there are no Harappan sites at all in that region? The southernmost limit of the Harappan regime is the upper reaches of the Godāvarī. There is no Harappan site south of that. Second, why were only a handful of the Dravidian-speaking people left behind in Baluchistan and not in the main area occupied by the Harappans, viz. the Indus-Sarasvatī valleys and even in Gujarat? In this context it may be well worth noting that some scholars are of the view that the Brahui-speaking Baluchis had migrated to that region from elsewhere instead of being the leftovers from a settled Dravidian-speaking population indigenous to that area. Some others even doubt an intimate relationship between Brahui and the Dravidian languages and hold that the former may well be regarded as 'Modern Colloquial Eastern Elamite'.

While the foregoing argument may be all right in countering the Dravidian hypothesis for the Harappan Civilization, by itself it does not lead us to any positive conclusion. We have, therefore, to examine other kinds of evidence.

A variety of arguments have been advanced to say that the Harappans are unlikely to be the Indo-Aryans. Here we shall consider the three most salient ones, viz. (1) 'glaring disparity' between the cultures represented by the Harappan remains and the Vedic texts; (2) absence of the horse from the former; and (3) chronological gap between the two.

Let us begin with the much emphasized disparity between the Harappan Civilization on the one hand and the civilization depicted in the Vedas on the other. It has been argued that the Vedic civilization was essentially rural and had no urban component whatsoever and since the Harappan Civilization is essentially urban, the two cannot be correlated. This view is based, to say the least, on an inadequate study and misinterpretation of the Vedic texts. These do refer to towns, fortifications, sea voyages and trade—all manifestations of urbanization.

The word *pur* occurs very frequently in the Ṛigveda and conveys the sense of the fortified town. Sometimes it is stated to have had even a hundred walls (*śatabhuji*), the word hundred evidently standing for a large number (as found, for example, at Dholavira, a Harappan site in Gujarat). Perhaps one may cite here the following from the Ṛigveda:

... varma sīvyadhvaṁ bahulā prithūni;
puraḥ kṛiṇudhavamāyasīradhṛiṣṭā ... (*RV* X. 101.8)

Herein the poet appeals to the gods: 'Stitch ye the coats of armour, wide and many; make iron[5] forts, secure from all assailants'.[6]

Likewise, there is ample evidence of sea voyages, seafaring ships and sea trade. To make the sea voyage easily possible, ships with three masts (*tirbandhur*) and/or ten oars (*daśāritra*) and even a hundred oars (*śatāritra*) were commissioned. The wealth thus achieved seems to have been tremendous, as may be seen from the following:

rāyaḥ samudrāṅśchaturo asmabhyam soma viśvataḥ;
ā pavasva sahasriṇaḥ (*RV* IX. 33.6)

[5] The word *ayas* used in the text stands for metal in general and not iron. At a later stage, two separate words were used, viz. *kṛiṣṇāyasa* and *lohāyasa*, denoting respectively 'black metal' i.e. iron and 'red metal' i.e. copper.

[6] Griffith, R.T.H., *The Hymns of the Ṛigveda* (Delhi: Motilal Banarasidass, 1973 [Reprint]).

'From every side, O Soma, for our profit, pour thou forth four seas filled full of riches thousandfold.'[7]

As regards the political set-up, well organized administration, etc., one may note terms like *rāṣṭra*, *rājā*, *jyeṣṭharāj*, *samrāṭ*, and *janarāj*, which refer to kingdoms and rulers of different statuses; terms for councils and assemblies such as *saṁsad*, *sabhā*, and *samiti*; and terms for various categories of administrative posts like *adhyakṣa*, *dūta*, *nidhāpati*, *rathaspati*, and *senānī*.

From the foregoing it would be abundantly clear that the Vedic society was neither nomadic nor even in a mere rural stage, as has been assumed by many. It had long passed those stages and was dealing with kings and kingdoms, was having an organized administrative machinery, had fortified towns and was engaged in both land and sea trade. Just as there were cities, towns, and villages in the Harappan ensemble (as there are even today in any society) there were both rural and urban components in the Vedic times. Where then is the 'glaring disparity' between the cultural levels of the Harappan and Vedic societies?

And now to the horse. It has often been stressed: 'No horse, no Aryans'. And rightly too, since it is difficult to visualize a material culture of the Aryans that does not include the horse, which figures so prominently in the Vedic texts. Hence the position has to be examined in some detail.

A terracotta figure found by Mackay in his excavations at Mohenjo-daro was identified by him as that of the horse. This identification has been accepted by many but not all. However, in recent years, a lot of new light has been thrown on the issue. Lothal has yielded not only a terracotta figure of the horse but also the second right upper molar of that animal. To recall what Bhola Nath of the Zoological Survey of India has stated, the tooth 'resembles closely with that of the modern horse and has pli-caballian (a minute fold near the base of the spur or protocone) which is well distinguished character of the cheek of the horse'.[8]

[7] Griffith, *op. cit.*, p. 483.

[8] Rao, S.R., *Lothal—A Harappan Port Town* (1955–62), Vol. II (New Delhi: Archaeological Survey of India, 1985).

Surkotada has yielded quite a few bones of the horse, which have been identified as such not only by A.K. Sharma but also by Sandor Bokonyi, an internationally recognized authority on the anatomy of the horse. To repeat one of his significant observations: 'The occurrence of true horse (*Equus caballus* L.) was evidenced by the enamel pattern of the upper and lower cheek and teeth and by the size and form of incisors and phalanges (toe bones). Since no wild horses lived in India in post-Pleistocene times, the domestic nature of the Surkotada horses is undoubtful.' Horse remains have been identified at Kalibangan too; and Bhola Nath also states that an earlier collection from Harappa examined by him did contain remains of the true horse. However, no horse bones have so far been reported from the current excavations at the site. Finally, attention must be drawn to the discovery of terracotta figurines of the horse by Jarrige and his colleagues in the Harappan levels at Nausharo in Pakistan. Thus, the horse has cleared the first hurdles, though no doubt one would like to have more and more examples.

To come to the chronological gap. As is well known, it is Max Müller's dating of the Ṛigveda that has become the basis for those who hold that the Vedic Aryans came to India from outside and that this event took place after the middle of the second millennium BC. However, Max Müller's method itself is questionable. In brief, assuming that the *Sūtras* belonged to c. 600–200 BC and assigning an ad hoc duration of two centuries to each of the preceding literary periods, he held that the Ṛigveda may be dated to c. 1200 BC. This ad-hocism may have had its value at a time when hardly anything was known in the West about the Vedic texts, but the results arrived at cannot be taken as the gospel truth. Indeed, later in his career Max Müller himself had begun to feel shaky about his dating and admitted: 'Whether the Vedic hymns were composed [in] 1000, or 1500, or 2000, or 3000 years BC, no power on earth will ever determine'.[9]

Quite in contrast to Max Müller, there are scholars who hold that the Rigveda is as early as the fourth millennium BC. Their thesis is based on astronomical calculations. For example, a passage in the

[9] Max Müller, F., *Physical Religion* (New Delhi: Asian Educational Services, 1979 [Reprint]).

Aitareya Brāhmaṇa refers to the shifting of the vernal equinox from Mrigaśiras to Rohinī, which event, according to these experts, would have taken place around 3500 BC. This wold place the Ṛigveda in the fourth millennium BC. Not being a student of astronomy, I am not in a position to offer any opinion on this dating. At the same time, I do not see any reason to reject it either, without a careful and unbiassed examination of this and other astronomical data provided by the Vedic texts.

Anyway, I would like to revert to archaeology and draw attention to the well-known Boghaz Keui inscription from western Asia. It is dated to the fourteenth century BC and refers to the Vedic deities Indra, Mitra, Nāsatya, and Varuṇa as being witnesses to a treaty between the Hittite king Suppiliuma and Mittani king Matiwaza. The question is whether these Indra-Varuṇa worshippers occupied the West Asian region first and then moved on to India or were they originally from India and its neighbourhood and later reached West Asia, or did they go to both these regions from a third place? Since we do not have so far any evidence of the Indra-Varuna worshippers of that vintage in any third place, the last-named alternative has to be kept on hold for the time being. Further, since the Indra-Varuṇa worshippers do not enjoy continuity in the West Asian region, greater chances are that they had gone to that region from the Indian side. A similar scenario is also suggested by another inscription found in that region, which refers to horse-training terms like *ekavartana*, *trivartana*, and *pañchavartana*, so specifically Sanskritic. Thus, the presence of Indra-Varuṇa worshippers, that is, the Indo-Aryans, in India has got to be well before the middle of the second millennium BC. How much earlier is anybody's guess.

We may now take up the geographical aspect of the issue. The texts concerned give a pretty good idea of the region occupied by the Vedic people. While in the east, the main life-stream was the Sarasvatī, the people were also familiar with the Yamunā and Gaṅgā. Moving westwards, almost all the rivers from the Śutudrī (modern Sutlej) to Sindhu (Indus) are mentioned: the Vipaś (Beas), Paruṣṇī (Rāvī), Asiknī (Chenāb), Vitastā (Jhelum), etc. Further west, we come across the Kubhā, Krumu and Gomtī, identified respectively with the Kabul, Kurram and Gomal, all being western tributaries of the Indus. While the *Aitareya Brāhmaṇa* refers to Gandhāra (modern

Kandahar region), the *Atharva Veda* mentions Balhika, which is none other then the Balkh area in Afghanistan. It is thus clear that the Vedic geography coincides with eastern and northern parts of present-day Afghanistan, practically the whole of Pakistan, and Panjab, Haryana, north-eastern Rajasthan and north-western Uttar Pradesh in India. In this context, it is important to note that this very region was the domain of the Harappan Civilization. In the north-west, we are familiar with the site of Shortughai in Afghanistan, which was a full-fledged seat of the Harappans (not a mere trade-contact site) and in the upper Gaṅgā-Yamunā *doāb* in the east we have the site of Alamgirpur. Thus, geography does not stand in the way of a correlation between the Vedic and the Harappan periods. As a matter of fact, it establishes an equation which ought to be of great significance if other factors also point that way.

In the context of this debate as a whole, one would like to refer to an important observation made by Hemphill and his colleagues:[10] 'As for the question of biological continuity within the Indus Valley, two discontinuities appear to exist. The first occurs between 6000 and 4500 BC and is reflected by the strong separation in dental non-metric characters between neolithic and chalcolithic burials at Mehrgarh. The second occurs at some point after 800 BC but before 200 BC. In the intervening period, while there is dental non-metric, craniometric, and cranial non-metric evidence for a degree of an internal biological continuity, statistical evaluation of cranial data reveals clear indication of interaction with the West specifically with Iranian Plateau.' It would thus be seen that although there was some interaction between the Iranian plateau and the Indus valley, there was basic biological continuity within the Indus valley from c. 4500 BC to c. 800 BC. In such a situation, how can one envisage the entry of hordes and hordes of Vedic Aryans who are supposed to belong to an alien, non-Harappan biological group, around the middle of the second millennium BC? The only large-scale entry points are either around 4500 BC or after 800 BC. Since even Max Müller's followers would hesitate to force the entry of the Aryans into India after the

[10] Hemphill, B.E., J.R. Kukacs, and K.A.R. Kennedy 'Biological adaptations and affinities of Bronze Age Harappan', in R.H. Meadow (ed.), *Harappa Excavation 1986–1990.*(1991), p. 137.

latter date (that is, after 800 BC), is it not time to rethink the entire issue? Could the Chalcolithic people of Mehrgarh, who in the course of time evolved into Bronze Age Harappans, themselves have been the Indo-Aryans? These Chalcolithic people had relationship with areas now comprising northern Afghanistan, north-eastern Iran, and even southern part of Central Asia—an area that may have been the habitat of the Aryans prior to the composition of the Ṛigveda.

From the foregoing rapid survey it would be clear that neither the alleged disparity between the Vedic and Harappan cultures is all that pronounced as it has been made out to be nor are geographical considerations a bar nor is the chronological gulf so wide as to deny the Aryans an early presence on the subcontinent. However, all this evidence, though fairly strong in itself, needs to be strengthened through more clinching data, which can come only from a satisfactory decipherment of the Harappan script. May we hope for the best?

11

The Indus-Sarasvatī Civilization

Beginnings and Developments

S.P. Gupta

The next article is on the concept of the Indus-Sarasvatī Civilization. S.P. Gupta is the inventor of this concept. It starts out from the discovery, by Rafique Mughal, of a very large number of Indus Civilization remains and sites in the dried-up river bed of the Sarasvatī river, in the Cholistan desert of Pakistan, and sites on the Indian side of the border that appear to be related. Because the Sarasvatī river is prominently mentioned in the Ṛgveda, Gupta proposes to replace the concept of the Indus or Harappan Civilization with that of the Indus-Sarasvatī Civilization, giving it a longer period, from 4000 to 1400 BC, than the generally accepted period of 2600–1900 BC for the urban phase. He upholds the alternative view that the Indus Civilization and the civilization of the Veda are one. His article is an extensive treatment of the archaeological evidence for the Indus-Sarasvatī Civilization concept. It is a major work, with full reference to the evidence, and many maps and illustrations. It is over a hundred pages, too long to reproduce here in full. I have abridged it, taking the framing discussion from the beginning and end, and omitting the long middle section.

[From 'The dawn of Indian civilization (up to c. 600 BC)', in G.C. Pande (ed.) (*History of Science, Philosophy and Culture in Indian Civilization*, ed., D.P. Chattophadhyaya, vol. I Part 1) (New Delhi: Centre for Studies in Civilizations, 1999), pp. 270–9, 339–51, 366–75.]

The Indus-Sarasvatī Civilization: The Beginnings

What is generally called the 'Indus' or the 'Harappan' Civilization and used as interchangeable terms for the fourth–third millennium BC Bronze Age Indian Civilization is here called the 'Indus-Sarasvatī Civilization'. The reason for the change in nomenclature lies in the most startling archaeological discoveries made during the last two decades by Rafique Mughal (Figure 11.1).[1]

These discoveries were made in that part of the Lost Sarasvatī basin, which lies in Cholistan deserts of Bikaner located in the Bahawalpur region of Pakistan, adjoining north-western Rajasthan (Figure 11.2). This has now firmly established the primacy of the Sarasvatī river over the Indus in terms of concentration of the Indus sites of different categories—camp sites, industrial sites, village sites, and cities. Here Mughal has found the remains of as many as 363 sites of this civilization (Figure 11.3). His conclusions were supported by similar discoveries made in India. J.P. Joshi, R.S. Bisht, Suraj Bhan, and others have discovered around 250 sites in the basin of the Sarasvatī and its several tributaries such as the Dṛṣadvatī, in north-eastern Rajasthan, Haryana, and western Uttar Pradesh (Figure 11.4).[2] Thus, there appears to be more than 600 sites on the Sarasvatī and its tributaries in India and Pakistan (Figure 11.5). And certainly there are many more awaiting the spade of archaeologists (Figure 11.6). But, on the other hand, there are not even 150 sites on the Indus and its tributaries, including those more than a dozen sites which Mughal has recently discovered in Punjab, some even near Harappa, and

[1] M.R. Mughal, 'The Harappan settlement systems and patterns in the Greater Indus Valley', *Pakistan Archaeology*, No. 25, pp. 1–72. Also *Harappa Excavations 1986–1990* (Prehistory Press, Wisconsin, 1991), ed. R.H. Meadow. Also B.B. Lal, *The Earliest Civilization of South Asia.* (Aryan Books, New Delhi, 1997), 1990.

[2] Joshi et al., 'The Indus civilization: A reconsideration on the basis of distribution maps', in *Frontiers of the Indus Civilization*, (eds) B.B. Lal and S.P. Gupta, pp. 511–30.

also those S.R. Dar of Lahore Museum has found near the Salt Range in Pakistan. We, therefore, argue that the Sarasvatī should also find a prominent place in the nomenclature of this civilization. Hence, in place of the old ones, this new name, the Indus-Sarasvatī, which in any case still retains the 'Indus', because well known sites, like Mohenjo-daro and Harappa are located in the basins of the rivers of the Indus-system. The total number of Indus-Sarasvatī sites comes to around 1400 on the current showing.

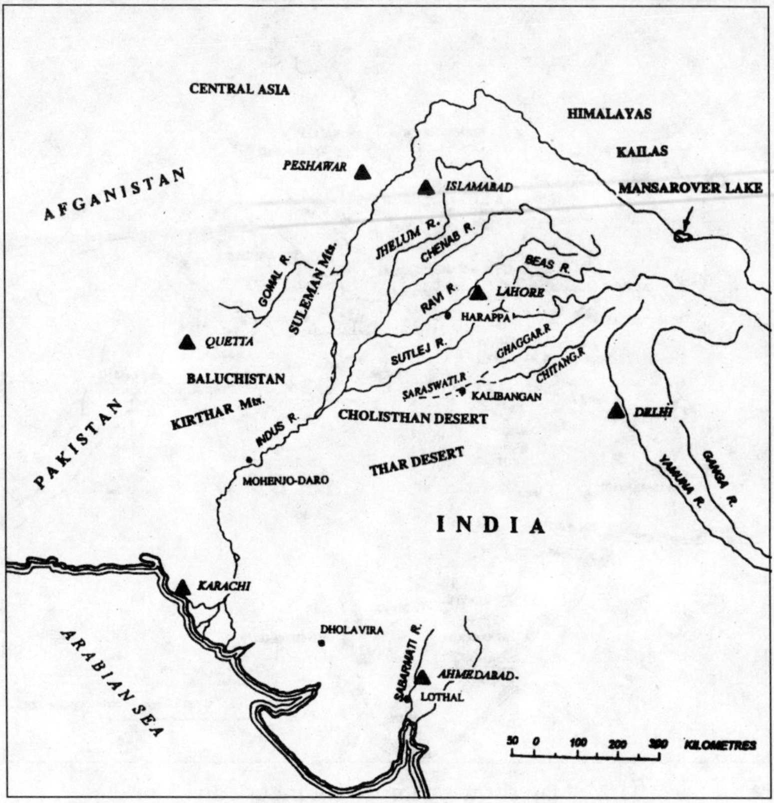

FIG. 11.1 Map showing important rivers and mountains

One thing more. It is common knowledge that it was on the banks of the Sarasvatī, now also called 'Sarasuti' (identified with Ghaggar and a few of its tributaries), that the hymns of the Vedas, the oldest literary texts in India, were composed. Sarasvatī, therefore, played an extremely important role in the making of the most ancient phase of the Indian civilization, called the Indus-Sarasvatī Culture-Complex, placed in the fourth and the third millennia BC.

The Indus and the Sarasvatī together played the same role in the making of the Bronze Age Indian civilization, which the Tigris and Euphrates played in the making of the Mesopotamian Civilization during the same period.

FIG. 11.2 Map showing important Indus-Saraswati sites

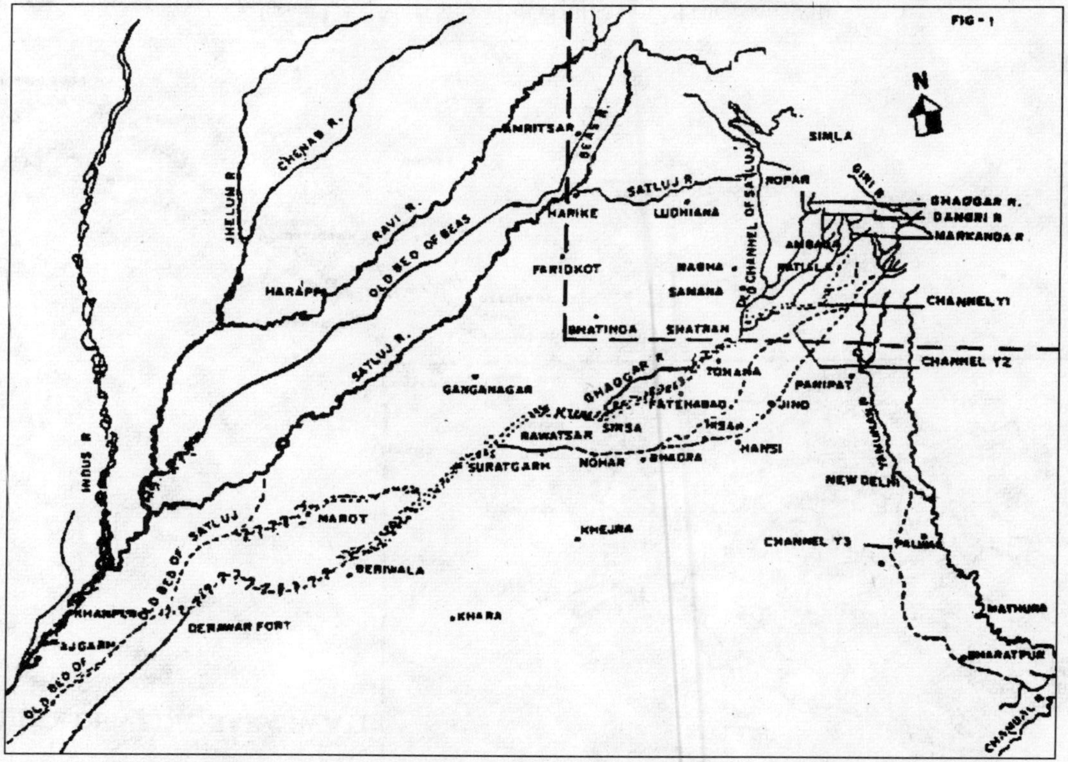

Fig. 11.3 Map showing present system and major palaeo-channels in north-west India

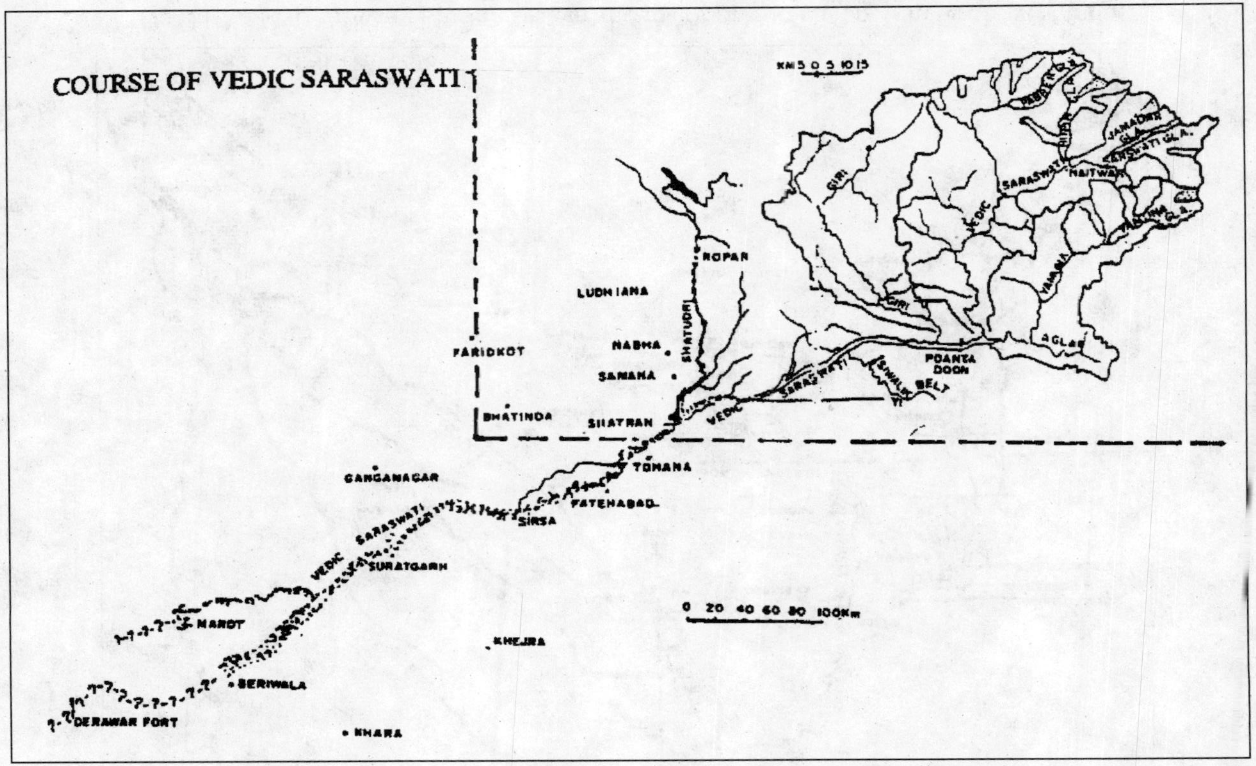

Fig. 11.4 Map showing courses of Vedic Sarasvatī

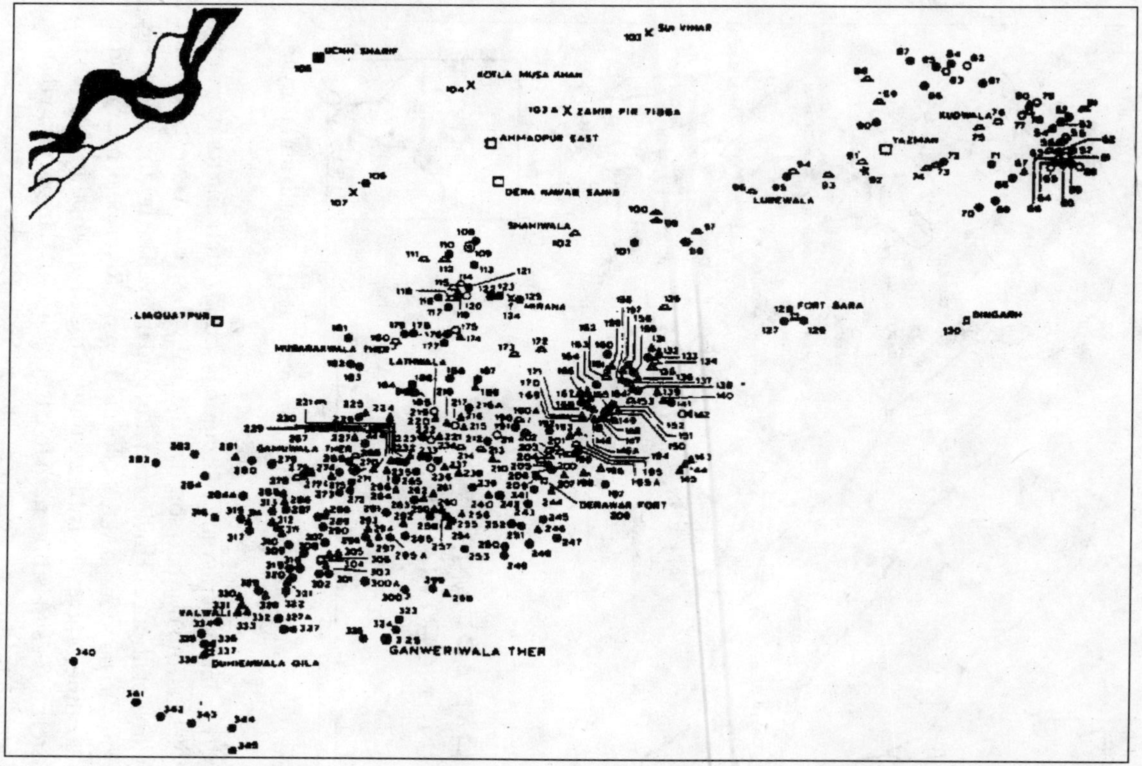

FIG. 11.5 Map showing concentration of Indus-Sarasvatī sites on Cholistan (after Mughal)

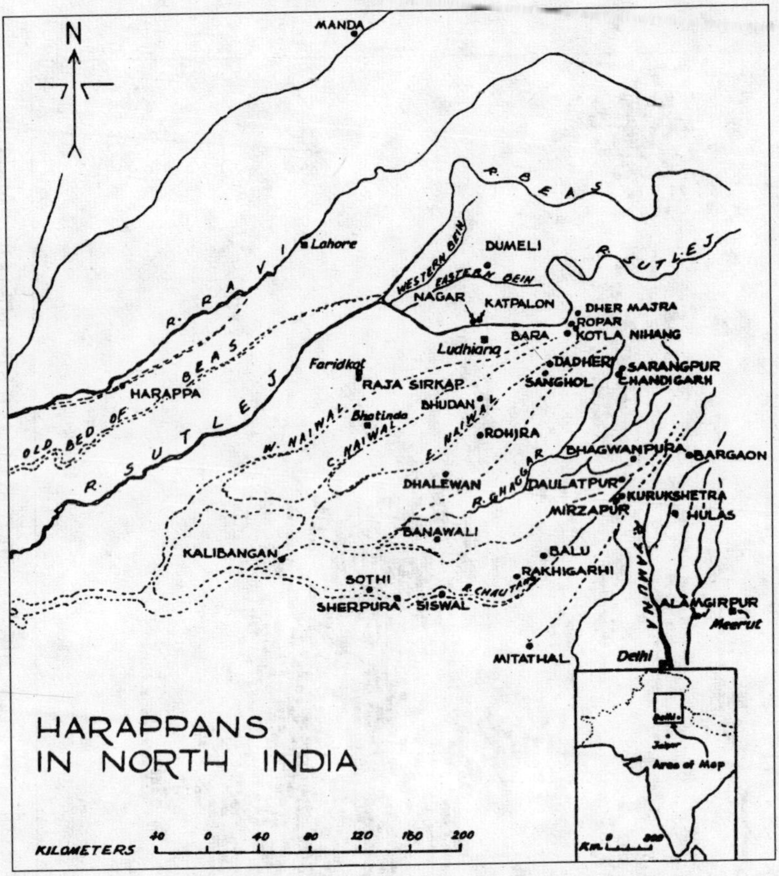

FIG. 11.6 Map showing Indus-Sarasvatī sites in Punjab and Haryana

The Indus-Sarasvatī Civilization is found extending for more than 1600 km from north to south and equally from east to west, covering an area of about 2.5 million sq. km and more. The northernmost site known to us so far is Manda, located on the River Beas near Jammu; the southernmost site is Bhagatrav on the River Tapti in Gujarat; the easternmost site is Bhorgarh in east Delhi and Alamgirpur in district Meerut; and the westernmost site is Sutkagendor, located on the ancient shore of the Arabian Sea, near the eastern border of Iran. The Indus-Sarasvatī Civilization was, therefore, around four times more in area coverage than any contemporary civilization, including the Egyptian and the Mesopotamian.

The sites belonging to the Indus-Sarasvatī Civilization are generally found located on rivers, either those still flowing like the Indus, or on the dried-up courses of old rivers like the Satluj, Sarasvatī, and Dṛṣadvatī. There are some sites in the sub-mountainous regions as well, like Mehrgarh and Nausharo on the Bolan Pass of the Kirthar mountains overlooking the lower Kachhi plains, although here also the source of water lay in a river, the Bolan. In Gujarat, on the other hand, the sites are located either on the rocky surfaces with seasonal rivers flowing nearby, like Dholavira on the Manhar in Kacch, or else on the banks of small rivers which joined sea with the hinterland, like Bhogao on which Lothal was located. In Sindh, some sites, like Ghazi Shah, are found on lakes as well, like Lake Manchhar. In recent years, some sites have been found on the ancient sea-coast as well, such as Bala Kot, Miri Kalat, and Sotka Khoh, in Pakistan, and Somnath, Bet Dwarka, etc. in India, all on the Arabian Sea. Even the islands were inhabited such as the Khadir in the Rann of Kacch where sites like Dholavira were established.

This shows that the Indus-Sarasvatī people developed a civilization, the kind of which could not be developed by any other contemporary people—neither in Egypt nor in Mesopotamia; it could overcome the barriers of seas and mountains besides large rivers, lakes, and deserts. This also shows that they had developed enough scientific and technological capabilities needed to overcome the seemingly insurmountable natural impediments.

The sites like Mohenjo-daro and Harappa, located on the large rivers like the Indus and the Ravi respectively, were always threatened by floods, sometimes so severe that the people had to erect high mud and mud-brick platforms to build the houses on top of them for safety as Mohenjo-daro and Chanhudaro. These cities suffered losses of men and materials several times during their existence. Kalibangan suffered similar losses due to earthquake and Kot Diji, Gumla, etc., due to fire. Thus, the Indus-Sarasvatī people kept on learning and improving skills in the field to town planning and house-building, particularly in those areas of Rajasthan, Sindh and Punjab which were under constant danger of being flooded.

Contrary to the popular understanding that all cities of the Indus looked alike, no two Indus-Sarasvatī cities are found identical in town planning, house-building, and water management system even though most of the sites are found protected by huge fortification walls and sharing common formal elements such as the division of the settlement in two (or more) unequal parts, the smaller of the two represented the so-called 'citadel', or the quarters of the political authorities, while the larger one represented the 'township', meant for the rest of the people as at Harappa, Mohenjo-daro, and Kalibangan. Interestingly enough, according to recent findings, Harappa (Fig. 11.7) had at least four distinct settlements, each one separately fortified with separate gateways, but one of them was the so-called 'citadel', located on a considerable height. Surkotada, on the other hand, had a single fortification encircling the entire township (Fig. 11.8). Banawali, on the other hand, had at least two rings of fortification walls (Fig. 11.9). Kalibangan had two units (Fig. 11.10), one considerably larger than the other, both separately fortified. Smaller sites, such as Allahdino near Karachi were not fortified at all. Internally also all cities were not planned on the so-called chess-board pattern, with east–west and north–south roads running. Although a part of Mohenjo-daro may have been planned like that, it was not done everywhere; Chanhudaro roads were oriented north-west–south-east and north-east–south-west. Still, most of the cities had major roads running in cardinal directions. In fact, most of the city sites, such as Harappa and Dholavira, have been found periodically growing or expanding as well as declining, at least spatially, leading to various forms of settlements: habitational uniformity and monotony in the Indus-Sarasvatī Civilization is indeed a myth created by scholars like R.E.M. Wheeler and following him repeated by most of textbook writers. The fact is that each Indus-Sarasvatī city was unique creation by the genius of its own people who had to face different sets of challenges, both natural and man-made, and not a single set of problems and predicaments.

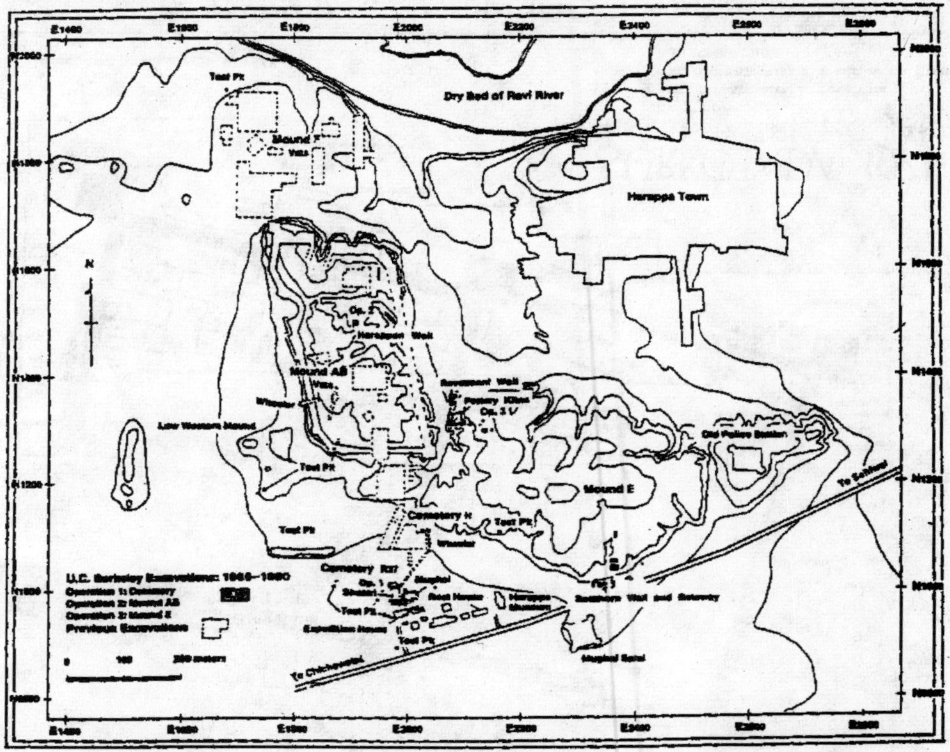

FIG. 11.7 Map showing different fortified areas of Harappa

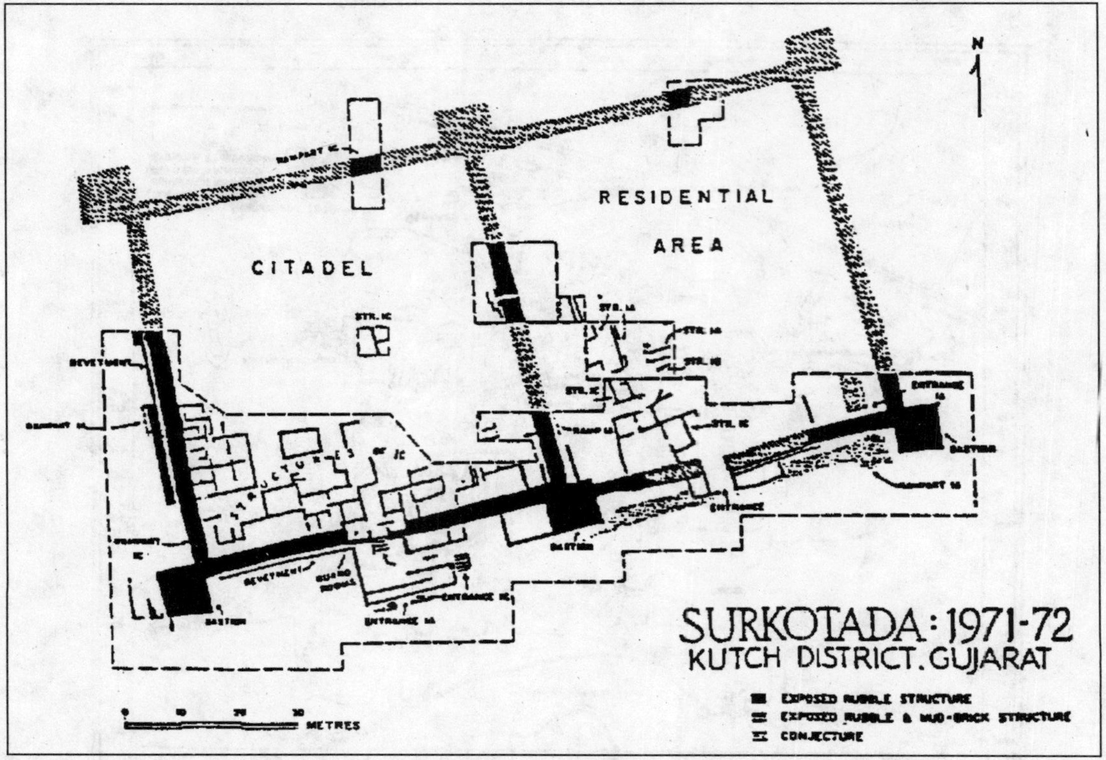

FIG. 11.8 Map showing the fortified areas at Surkotada

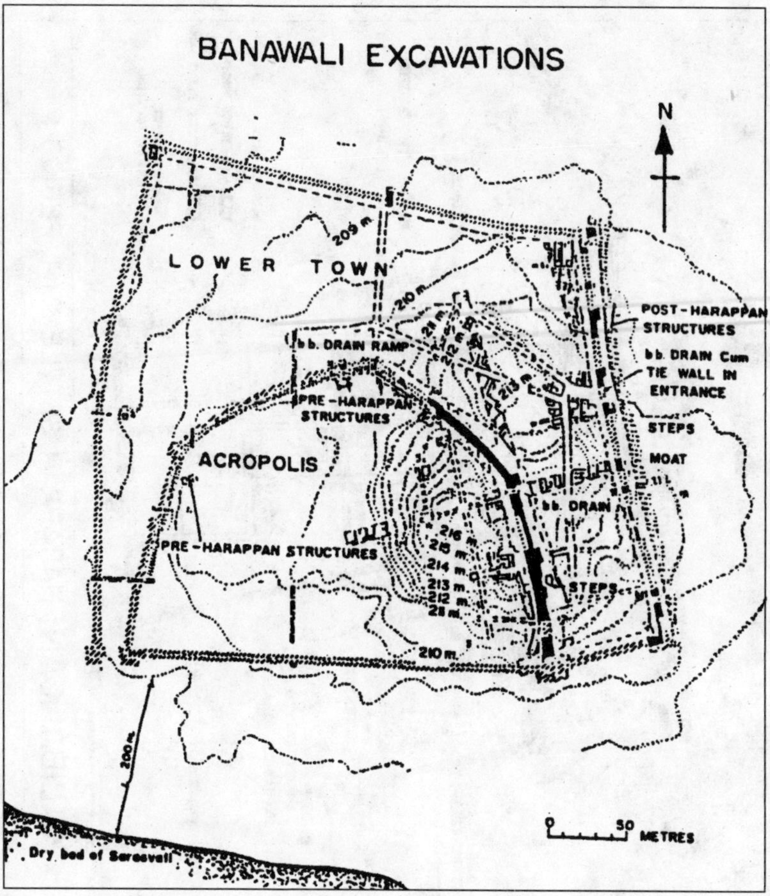

FIG. 11.9 Map showing the fortified areas at Banawali

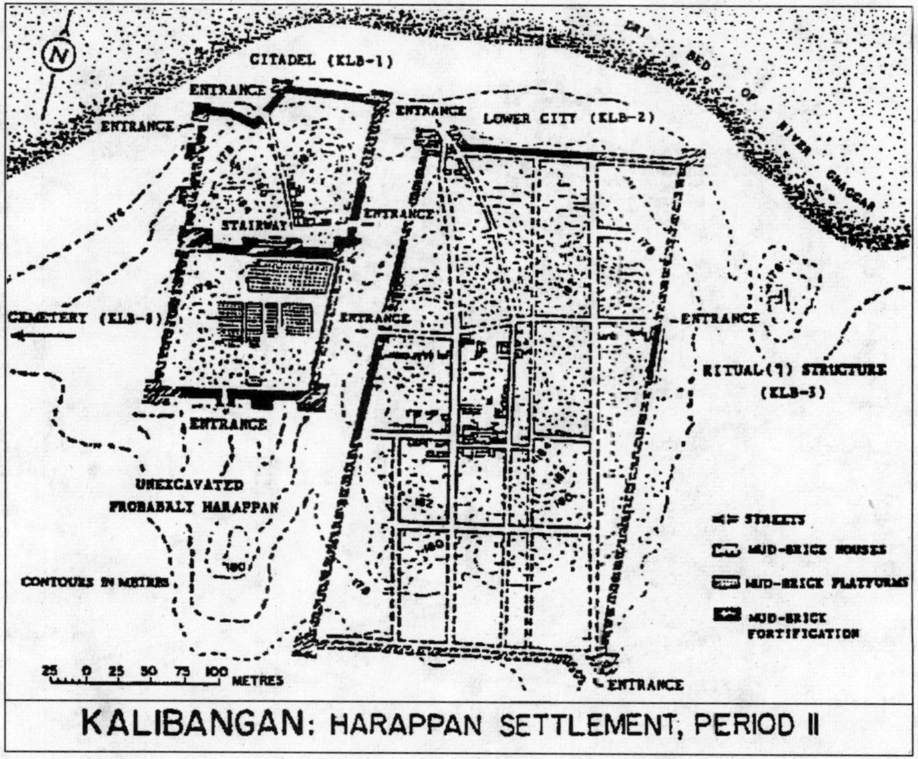

FIG. 11.10 Map showing the fortified areas at Kalibangan

Broadly, the Indus-Sarasvatī Civilization in now bracketed between 4000 and 1400 BC, which has substantially changed the proposition made by Wheeler and others in the past; according to them, the bracket was between 2500 and 1500 BC; according to one view it was only 2300 and 1700 BC. The new chronology based on new discoveries and fresh understanding of the past is divisible as follows:

The Formative Phase of the Indus-Sarasvatī Civilization (Sites: Miri Kalat, Balakot, Mehrgarh, Jalilpur, Harappa, Hakra Basin, Kunal, Padri, etc.)	4000 BC–3500 BC
The Early Phase of the Indus-Sarasvatī Civilization (Sites: Kot Diji, Rehman Dheri, Kalibangan, Sothi, Kunal, Banawali, etc.)	3500 BC–2800 BC
The Period of Transition (Sites: Harappa, Rehman Dheri, Amri, Dholavira, Surkotada, etc.)	2800 BC–2600 BC
The Mature Phase of the Indus-Sarasvatī Civilization (Sites: Harappa, Mohenjo-daro, Lothal, Kalibangan, etc.)	2600 BC–1900 BC
The Late Phase of the Indus-Sarasvatī Civilization (Sites: Cemetery 'H' at Harappa, Jhukar, Hakra Basin sites, Yamuna Basin sites, etc.)	1900 BC–1500 BC
The Final Phase of the Indus-Sarasvatī Civilization (Sites: Bhagwanpura, Dadheri, Dholavira, etc.)	1500 BC–1400 BC

(These are only broad chronological brackets of different stages of the beginning and the end of the Indus-Sarasvatī Civilization and are based upon calibrated radiocarbon dates.)

The land covered by the people of the Indus-Sarasvatī Civilization is generally semi-arid although it encompasses a variety of regions—from the dry and cold hilly tracts of the Kirthar and the Suleiman in the north-west to the dry and arid zones of Sindh and Rajasthan in the south and the east, respectively. The climate in the third millennium BC was in all probability the same as now; except perhaps for a very short period of slightly higher precipitation, a theory not accepted by all. But local hydrological changes did occur in certain regions, which affected the course as well as the volume of water in some perennial rivers. For example, during prehistoric times, tectonic upheavals in the sub-Himalayan zone as well as Haryana and Rajasthan made the Sarasvatī shift its course several times, even divided its channel into more than one, all behaving like *wadi*s (seasonal streams) and tributaries. One of the latest in the series created the Ghaggar-Hakra channel, called 'Sarasvatī Channel', between 10,000 and 5000 BC, after which aridity had set in, which is not yet over. It was fed by the glacier 200 km north of Adi Badri. Around 2000–1900 BC, a shift took place due to which the Ghaggar-Hakra-Sarasvatī water merged itself in the Yamuna through the Dṛṣadvatī Channel. On the other hand, the Satluj, a tributary of the Ghaggar-Sarasvatī channel shifted itself drastically northwestward and merged its water in the Beas.[3] All this because of the neo-tectonics in Haryana-Rajasthan. While this event of nature made the Ghaggar-Hakra-Sarasvatī channel cry for more water, the same event as well as neo-tectonic upheaval that occurred during the same time in southern Sindh, including the Karachi region, brought about unprecedented floods in the Indus as has been recorded at sites like Sehwan, Chanhudaro, and Mohenjo-daro. (Fig. 11.11).

In the past, scholars like Marshall and Wheeler[4] had surmised that the climate in Rajasthan, Sindh, and Punjab, the epicentre of this civilization, according to their views, was considerably wet throughout the 'Indus Period' because the seals as well as terracotta, stone, and bronze objects show the presence of rhinoceros, tiger,

[3] Yash Pal et al. (1984), 'Remote sensing of the "lost" Sarasvatī river', in *Frontiers of the Indus Civilization*, pp. 491–8.

[4] R.E.M. Wheeler, *The Indus Civilization*, Cambridge, 1968.

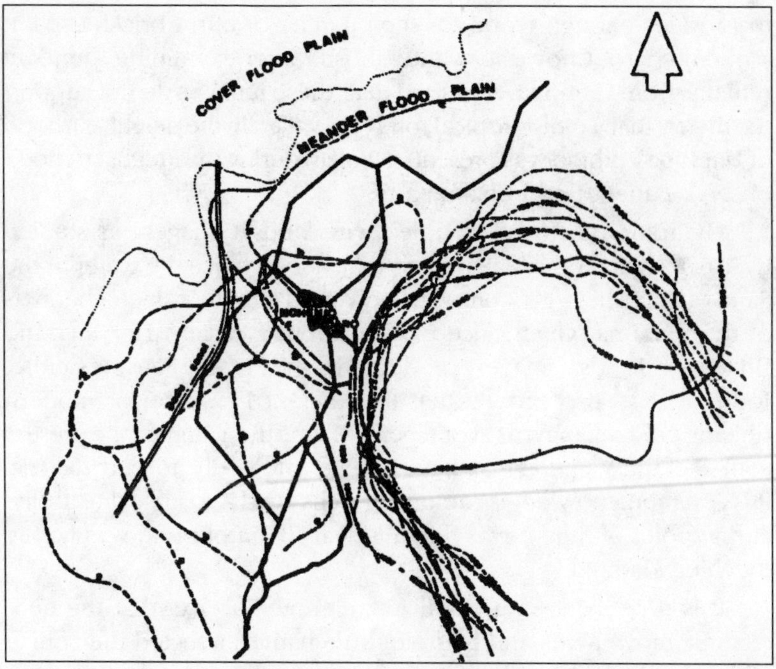

FIG. 11.11 Map showing the shifting of Indus-bed during the last 7000 years

buffalo, crocodile, etc. which live in water or slush of the marshy lands. They had also argued in favour of their theory on the basis of the presence of millions of burnt bricks at Mohenjo-daro and Harappa which, according to them, must have required ample number of trees to be felled and burnt for fuel in the kilns. However, scientific studies hardly support this theory even though some feel on the basis of pollen studies conducted by Gurdip Singh at Sambhar and other lakes, that the Mature Phase of the civilization had witnessed a little more rainfall than that of this day. But Rajasthani lakes appear to have dried from 5000 BC itself. Raikes and Dyson[5] rightly believe that only 400 acres of gallery forest along the Indus were sufficient

[5] Raikes, R.L. and R.H. Dyson, 'The prehistoric climate of Baluchsitan and the Indus valley', *American Anthropologist*, vol. 63, No. 2, pp. 256–81, 1961.

to produce enough wood for the quantity of burnt bricks used at Mohenjo-daro. Chowdhury and Ghosh,[6] after examining the plant remains from Harappa, observed that 'these remains do not support the theory that a moist tropical forest prevailed in the neighbourhood of Harappa'. 'Rhino was present in Punjab during the Mughal period,' observe Banerjee and Chakrabarti.[7]

Hydrological studies coupled with landsat imagery as studied by Yash Pal and others also show that at least twice the water of the Sarasvatī may have got completely diverted into the palaeo-channels of the Yamuna which once passed through eastern Haryana and Bharatpur. Landsat imagery produced by the Remote Sensing Centre, Jodhpur, has also proved that the ancient Dṛṣadvatī or modern Chitang or Chautang was at one point of time the Yamuna; the present course of the Yamuna may have been created only around 2000 BC. It is common knowledge Yamuna had changed its course drastically; at one point of time it was flowing near Bharatpur and was hardly touching Mathura.

It is now increasingly realized, as noted above, that the neo-tectonic movements and hydrological changes affected the course of the river Satluj as well—what was once a tributary of the Sarasvatī-Ghaggar had, at one time, after 1900 BC, become a part of the Indus system. Mughal has recently found more than a dozen Mature Indus-Sarasvatī sites on the old, now dried up, channel of the Satluj but none on the banks of the present-day channel of the Satluj (pers. comm.).

It goes a long way to prove that the oral tradition, according to which at Prayag or Allahabad it is the confluence of three rivers—the Gaṅgā, Yamunā, and Sarasvatī —and not only the first two, is not a myth since it is based upon scientifically supported facts; the

[6] K.A. Chowdhury and S.S. Ghosh, 'Plant remains from Harappa', *Ancient India*, No. 7, pp. 3–19, 1951.

[7] S. Banerjee and S. Chakrabarti, 'Remains of the great one-horned rhinoceros from Rajasthan', *Science and Culture*, p. 430, 1973.

[8] Gurdip Singh, 'The Indus valley culture' (seen in the context of Post-Glacial climate and ecological studies in North-West-India), *Archaeology and Physical Anthropology in Oceania*, 6(2), pp. 177–89, 1971.

Sarasvatī is in fact called in sacred Sanskrit literature as *vilupta nadī* or completely hidden or lost river.

The history of the Sarasvatī is, however, being constantly studied. Recent studies made by Ghose, Kar, and others[9] prove that in all likelihood, the original course of this river, of the prehistoric period, flowed through the Pañchabhadrā catchment area in the north-western Aravallis, and after flowing some distance joined the channel of the Luni, eventually emptying itself in the Great Rann of Kacch. However, due to neo-tectonic movements, its course shifted in north-westerly direction, first through the Jaisalmer region and, after some time, through the present-day Ghaggar-Hakra-Sarasvatī channel. But at what point of time the Sarasvatī left the Luni channel and adopted the present-day Ghaggar-Hakra channel in the Bikaner region is yet to be worked out, but one thing is absolutely clear: during the fourth millennium it flowed past Banawali, Kunal, Kalibangan and entered the Bikaner-Bahawalpur region of Pakistan. In other words, the Luni and Jaisalmer stages of the Sarasvatī were of the Stone Age period while the Ghaggar-Hakra stage is of the Bronze Age.

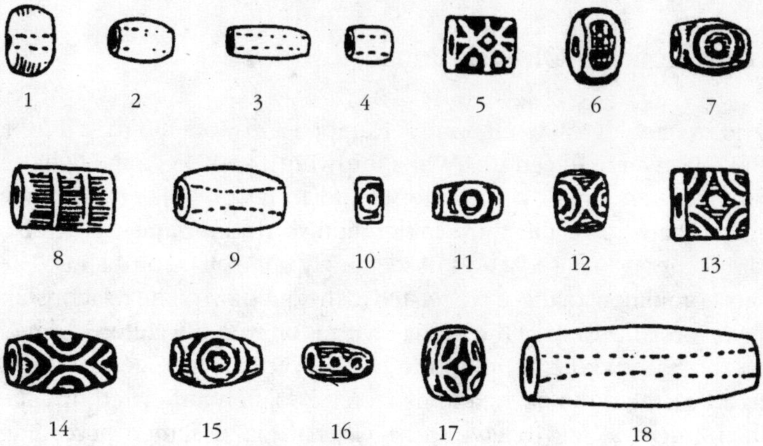

FIG. 11.12 Etched carnelian beads from Shadad, Iran

[9] B. Ghose et al., 'The lost courses of the Sarasvatī river in the Great Indian Desert: New evidence from Landsat imagery', *The Geographical Journal*, vol. 145(3), pp. 446–51, 1979.

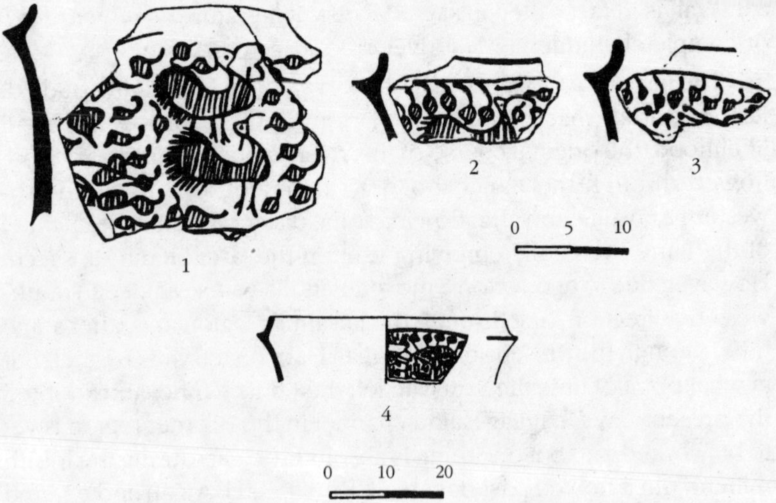

FIG. 11.13 Indus-Sarasvatī pottery at Shortughai, Afghanistan

...

New Light on Old Problems

The archaeological work done at Harappa and Mohenjo-daro during the mid-twentieth century, while throwing a very welcome light on a completely unknown chapter of Indian history, viz., the Bronze Age urbanism of the third millennium BC Indus-Sarasvatī, it also simultaneously raised a host of seemingly unresolved problems. The most prominent of these are related to the question of the relationship or non-relationship of the Indus Civilization with the culture formed by the Early Vedic people in India. Till recently, the general view had been that the two cultures were absolutely unrelated; in fact, the former was said to have ended when the latter started, according to Marshall, Wheeler, and others, for the reasons set out below.

The Vedic hymns were supposed to have been composed after 1500 BC and compiled in the form of books between 1200 and 1000 BC. This view was propounded, though not insisted upon by Max Müller in the mid-nineteenth century and accepted by many scholars, both foreign and Indian, without much questioning. On the other hand, the Indus-Sarasvatī Civilization was believed to have belonged to the period between 2500 and 1500 BC, a view propounded and insisted upon by Mortimer Wheeler in 1964 and accepted by many scholars with hardly any modification at either end.[10] This has been completely modified. As shown earlier, the bracket is 4000 BC–1400 BC.

The Vedic people were equestrian, domesticating and using horses in their everyday lives while the Indus-Sarasvatī people were not using this animal in any form according to these authors; the two were, therefore, entirely different from each other. In fact, they were opposed to each other as enemies, they opined.[11] But the bones of the domesticated horses have been found at several places as will be shown a little later.

The Vedic literature abounds in references to cattle, particularly the cow, which, according to these authors, implies that the Vedic people were primarily nomadic in habit and pastoralists in occupation. On the other hand, the Indus-Sarasvatī people were primarily not only agriculturists but also city-dwellers engaged in manufacturing a variety of goods and in long-distance trade; the two were, therefore, entirely different people culturally also, according to them.[12] But this is not true. The Vedic people were also metallurgists and they engaged themselves in long-distance trade as will be shown shortly.

The hymns of the Vedas were composed in the basins of the Sarasvatī and Dṛṣadvatī as per the internal evidence of the Vedic literature, while the Indus-Sarasvatī people generally lived in the basins of the Indus and some of its tributaries; therefore the two could not be the same people, they argued.[13] But it is not true. There are many times more sites on the Sarasvatī than on the Indus as will be shown a little later.

The Vedic people were not only nomadic people using horse-driven chariots for wandering, they were also a martial people

[10] Wheeler, *op. cit.*

[11] J. Marshall, *Mohenjodaro and the Indus Civilization* (London), 1932.

[12] R.S. Sharma, 'Who were the Aryans?', in *Miscellany*, 19 December, pp. 4–5, 1993.

[13] Wheeler, *op. cit.*

engaged in warfare, destroying fortified townships under the command of Indra, the supreme Vedic god, while the Indus-Sarasvatī people were peace-loving town dwellers and traders, maintained Wheeler; others simply repeating what he said.[14] But this is not true. The Vedic people lived in a variety of houses in cities as will be shown.

Wheeler also proposed the theory that in the formation of the Indus-Sarasvatī cities, the Mesopotamian cities had a lot to contribute. The very idea of a city came from Mesopotamia, since he refused to believe that there were earlier evolutionary stages of this civilization in the Indus valley;[15] others questioned him only rarely during his lifetime. It is not true since there is now ample archaeological evidence to show that the Indus-Sarasvatī cities grew out of Indus-Sarasvatī townships and not modelled after the Mesopotamian cities.

Marshall, Wheeler, and others also said that while the Vedic people used iron in their everyday lives, the Indus-Sarasvatī people had no knowledge of this metal, hence they were not the same people. But this is also not true since the Ṛgvedic people knew metals (*ayasa*) but not iron. Thus many of these propositions have, of late, not been found acceptable when the evidence produced was re-scrutinized. For example, Indra's invasion of the Indus-Sarasvatī cities like Harappa, the massacre of the Indus-Sarasvatī people by the invading armies of the Vedic Aryans at Mohenjo-daro,[16] the end of the Indus-Sarasvatī Civilization caused by the barbarous inroads of the Aryan tribes coming from the west,[17] particularly from Central Asia, and descending down to the plains of Punjab in their horse-driven chariots, as warlike nomadic people. They came in one wave or several waves, pushing out the original inhabitants because of their better weaponry and making them flee towards the southern states of India where Dravidian languages are spoken.[18] This

[14] Ibid.

[15] Ibid.

[16] G.F. Dales, 'Mythical massacre at Mohenjo-daro', *Expedition*, vol. 16, No. 3, pp. 37–43, 1964.

[17] Piggott, S., *Prehistoric India* (Pelican, London), 1951.

[18] A.D. Pusalkar, 'The Indus civilization', in (ed.) R.C. Majumdar, *The Vedic Age* (Bombay), pp. 172–202, 1952.

somewhat overdramatized scenario, skilfully sketched by the older writers and presently echoed by scholars like Asko Parpola, has now been replaced by a more sober and realistic scenario, thanks to the painstaking researches done by the present generation of scholars in India and abroad. For example, Bhagwan Singh has shown that the Vedic society had a number of craft-specialists and metallurgists who were engaged in 'long-distance' 'sea' and 'land' trade and commerce. It is based upon the internal evidence of the Vedic literature itself. His book *The Vedic Harappans* has innumerable references to this fact. Let us look at the problem afresh.

FIG. 11.14 Indus-Sarasvatī style seals from Altyn Depe

FIG. 11.15 Indus-Sarasvatī seal from Shortughai, Afghanistan

CHART 11.1 Indus-Saraswati Civilization: Stages of Development (4000 BC–1500 BC)

Period	*Approximate Time Bracket*	*Region and Cultures*					
		Punjab	*Sindh*	*Rajasthan and Cholistan*	*Haryana*	*Gujarat*	*Baluchistan*
Late Period	1900 BC to 1500 BC	Cemetery–H Nagar Dadheri Katpalon Sanghol—I	Jhukar	Kudwala Lurewala Gamanwala Siddhuwala Shahiwala	Mithathal–IIB Bhagwanpura–IB	Dholavira–VI Kuntasi–II Surkotada–IC Rojdi Lothal B	Mehargarh–VIII Sibri
Mature Period	2600 BC to 1900 BC	Harappa–III C B A	Mohenjo-daro (Upper Levels) Balakot–II	Kalibangan–II Ganeshwar–II Ganweriwala	Banawali–II Kunal IC	Dholavira–IV Kuntasi–I Surkotada IA–IB Padri II Rojdi Lothal A	Nausharo–II
Transition Period	2800 BC to 2600 BC	Harappa–II Kot Diji B	Mohenjo-daro (Intermediate Levels) Balakot–II (Lower Levels)	Kalibangan (I–II Overlap)	Banawali–IC Kunal IB (Upper Level)	Dholavira–III Surkotada–IA (Lower Levels)	Nausharo–II–IC

(Contd)

Period	*Approximate Time Bracket*	*Region and Cultures*					
		Punjab	*Sindh*	*Rajasthan and Cholistan*	*Haryana*	*Gujarat*	*Baluchistan*
Early Period	3500 BC to 2800 BC	Kot Diji–I Harappa–I	Kot Diji–I Mohenjo-daro (Lower Levels) (Pre-Defence)	Ganweriwala Kalibangan–I Ganeshwar–I Sothi Culture	Kunal IB Kot Diji Banawali IA–IB	Dholavira–I–II Padri–I	Mehrgarh V–VII Nausharo IA & B
Formative Period	4000+ BC to 3500 BC	Pre-Harappa–I 'Ravi Culture' (Pre-Kot Diji) Level Jalilpur–I	Amri Culture Miri Kalat–II Balakot–I	Ganweriwala Hakra Culture Lathwala–I Bhostanwala Ambrawali Chikrala	Kunal Culure Kunal–IA	Padri I Loteshwar	Mehrgarh–IV–V

Backdrop

It is now more or less clear that, around 8000 BC, Late Stone Age nomadic hunters and gatherers started settling down in the hills and the piedmont regions of Afghanistan and Baluchistan. The first permanent villages of these people started domesticating cattle, sheep, and goats as well as cultivating cereals like barley and wheat, ushering in the era called Neolithic whose economy was based on agriculture and animal husbandry. Civilization now begins in this part of the world, since sedentariness is the prerequisite for the growth of human management skills which alone leads to various innovations, making the community life of a people change its socio-economic and cultural character from somewhat self-sufficient village units to a highly complex and interdependent city network. There is now ample archaeological, palaeozoological, and palaeobotanical, evidence to prove that between 8000 BC and 6000 BC, sedentariness became a permanent feature of the lifestyle of a people who chose the wide terraces of the Bolan river in the piedmont of the Kirthar mountains where the river meets the plains of northern Sindh to live on; the place is known as Mehrgarh.[19] Between 6000 BC and 4000 BC, these people developed copper and bronze metallurgy as well as craftsmanship in bone, stone, and terracotta, besides a belief-system manifested in the formal disposal of the dead, imagery and symbols, leading to long-distance trade and commerce as well as development of rites and rituals connected with the belief-systems. From 4000 BC onwards we see the movement of these people towards the Indus basin and hilly lowlands of southern Baluchistan; this is well attested at sites like Ghazi Shah, Amri, Miri, Kalat, and Mohenjo-daro.[20]

The date 4000 BC is very crucial in Indian history from yet another point of view. We find the birth of the first villages in the plains of the Indo-Gangetic divide through which also flows the Sarasvatī and its tributaries, such as the Dṛṣadvatī, as well as the tributaries of the

[19] J.F. Jarrige, 'Excavations at Mehrgarh: Their significance for understanding the background of the Harappa civilization', in (ed.) G.L. Poesshl, *Harappan Civilization*, pp. 79–84, 1982.

[20] Shashi Asthana, *Pre-Harappan Cultures of India and the Borderlands* (Books and Books, New Delhi), 1985.

Indus like the Ravi, Satluj, and Beas. At sites like Harappa and Jalilpur in Punjab and Kunal in Haryana, there are indications that Neolithic-Chalcolithic villages, going back to 5000–4000 BC, with clusters of huts were established there.[21] The 'Hakra Culture' sites in Bahawalpur region, along the lost Sarasvatī, also belong to this category.

In the region around Taxila, a similar socio-economic change seems to have occurred. At sites like Sarai Khola we have definite evidence of Neolithic-Chalcolithic villages.[22] In Bannu valley, there are the remains of the early fourth millennium Neolithic villages at sites like Lewan and Sheri Khan Tarakai.[23]

In the Gomal valley also, the early fourth millennium levels have yielded evidence of Neolithic-Chalcolithic villages at sites like Gumla.[24] In southern Sindh too, there were Neolithic-Chalcolithic villages at sites like Balakot and Miri Kalat during the early fourth millennium.[25] In Gujarat also, both northern and southern, we find Neolithic-Chalcolithic villages at sites like Loteshwar and Padri, going back to the early fourth millennium.[26]

All this clearly shows that, in the process of the formation of the Indus-Sarasvatī Civilization, which was typically a lowland cultural phenomenon, not one but several regions were directly or indirectly involved, as has been pointed out by Mughal.[27] The usual American perception (of scholars like Possehl) that the highland Baluchi cultures, such as the Quetta culture with roots in Iranian Neolithic

[21] S.P. Gupta, *The Indus-Sarasvatī Civilization* (Pratibha Prakashan, New Delhi), 1996.

[22] M.A. Halim, 'Excavations at Sarai Khola, Pt. II', *Pakistan Archaeology*, No. 8, pp. 1–112, 1972.

[23] F.R. Allchin et al. (eds), *Lewan and the Bannu Basin: Excavation and Survey of Sites and Environments in North-West Pakistan*, 1986.

[24] A.H. Dani, 'Excavation in the Gomal Valley', *Ancient Pakistan*, vol. 5, pp. 1–77, 1971.

[25] G.F. Dales, 'Reflections on four years of excavations at Balakot', in (ed.) A.H. Dani, *Indus Civilization: New Perspectives*, pp. 25–32, 1981.

[26] V.H. Sonawane and P. Ajithprasad, 'Harappan culture and Gujarat', *Man and Environment*, vol. XIX, Nos 1–2, pp. 129–40, 1994.

[27] Mughal (1990), *op. cit.*

cultures of the Zagros mountains, and the Iranian Bronze Age cultures were primarily responsible for the birth and early growth of the Indus-Sarasvatī Civilization, therefore, requires serious reconsideration since the pre-4000 BC cultures leading to the 4000 BC settlements are now locally available in Punjab, Haryana, Rajasthan, and Gujarat, particularly at Harappa, where a four-metre deposit of handmade black painted red ware with mud-brick houses was found in early 1996.

Our view is that the roots of urbanism go deep into the Chalcolithic villages. It occurred during the early fourth millennium BC at various places and not one. In other words, priority in terms of chronology alone does not prove that Mehrgarh alone civilized the whole Indus-Sarasvatī region, extending from southern Gujarat to Haryana, Punjab, and beyond. In fact, the Mehrgarh pottery, copper objects, shell items, etc. are not found at sites like Padri, Nagwada, Jalilpur, and Sarai Khola. Although we are not at all sure about the founders of the first Chalcolithic villages in the Trans-Indus regions, such as Harappa, it is important to note that at least a thousand years prior to the growth of urbanism in the Indo-Gangetic divide, there were Chalcolithic cultures which eventually developed into the Indus-Sarasvatī Civilization.

The process of change was, however, neither unilinear nor uniform although, when we take the overall picture and leave aside the details, we see directional changes which created a pattern in which some sites remained 'resource areas' for the raw materials needed by the craftsmen; some sites developed as 'manufacturing centres', some sites remained camp-sites of the migrating labour, perhaps; some sites developed as small townships playing a vital role in developing trade routes for internal trade, both river-borne and land-borne; some sites developed as large cities with centres of multiple activities, including manufacturing, trading, and political(?) activities, while some other sites developed as cities of moderate sizes but engaged in import and export business through seaports. The following example noted by Mughal testifies that this was so. It concerns sites he explored along the lost Sarasvatī in the Bikaner deserts called Cholistan.[28]

[28] Ibid.

The Cholistan has given a good sample size of 414 sites among which 264 sites belong to Early, Mature and Late Harappan Periods of the Indus Civilization. In addition, 99 sites represent an earlier period called Hakra while 14 sites belong to the Painted Grey Wares of the first millennium BC, making a total of 337 sites.

All the sites are not settlements but as observed on the surface fall into several distinct categories: industrial, where craft related activities and kilns for firing of pottery and other materials are concentrated; multifunctional sites combining settlements with specialized activity areas in or near the settlements; purely habitational sites; camp sites marking temporary occupation by the herders and grazers; and two cemetery sites. All the sites are located along or near the changing course of the Hakra River which ultimately dried up around the beginning of the first millennium BC. The area now consists of wide open and level mud flats partially covered with drift sand that has advanced 30 to 35 kilometers eastwards from the original limits of the Thar Desert.

Therefore, there is no single-site origin of the Indus-Sarasvatī Civilization; in its origins, many people, many centres, many craft specializations, many mining activities, many trade routes, and many talents of management of long-distance trade and travel got involved in a network of systems dealing with politics, municipality, commerce, and beliefs. And this picture is also reflected in the Vedic literature. This is crucial. Very crucial indeed from the point of view of correlation between archaeology and literature because without this we shall never reach the truth.

The sole reason why the truth was not revealing itself to us in this context was simple enough: the misrepresentation of the economic character of the Vedic society by the scholars of literature, that the Vedic society was 'pastoralist', there was neither the craft-specialization in it nor trade and commerce. Max Müller called it 'most primitive'. Hence, even B.B. Lal suggested in 1951 that the Vedic society is reflected in the Painted Grey Ware villages dated to 1100–600 BC. But once this false shell is broken, the dichotomy between the Indus-Sarasvatī society and the Vedic society completely vanishes. This we will show now. First, the question of the presence or absence of the horse on the Indus-Sarasvatī sites.

The Horse in the Indus-Sarasvatī Civilization

More than twenty years ago, A.K. Sharma[29] identified bones of domesticated horse (*Equus caballus* Linn.) coming from the stratified deposits of Surkotada, a Mature Harappan or Indus-Sarasvatī site in Gujarat excavated by J.P. Joshi. He published these findings in *Purātattva* No. 7 (1974). The bones found include leg bones, hoofs, phalanx, molars, incisors, and cannon bones (Plate 1). However, his views remained a suspect in the eyes of disbelievers as noted earlier, till 13 December 1991 when the same bones were re-examined by Dr Sandro Bokonyi from Budapest, an internationally recognized archaeo-zoologist, specializing in horse bones. He declared that the bones belonged to the 'true domesticated horses', *Equus caballus* Linn. This has, therefore, set at rest the controversy raised by the observations of Richard Meadow who had not personally examined the bones in question but still felt (1986) that the Surkotada bones may not have belonged to the true horse. It is significant to note that bones of *Equus caballus* Linn. were found at the sites not just from a single layer of a single level; they were found by the excavator in all the levels, from the bottom to the top, spanning the entire period of the Mature Indus-Sarasvatī Civilization of the third millennium. The full scientific report on the excavation by J.P. Joshi was published by the Archaeological Survey of India in 1990 under the title *Excavations at Surkotada 1971–72 and Explorations in Kacch.*

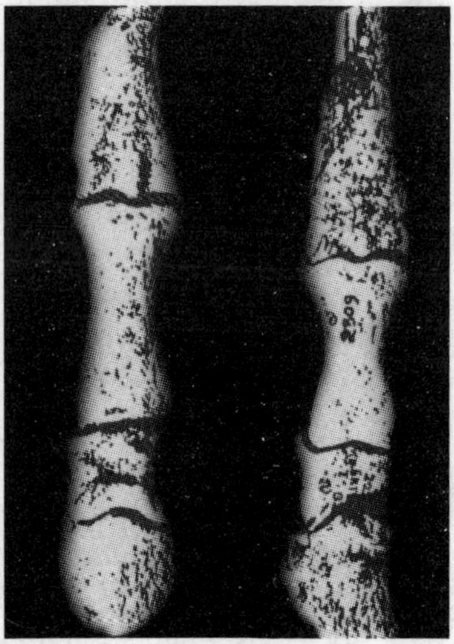

PLATE 1 Surkotada: Leg bones of a domesticated horse

[29] A.K. Sharma, 'Evidence of horse from the Harappan settlement at Surkotada', *Purātattva*, No. 7, pp. 75–6, 1974.

Fortunately, this did not remain a unique find because if it had been, it would have led to several speculations such as the possibility of a 'one-time import of domesticated horses at one of the Indus settlements'. In 1979, S.R. Rao[30] found the bones of domesticated horses in his excavations at Lothal, also in Gujarat, from the Mature Indus-Sarasvatī as well as Late Indus-Sarasvatī levels. He found even a terracotta figurine of the horse in Lothal (Plate 2).

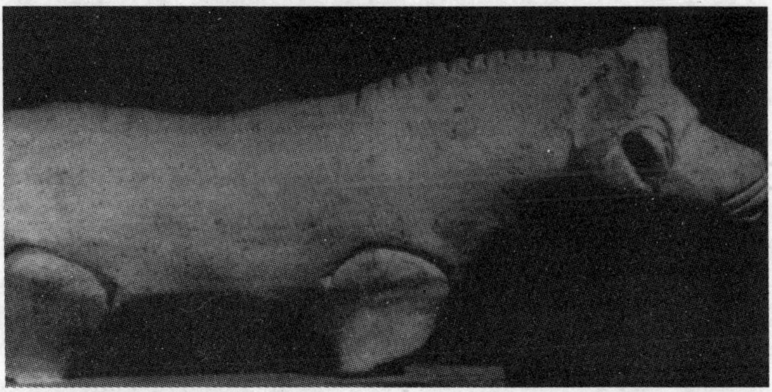

PLATE 2 Lothal: Terracotta figurine of a horse

Surkotada and Lothal are not the only Indus-Sarasvatī sites where the true horse was in use. Bhola Nath, the archaeo-zoologist of the Zoological Survey of India had, as far back as 1953 identified the bones of domesticated horse within a large collection of animal bones from Area G of Harappa in Punjab.[31] Bhola Nath, in fact, identified the bones of *Equus caballus* Linn. from yet another Mature Indus-Sarasvatī site, Ropar,[32] near Ambala in Punjab, excavated by Y.D. Sharma in 1953.

[30] S.R. Rao, *Lothal: A Harappan Port Town*, 1955–62, Memoir of the Archaeological Survey of India, No. 78, 1985.

[31] Bhola Nath, 'Remains of horse and elephant from prehistoric site of Harappa, West Pakistan', *Proceedings of First All India Congress of Zoologists*, vol. 2, Scientific Papers, pp. 1–14, 1953.

[32] Bhola Nath, 'Advances in the study of prehistoric and ancient animals in India—Archaeology review', *Records of the Zoological Survey of India*, vol. 61, pp. 1–13, 1968.

That Kalibangan in Rajasthan, another Mature Indus-Sarasvatī site, excavated by B.B. Lal also yielded bones of domesticated horses became quite clear when not only A.K. Sharma but also the archaeo-zoologists of the Zoological Survey of India confirmed in writing on 30 November 1992 that, among the bones of many species of animals and birds found there, the bones of *Equus caballus* Linnaeus occur as well.[33]

In 1972–3 the Indus-Sarasvatī site of Malvan in Gujarat was excavated by J.P. Joshi and F.R. Allchin.[34] A.K. Sharma, who also participated in the excavations, identified bones of the domesticated or true horse from this site as well (specimen nos 63 and 25 are lumbar vertebra of *caballus* Linn.).

It may be recalled that, as early as 1938, Mackay[35] found a terracotta horse figurine at Mohenjo-daro. Wheeler also noticed horse bones too at Mohenjo-daro as early 1968.[36] He rightly observed: 'It is likely enough that camel, horse and ass were in fact all familiar features of the Indus caravans.' The caravans did indeed regularly cross the highlands of Gujarat and the lowlands of Sindh, Punjab, and Rajasthan. In other words, the horse was widely domesticated and used in India during the third millennium BC over most of the area covered by the Indus-Sarasvatī Civilization. Archaeologically this is most significant since the evidence is widespread and not isolated. During the second millennium BC, the presence of the horse at Pirak in Baluchistan is also well known.

Unfortunately, the horse has become a bone of contention between two groups of historians dealing with the 'Aryan Problem' in India, the so-called Nationalists and the so-called Marxists. The former, basing their views on the archaeological findings, maintain that the people of the Indus-Sarasvatī Civilization may have been the Vedic Aryans who are known in history for their chariots driven by horses, while the latter hold that the archaeological findings are

[33] A.K. Sharma, 'The Harappan horse was buried under the dunes of ***', *Purātattva*, No. 23, pp. 30–5, 1993.

[34] J.P. Joshi and F.R. Allchin, *Excavations at Malvan*, Archaeological Survey of India, New Delhi, 1995.

[35] E.J.F. Mackay, *Chanhudaro Excavations 1935–36* (New Delhi), 1943.

[36] Wheeler, *op. cit.*

'minor', 'limited', and 'marginal', and hold onto the age-old view that the people of the Indus-Sarasvatī Civilization were not horse-users, hence could not be the Vedic Aryans. To say the least, this is a strange logic. For the scientists, Indus-Sarasvatī people were definitely horse-users, whether they were Vedic Aryans or not hardly concerns them. But Marshall certainly erred grossly when he observed that the Indus people could not be Vedic Aryan because they were not familiar with the horse, let alone its users. Incidentally, in the Vedas the people are never called *aśvārohīs*, that is, horsemen, they are credited only with chariots driven by horses. They ate sheep, etc. but not horse meat or camel meat. Hence, it is not surprising that the horse and camel bones are only rarely found in excavations.

Recently Bhagwan Singh[37] has made a very plausible suggestion with regard to the process of domestication of the horse, on the basis of biosphere, Vedic references, and archaeology. He starts with the observations made by Sandor Bokonyi in his letter dated 13 December 1991 to the Director-General, Archaeological Survey of India, M.C. Joshi:

(i) I can verify the supposition of A.K. Sharma concerning the occurrence of domestic horse in the site (Surkotada).

(ii) The occurrence of true horse (*Equus caballus* L.) was evidenced by the enamel pattern of the upper and lower cheek and teeth and by the size and form of incisors and phalanges [toe bones].

(iii) Since no wild horses lived in India in post-Pleistocene times, the domestic nature of the Surkotada horses is undoubtful. *This is also supported by an inter-maxilla fragment whose incisor tooth shows clear signs of crib biting, a bad habit only existing among domestic horses which are not extensively used for war.*

(iv) These horses were obviously imported from horse-domestication centres recently discovered in Soviet Central Asia whose distance was essentially shorter from India than from those in the Ukraine known since the mid-1960s.

[37] Bhagwan Singh, *The Vedic Harappans* (Aditya Prakashan, New Delhi), pp. 58–9.

(v) Since horse bones represent adult individuals, one can rightly suppose that the main exploitation of these horses was work (thus they were riding, pack or draught animals); nevertheless their meat was also eaten.

(vi) Besides horse bones, the overwhelming majority of equid remains are teeth and bones of the khur, the Indian wild half-ass (*Equus hemionus* khur) that once lived in great numbers, and is still existing sporadically in Kacch.

Bhagwan Singh[38] then goes to put forward his own hypothesis:

We visualise three stages of use of equids by the Vedic Aryans or the Harappans. Firstly, they exploited the onager available in their surroundings. They called this beast *aśva* as it moved faster than the other animals known to them. At the second stage, in the course of their trade they came to know of the Kacch ass. At earlier stages they considered even the goat, *ajaśva*, and spotted deer, *prasadasva*, among the fast animals, the former being the vehicle of Agni and the latter that of the Maruts. At the third stage, when a more energetic breed, the steppe horse, was introduced, the appellation was transferred to it as it was faster than the ass. But it continued to be used for quite some time for the ass as well. *Aśvatara* stuck to its ground and continues to be used for mules in Sanskrit even today. It is notable that this cross-breed was considered sturdier than the 'horse' known to the 'horse-riding' Aryans. However, when *aśva* became an exclusive term for the horse, *khara, raśabha, gardabha*, etc. were affixed distinctively to the ass. It is interesting that *khara* (cf. *prakhara*) and *raśabha* (f. *sar/ras*, Eng. rush, rash—onomatopoeic stems derived from the whizzing sound of wind and transferred to other fast-moving beings and things, including water) also refer to the speed of the animal.

'It appears that the Rann of Kacch with islands known for the wild ass (*Equus hemionus* Khur) was somewhat deeper during the Vedic or Harappan days and as such its ports were accessible through the naval route. R.S. Bisht writes, 'Traditions has it that it was once an extension of the Arabian Sea and was utilised for maritime trade through its various ports perched along both its banks—the southern and northern. The ships of the renowned merchant Jagdu Sha, carrying gold and miscellaneous provisions, are said to be sailing from port to port in the Rann'.

[38] Ibid., pp. 62–3.

The fact that the Vedic people imported the 'horse' from Kacch is supported by Vedic literature which is full of references to the *aśva* owing its birth to water or sea. *Uccaiḥśrava*, the *aśva* emerging from the churning of the sea of milk or *kṣīrasāgara*, is the ass found as a wild animal in Kacch. It may be pointed out that Khirsar was a port in Kacch and it has a mound of Harappan times. It is all the more important for us that another name of Khirsar is 'Ghodewali wadi', the town (marketing centre) of horses.

I am sure the book entitled *The Vedic Harappans* by Bhagwan Singh will be an eye-opener to all the archaeologists who have very little knowledge of Vedic Sanskrit and Vedic literature.

The Indus-Sarasvatī Civilization and the Vedic Culture: A Reappraisal

Once it is clear that the Indus-Sarasvatī urbanism was a product of a developing culture-process of indigenous origin, we may return to our earlier issues and deal with a few specific issues, particularly those on the basis of which the Indus-Sarasvatī Civilization was once considered non-Vedic, a view which has now been found to be invalid.

The basic issue is the economic character of the Vedic society, as noted earlier. Undoubtedly, the source to reconstruct it is the Vedic literature itself. Bhagwan Singh has pursued this study. He used partly the linguistic approach and partly the contextual approach. The conclusions arrived at have indeed been startling. The economic character of the Vedic people has emerged as a strong combination of rural and urban elements and not just pastoral or agricultural pastoralism. The thrust of present-day arguments in favour of the theory of Vedic and Harappan or Indus-Sarasvatī identity rests on the major grounds set out below.

It is common knowledge that the Indus-Sarasvatī people or the Harappans were enterprising traders and that they had overseas contacts with the Persian Gulf countries like Oman, Bahrain, Failaka, and Sumer since the Indus-Sarasvatī seals and sealings, pottery, beads, copper tools and ingots, weights of chert, etc., have been found at more than a dozen sites in these countries. Do we then get any reference to sea trade in the Vedic literature, even through the Vedic seers may have been least concerned with these activities? The answer is in the affirmative; there are indeed several references to sea (*samudra*) and traders (*paṇis*) engaged in sea-borne trade. *Navaḥ samudriyaḥ, śata-aritra* are among such terms which clearly indicate it. So much so that even piracy is mentioned. Fights on boats are mentioned. Attacks on boats laden with goods by unscrupulous people in order to capture them finds clear mention (ṚV.I. 36.18, 61;II;IV,196). *Ugradeva, Navavastva, Bṛhadratha, Turviti*, the *Yadus* and *Vayya* had tough encounters with pirates, notes Singh.

Trade with distant lands presupposes the emergence and consolidation of an internal trade network. At Dholavira we have a signboard with ten letters (Plate 3), obviously used for trading purposes. Does the Vedic literature throw some light on it? Yes, it does. Rivers, boats, goods on boats, movement of traders, monies and money transactions, including interest on loans, find ample references in the Vedic literature. Terms like *Vaṇika, Vaiśya, Vadinjaya*, and *krinati*, clearly show that trade, traders, and monies did play their part in the everyday life of the Vedic people. References to *ratha*s driven by horses, and carts driven by bulls, when seen in the light of terms used for fast-moving camels, donkeys, mules, etc. also establish the fact that the land routes were used by traders. This is not the place to go into details of sea-borne, river-borne, and overland long-distance trade, with all the hazards involved in it, described in the Vedic literature; what is important to note here is that those who emphasize cattle-keeping as the only mode of economic life of the Aryan society dishonestly suppress the references, which prove that the Vedas were quite clearly aware of the contemporary long-distance internal and external trade.

The Indus-Sarasvatī people are known for their variety of houses in cities. The question is whether the Vedic people were aware of such things. *Sarma, trivarutha sarma, sahasra-sthūna sarma, dhama, kṣaya, gṛha, sadana, vastu, vasati, durya, chardi, bhuvana*, are only a few of the terms they used for houses. This shows that a variety of houses were built in the Vedic settlements. Do the nomadic cattle-keepers make such a variety of houses in any part of the world? Perhaps, not. There are examples of all these types at Dholavira (Plates 4–6).

PLATE 3 Part of the sign board inscription

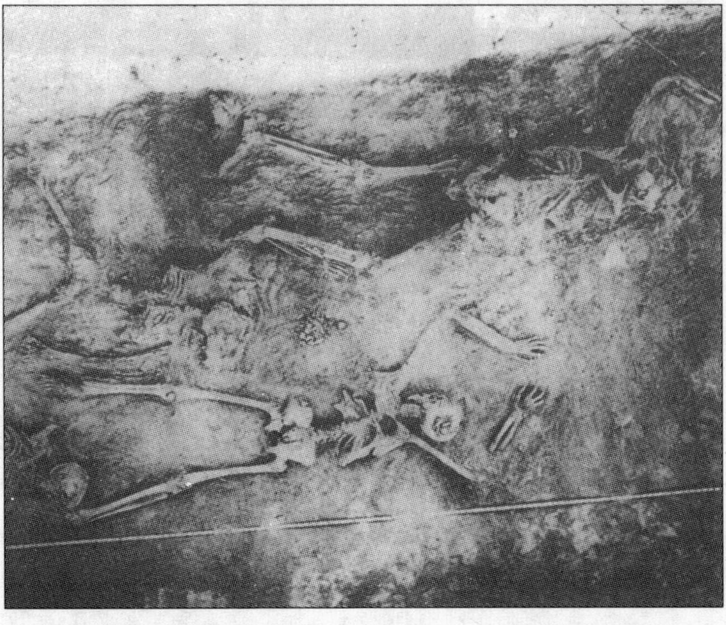

PLATE 4 Dholavira—East-west running street of the middle town

PLATE 5 Dholavira: North gate of citadel

PLATE 6 East gate of citadel showing architectural members

It is common knowledge that the *yajña-kuṇḍa*s were built with bricks, both burnt and unburnt. We are made to believe, rightly observes Singh, that those 'who used the bricks in religious architecture did not use them in the house-building'. Kosambi once observed in a most curious manner that parts of the Ṛgvedic *ṛcā* (122.13), where bricks are mentioned, must have been composed in Mesopotamia. 'In his view', further observes Singh, 'the cattle-keeping nomadic Vedic people should not be expected to use bricks.' Such curious arguments may have suited the Marxist historian in him but it does not suit an unbiased sober scholar of history. In the Brāhmaṇas, for example, the *Śatapatha* (1.2.22; 1.1.1–9), the term *iṣṭaka* for bricks has been used repeatedly. In fact, the people appear to be quite aware of cities as well as the adverse cultural effects of city life on human beings.

Once it becomes reasonably clear, as Bhagwan Singh has made out, that the Vedas do contain enough material which shows that the authors of the hymns were fully aware of cities, city life, long-distance overseas and overland trade using seals and sealings, such as at Dholavira (Plate 7), which had characterized the Indus-Sarasvatī urban civilization, it becomes easier for us to appreciate the theory that the Indus-Sarasvatī and Vedic civilizations may have been just the two complementary facets of one and the same civilization. And this, it is important to note, is not a proposition invalidating the cattle-keeping image of the Vedic Aryans. After all, all ancient civilizations had both the components, the village and the city, and numerically villages were many times more widespread than the cities. In India currently there are round 650,000 villages but hardly 6000 towns and cities put together. If, therefore, during the Indus-Sarasvatī times there were more villages than cities and townships, it should not at all surprise us. Plainly, if the Vedic literature reflects primarily village life and not urban life, it does not at all shock us because the Vedic literature was primarily written for and written by hermits living in relative isolation which ambiance was generally to be preferred when offering prayers to the gods. In fact, for this very reason, the manner in which the *ṛṣi*s told the story of trade and commerce, cities and city-life, etc. is not as direct as a Gazetteer might tell it; it is indirect, it is incidental, it is couched in simile. In other words, the Vedas are to be 'decoded' in a sense, and it is not difficult to do it. Scholars like

Bhagwan Singh and Subhash Kak have done it in order to cull out the references which throw a flood of light on the real nature of the Vedic Aryan vis-à-vis the Indus-Sarasvatī Civilization.

The Myth of Massacre of Mohenjo-daro and Aryan Invasion of the Indus-Sarasvatī Cities

'It seems better, as the evidence stands, to accept the identification and to suppose that the Harappans of the Indus valley in their decadence, in or about seventeenth century BC, fell before the advancing Aryans in such fashion as the Vedic hymns proclaim.'[39]

PLATE 7 Dholavira: Indus-Sarasvatī seals and sealings (first top left is from the early levels of Indus-Sarasvatī period, i.e., Stage III)

Curiously enough, while propounding the theory of destruction of the Harappan or the Indus-Sarasvatī towns as well as the Indus-Sarasvatī Civilization by the invasion of the Aryans, Wheeler combined different kinds of evidence picked up selectively from different sites. Thus, he combined evidence of skeletons found strewn in a

[39] Wheeler, *op. cit.*, 132.

disorderly manner in the streets and houses of Mohenjo-daro with the so-called mud-brick defences of Harappa. Besides the fact that this is a faulty methodology, the theory of the defence and Aryan invasion could be conceived only in warlike activities and use of military weapons by the Indus-Sarasvatī people. And this has been highly questionable right from the time of Marshall (1931) who first proposed the invasion theory, though the invasion he had in mind was made by the Baluchi nomads and not by the Aryans.[40] Wheeler himself had candidly admitted the absence of military outfits in Harappan towns.[41] Still he suggested that small domed pieces of copper, each perforated with two holes, were sewn onto a garment and used as an equivalent of mail, but there is no supporting evidence and neither body-armour nor helmets (well-known in Early Dynastic Sumer), nor indeed shields, can at present be attributed to the Indus-Sarasvatī people.

He further states that it is 'true, the military element does not loom large amongst the extant remains, but it must be remembered that at present we know almost nothing of the civilization.'[42] In fact, the implements of copper found so far in the Indus-Sarasvatī towns are, by and large, domestic in nature. Moreover, where are the remnants of the weapons of war supposed to have been used by the invading Aryans? Can their absence be justified in the case of the invaders as well? Similarly, if the invasion by the Aryans was the cause of the destruction of the Indus-Sarasvatī culture, where are the remains of the Aryans at the Indus-Sarasvatī sites? The Aryans cannot be said to have destroyed the Indus-Sarasvatī people simply in a fit of temper or for the sake of pleasure. The onslaught must have had a certain aim behind it and the principal aim of an invader is generally loot or the occupation of the site, at least temporarily. The Aryans cannot be believed to have been interested only in collecting booty from various places and abandoning the sites when it is clear from the early Vedic literature that the *saptasindhu* or the Punjab-Haryana region was their homeland. Indications of people,

[40] Marshall, *op. cit.*

[41] Wheeler, *op. cit.*, p. 73.

[42] Ibid., p. 72.

other than the Indus-Sarasvatī people, occupying the same site immediately after its destruction, in an almost overlapping manner, are not available from the sites representing the mature Indus-Sarasvatī culture; even the Cemetery 'H' complex at Harappa was separated from the Harappan levels by more than a metre and a half of deposit of debris which,[43] of course, is only partially true. Dales is, therefore, right in raising some of the following most pertinent questions:

Where are the burned fortresses, the arrow-heads, weapons, pieces of armour, the smashed chariots and bodies of the invaders and defenders? Despite the extensive excavations at the largest Harappan sites, there is not a single bit of evidence that can be brought forth as unconditional proof of an armed conquest and the destruction on the supposed scale of the Aryan invasion.[44]

This brings us to the 'massacre' of people at Mohenjo-daro, since, as said at the outset, Wheeler combined the supposed evidence of the destruction of fortifications with the skeletons found spread helter-skelter at this site (Plate 8). Wheeler himself was not sure if the evidence was sound since he clearly states that, 'unfortunately, the older excavations did not record stratification with any regard to precision, and in the absence of precise record it cannot be affirmed without shadow of doubt that the skeletal remains were not contemporary'.[45] That all the skeletal remains were not contemporary to each other as the product of a single tragedy had been conclusively proved by Dales, at least four years before Wheeler reluctantly accepted the position.

What of these skeletal remains that have taken on such undeserved importance? Nine years of extensive excavations at Mohenjo-daro (1922–31)—a city about three miles in circuit—yielded the total of some 37 skeletons, or parts thereof, that can be attributed with some certainty to the period of the Indus Civilization. Some of these were found in contorted positions and groupings that suggest anything but orderly burials. Many are either disarticulated or

[43] Ibid., p. 84.

[44] Dales, *op. cit.*, p. 38.

[45] Wheeler, *op. cit.*, p. 129.

incomplete. They were all found in the area of the Lower Town—probably the residential district. Not a single body was found within the area of the fortified citadel where one could reasonably expect the final defence of this thriving capital city to have been made.

At Dales commented, 'It would be foolish to assert that the scattered skeletal remains represent an orderly state of affairs, since there is no conclusive proof that they even belong to the same period of a single tragedy.'

PLATE 8 Mohenjo-daro: Skeletons of the people caught in floods

The fact of the matter is that, except for two, no skeleton bears marks of cut by a sharp-edged weapon and close examination of the two cases of cut marks by Professor K.A.R. Kennedy has shown that the wounds were completely healed, a process which takes around three months time. Clearly enough, no one died in a warlike situation as visualized by Wheeler.

So much about the myth of 'massacre at Mohenjo-daro'. But then how to explain the evidence of skeletons found in its streets. Simple enough. They were the victims of repeated floods which the city experienced from the Indus. They belonged to different periods of time and they are found embedded in silt and clay.

Artisans and Their Craft-Specializations in Vedic Society[46]

That the artisans enjoyed a respectable position in the Vedic society is clear from the deification on some of the professions:

Aśvins	surgeon, charioteer, sailor
Uśa/Urvaśi	dancer
Ṛbhus	fabricator, seal-maker
Tvasta	carpenter, fabricator
Pusa	guard, guide
Agni/Brāhmaṇaspati	priest
Maruts	peasants, miners, traders, warriors
Rūdra	therapist, physician
Varuṇa	navigator
Vāstospati	architect, mason
Viśvakarmā	carpenter, architect
Viśvarūpa	potter, fabricator
Sarasvatī	artist, poet
Sinivali	entertainer

These artists and professionals are not only praised as *satyamantra*—one whose words are true, *vistvi*—innovative, *sami*—laborious, *suracakṣas*—far/sharp-sighted, and *vidmanapas*—skilful artisans, but there are also clear suggestions in that despite their low position in the social order, they had a special status which evoked respect.[47]

These craftsmen are appreciated time and again for their wondrous command over the crafts which produced marketable

46 What follows is from Bhagwan Singh, *op. cit.*

47 *martash santah amrtavamanasuh* (I.110.4)

goods and therefore fetched huge profits.[48] It is not due to liberal attitude of the Vedic people but due to the material conditions prevailing in those days. If a society advances in the field of science and technology, specialists enjoy a respectable position due to greater emphasis on quality and quick supply of demands. As a result, demand for highly skilled artisans increases in the society. When there is a setback, they suffer accordingly, both socially and economically. So we do not feel surprised to find the Aśvins and the Ṛbhus offered *Soma* with Maruts and Indra for they are adding to the prosperity of their clients.[49] But as *pañcajanas* or *pañcākrstis* they are mentioned almost without the passion visible in the case of Ṛbhus and Aśvins and Tvasta, reminding of equally rhetorical references of *saptasindhavaḥ* or the seven rivers in contrast to verses on Sarasvatī, Sindhu, Vispāsā, and Sutudri. However, doubt may not be cast on diversification of human endeavours and specialization of crafts with a long history and enviable competence. We know how exquisite most of the Harappan products are. But if we have a look at the words of appreciation showered on them in the Ṛgveda we are amazed to find that the quality of Harappan products and the words of admiration in the Ṛgveda match perfectly.

Ṛgvedic language has a rich vocabulary evolved in the course of technical development and appreciation of art work. We come across scores of words in extra-industrial contexts which derive their significance from the qualities and defects of such products. Even a cursory glance at this terminology is sufficient to convince that the

[48] 'Wealth from the Rbhus is most glorious in renown, that which the Heroes, famed for vigour, have produced .... Great store of wealth and mainly power hath he obtained from Vaja, Vibhvan, Rbhus have looked kindly on .... Fashion us, O Rbhus, power and splendid wealth .... Bestowing on us here riches and offspring, here fashion fame for us befitting heroes. Vouchsafe us wealth of splendid sort, O. Rbhus, that we may make us more renowned than others' (IV.36.6, 6, 8, 9).

[49] *ayam vam madhumattamah sutah rtavrdha*
tamasvina pibatam tiro-ahayam dhattam ratnani dasuse ...
asvina madhumattatamam patam somamrtavrdha
athadya dasra vasu bibhrata dasvamsam upagacchatam

artisans and their clients were meticulous in taking note of the minutest flaws in the article produced, sold, and purchased:

akertaruk (X.84.4)	possessing unimpaired splendour, showing no scratch
aketu (I.6.3)	shapeless, unrecognizable
akharva (VII.32.13)	not shortened or mutilated
agnibhrajas (V.54.11)	possessing fiery splendour
agniśriyaḥ (III.26.5)	having the brightness of Agni
atirocamana (X.51.3)	surpassing others in shine/polish
atividdha (VII.96.2)	pierced or drilled badly
atisarp (VIII.102.21)	to pass through
anva (IX.10.5; 91.3)	fine interstice or hole
anvi (IX.1.7)	pierced
anvya (IX.14.6; 15.1;26.1)	penetrable
ataptatanu (IX.83.1)	unfired, unbaked
atrdila (X.94.11)	having no interstices
adabdhadhiti (VI.51.3)	whose works are unimpaired
adbhuta kratu (VIII.23.8)	possessing wonderful intelligence
adhivikartana (X.85.35)	the act of cutting off or cutting asunder
anabhimlata varṇa (II.35.13)	unfaded colour or brightness, glaze
anabhisasta (IX.88.7)	blameless, faultless
anavadyarūpa (I.123.8; II.27.2)	of faultless shape, form
anavadyarūpa (I.152.4)	not united but spreading all around
anaviddha (VI.75.1)	uninjured, unpierced
arepa (V.53.3; 63.6; X.78.1)	spotless
aśreman (III.29.13; X.8.2)	faultless, perfect
akṛta (VIII.10.1)	arranged, built
ākṛti (X.85.5)	constituent part, shape, form
atrda (VIII.1.12)	to divide, pierce
ama (III.30.14; IV.3.9)	unbaked, unannealed

aripra (VII.47.1; 90.4; X.120.9)	plain, unslipped, pure clean
krtnu (I.92.10; VI.18.5)	artificer, mechanic
kṛtṛma (II.15.8; VIII.21.3)	artificial
komya (I.171.3)	polished
cakṣma (II.24.9)	graceful, appealing
caru (I.24.1; II.27.8; V.3.3)	beautiful, agreeable
tridila (X.94.11)	pierced, porous
tridhātu (I.34.6; III.26.7; IV.42.4)	alloy (bronze) made of three metals
trivartu (VII.101.2)	threefold
trivisti dhatu (I.102.8)	alloy
prama (X.130.3)	measure, estimate
mlata (VIII.55.3)	tanned
mrda (VI.53.3)	soft
randhra (VIII.7.26)	hole, aperture
ripa (II.32.2; X.79.3)	to smear, to adhere to
ripta (I.162.9)	smeared
ripra from p. 122	dirt, impurity
ripravaha (X.16.9)	removing impurity
vivartana (I.162.14)	revolution
vidujambha (III.29.13)	strong-toothed
sukrta (I.35.11)	well made
sri (IX.71.4; X.61.3)	to mix, shuffle

Passing through such words we are regularly reminded of the care and skill of Indus-Sarasvatī artisans, of the shape, lustre, and polish of their ceramic wares and seals, of the fine drilling of the beads, and of the perfect fixture of their chariots and boats. Now we may examine some of the areas of expertise.

The most important development in transition from Neolithic to Chalcolithic was the introduction of metals. It transformed the primitive agricultural subsistence pattern into advanced agriculture with animal power for traction and metal related trade-cum-industrial network. This again led to emergence of procurement-cum-distribution centres with concomitant developments culminating in urbanization. In the Neolithic society there was hardly any space for whole time craft specialization as there was nothing which everyone could not do reasonably well. But with the introduction of metallurgy, no society could survive without a section of it devoting itself entirely to mining, smelting, and transporting the ore and followed by other sections engaged in making tools, implements, and ornaments. Specialization became more pronounced with non-availability of mineral ore nearby. Thus division of labour and professional expertise.

12

Archaeology and Language

Colin Renfrew

Colin Renfrew's book, *Archaeology and Language*, is often cited by proponents of the alternative view. His work gives partial support to that position, and Renfrew comes to it by a completely independent path. He is an eminent British anthropologist who has no stake in the political controversies within India. This gives his work a special importance in the Aryan debate, and so we need to examine it closely.

Renfrew's book is about the archaeology of the dispersal of Indo-European languages. He proposes a new, 'wave of advance' model to explain the spreading of Indo-European languages. According to him, the languages spread with the first spread of agriculture—the 'Neolithic revolution'—and the success of the languages has to do with the population growth that follows the invention of agriculture, leading to a steady pressure for territorial expansion, against less populous non-agricultural peoples. This leads him to locate the point of origin for Indo-European in Anatolia (Turkey), and to push the date for the beginning of the dispersal back by several thousand years, to before 6500 BC. This is opposed to the general opinion which puts the beginnings of Indo-European spread in about 2400–2000 BC, well after the Neolithic revolution.

The book is mainly concerned with Europe, but Renfrew devotes Chapter 8, 'The early Indo-Iranian languages and their origins', to Iran and India. We give here an excerpt from that chapter relating to India. In this excerpt, Renfrew proposes, as Hypothesis A, that the Indo-Aryan Sanskrit speakers came to India through the early spread of agriculture, whence they are the creators of the Indus Civilization. But, as he says, 'the evidence is not completely persuasive', so he also offers a second possibility, less favourable to his overall argument, which he calls Hypothesis B. It is an updated version of the standard view, by which Sanskrit-speakers enter India from without after the fall of the Indus Civilization. The evidence for the use of horses and chariots figures importantly in Hypothesis B.

In evaluating the bearing of this argument on the Aryan debate, readers need to know that Renfrew's main argument about a very early spread, through agriculture, of Indo-European languages, is controversial and has not won much support among archaeologists and linguists. They also need to observe that Renfrew is undecided as between Hypotheses A and B or, in our terms, the alternative view and the standard view. Finally, they need to note that both Hypotheses A and B assume that Sanskrit came to India from outside, from a centre in Turkey. Thus Renfrew does not support the idea that Sanskrit or Indo-European is indigenous to India, and gives only tentative support to the idea that Sanskrit is connected with the Indus Civilization.

[From *Archaeology and Language: The Puzzle of Indo-European Origins* (London: Jonathan Cape, 1987).]

Hypothesis A: Neolithic Aryas?

The time has now come to grasp the nettle. I can suggest one interesting way of relating the early languages of India and Iran to those of Europe. As we shall see, the evidence is not completely persuasive, and it is necessary to think of an alternative hypothesis, which is set out as Hypothesis B. However, both have the merit of offering some mechanism for the language displacement involved.

The first, and in some ways the simplest, answer is to suggest that the arrival of Indo-European speakers in the Indian subcontinent was quite analogous to that in Europe. Recent archaeological work in Pakistan has given very early evidence for farming there of a kind simply not previously available. The French archaeologist, Jean-François Jarrige, has conducted an outstandingly successful excavation at the site of Mehrgarh in Baluchistan (west Pakistan),[1]

[1] Jarrige, J.F., 'Continuity and change in the north Kachi Plain (Baluchistan, Pakistan) at the beginning of the second millennium BC' (Unpublished paper delivered in Cambridge on 24 April 1985).

and there is now evidence for the cultivation of cereal crops (six row barley, einkorn, emmer and, bread wheat) preceding 6000 BC.

It is not yet altogether clear that Baluchistan lay outside the primary zone for the domestication of these and other species. It would be perfectly possible to argue for the Zagros mountain loop of the four primary zones to extend eastward to west Pakistan. It is possible instead that some sort of wave of advance operated to south and east as well as to north and west from the primary zones in and near east Anatolia, although of course modified by the terrain. We have already seen how rapidly Europe adopted farming under the influence of this wave of advance. In this way it might be argued that, from the very earliest farming times, as represented by Mehrgarh and by other sites later, an early Indo-European language was spoken in the Indus valley and in areas to the north and west.

Despite Wheeler's comments, it is difficult to see what is particularly non-Aryan about the Indus Valley Civilization, which on this hypothesis would be speaking the Indo-European ancestor of Vedic Sanskrit. Certainly there are elements of continuity from the Indus Civilization onto its aftermath. The main disruption was the ending of urban life, but as Raymond Allchin has emphasized,[2] the rural life of northern India, and what is now Pakistan, carried on little changed.

There are, in particular, some suggestions that the religion practised in the Indus valley may have had its effect on the later Hindu religion. The 'great bath' at Mohenjo-daro may well have had ritual purposes,[3] which reminds us today of the various Hindu ceremonies of purification. Among the few major stone objects from the Indus valley sites are shaped stones, which many observers have pointed out may hold a phallic significance,[4] but they also resemble quite closely the lingam, the sacred stone dedicated to the Lord Shiva

[2] Allchin, F.R., 'The legacy of the Indus civilisation', in G.L. Possehl (ed.), *Harappan Civilisation, a Contemporary Perspective* (Warminster: Aris & Phillips, 1982), 325–34.

[3] Allchin, B. and F.R. Allchin, *The Rise of Civilisation in India and Pakistan* (Cambridge: Cambridge University Press, 1982).

[4] Marshall, Sir J., *Mohenjo-daro and the Indus Civilisation* I (London: Probsthain, 1931).

in modern Hindu practice. There are other indications, for instance the seated figure, in yoga position, seen on an Indus valley sealstone[5] has been equated by some with representations of the Lord Shiva himself. Of course, continuity of cult need not indicate continuity of language, but there is no inherent reason why the people of the Indus valley Civilization should not already have been speaking an Indo-European language, the ancestor of the Ṛigveda.

Raymond and Bridget Allchin have recently considered the case for 'pre-Vedic' movements into the plains of India and Pakistan, pointing to distinctive fireplaces at the site of Kalibangan,[6] which may be interpreted as ritual hearths.[7]

Such 'ritual hearths' are reported from the beginning of the Harappan period itself. It has been suggested that they may have been fire altars, evidence of domestic, popular and civic fire-cults of the Indo-Iranians, which are described in detail in the later Vedic literature. It may then be an indication of culture contact between an early group of Indo-Aryans and the population of the still flourishing Indus Civilization.

The Allchins do not suggest that the Indus Civilization itself should be regarded as Indo-European-speaking, simply that elements within it may already be recognized which are later characteristic of Indo-Aryan culture, as seen in the Ṛigveda. Their arguments in favour of Indo-Aryan features back in the Harappan period could certainly be taken in support of Hypothesis A.

Since the development of the civilization can quite plausibly be traced right back to early roots in the finds at Mehrgarh, the origin of the Neolithic there is of the greatest relevance. The difficulty, of course, is that the area in question is a long way south and east of the recognized early farming centres in the Zagros.

This view would certainly have the merit of linking the spread of the Indo-European languages to the south-east with the same basic mechanism as in the north-west. And of course the Old Iranian

[5] Agrawal, D.P., *The Archaeology of India* (London: Curzon, 1982).

[6] Thapar, B.K., 'Synthesis of the multiple data as obtained from Kalibangan', in D.P. Agrawal and A. Ghosh (eds), *Radiocarbon and Indian Archaeology* (Bombay: Tata Institute, 1973), 264–71.

[7] Allchin and Allichin, *op. cit.*

language is also Indo-European. One difficulty, of real significance, is that there are said to be very few loanwords which might be identified as Indo-European in the early languages recorded in Mesopotamia. Had there been such early contact between them and these early Indo-European languages to their east, then there might have been indications already in them. The proto-Elamite tablets from the south Iranian site of Tepe Yahya are likewise a counterargument to early Indo-European being spoken in that area, although proto-Elamite may have been a later introduction there.

On the other hand, the Soviet archaeologist, V.M. Masson,[8] has suggested that the seals which he recovered from the site of Altyn-Tepe in Turkmenia, far up north near the Caspian Sea, are of proto-Indian type. Since he accepts the Russian decipherment for the Indus valley script, which claims that the language is Dravidian, he comes to a very different conclusion from the one put forward here. But if we accept the observation that the Altyn-Tepe seals and those of the Indus are similar, and that this has linguistic implications, we could certainly take the alternative view that the accompanying language in each case was proto-Indo-European. This is not difficult to accept for the sites in Turkmenia, for there one sees a good degree of continuity back to the period of the earliest farming at Djeitun, and there are indications that these farming origins are related to those further to the west including those of our Indo-European-speaking farmers in East Anatolia. As the Soviet authors V.M. Masson and V.I. Sarianidi put it:[9]

> It has now been established beyond any doubt that the people who adopted the Djeitun culture maintained connections with the early agriculturalists of the Near East .... In the Iraqo-Iranian zone the best documented [area] is the Zagros Mountain region—Jarmo, Sarab and Tepe Guran: this offers the clearest analogies to the Djeitun culture, especially in flint implements and pottery, though there are also important differences which distinguish the two cultures.

[8] Masson, V.M., 'Seals of a Proto-Indian type from Altyn-depe', in P.L. Kohl (ed.), *The Bronze Age Civilisation of Central Asia, Recent Soviet Discoveries* (Armonk, N.Y.: M.E., Sharpe, 1981), 149–64.

[9] Masson, V.M. and V.I. Sarianidi, *Central Asia, Turkmenia before the Achaemenids* (London: Thames & Hudson, 1972).

Hypothesis A, then, would carry the history of the Indo-European languages in north India and Iran back to the early Neolithic period in those areas. The decisive process of dispersal would, as in Europe, be the demographic changes which accompanied the development of early farming. It might be possible also to link early Turkmenia with this process.

All of this, it must be admitted, is very hypothetical indeed. A much more comprehensive view is needed of the contemporaries of early Mehrgarh, and of the early Neolithic in Baluchistan generally, before the hypothesis can be further advanced. If Baluchistan itself turns out to be within the primary zone of early agriculture, as is perfectly possible, the argument may become more difficult.

It should be noted, moreover, that the Old Iranian language as seen in the *Avesta,* and Vedic Sanskrit, as seen in the Ṛigveda, are very close: so close that they are generally considered to belong to a single, Indo-Iranian branch of the Indo-European family. Without placing too much reliance on the actual absolute figures produced by glottochronology, we may note that the lexicostatistician, Norman Bird,[10] has reported a strong co-occurrence of Indic with Iranian words: 85 per cent of Iranian words from his list have Indic equivalences. At first sight this is an exceedingly high figure, although we should note that 77 per cent of Hittite words in the list have co-occurrences with Indic roots also. If Vedic Sanskrit and Old Iranian are really to be considered as very closely related, this would imply a higher degree of recent interaction than might result from the straightforward pattern of an early wave of advance spread of agriculture. Some degree of continuing contact after the spread of early farming would be necessary to produce this degree of linguistic affinity. Fortunately the various links between the cultures of the Iranian plateau in the succeeding periods are becoming increasingly clear. There are indications of settlements of the Indus valley culture on the banks of the Amu Darya river in northern Afghanistan, and graves of Bronze Age Turkmenian type has been reported from near the site of Mehrgarh in Baluchistan.[11] Of course, these are some four

[10] Bird, N., *The Distribution of Indo-European Root Morphemes* (Wiesbaden: Otto Harrassowtiz, 1982).

[11] Jarrige, J.F., 'The antecedents of civilization in the Indus valley', *Scientific American,* 243 (2), 122–33, 1980.

thousand years more recent than the earliest farming discoveries there. But it is clear that there were continuing interactions in Afghanistan and on the Iranian plateau, and a continuing community of Indo-European languages in that area is not improbable. It would be from this complex that, at a rather later date, the horse-riding nomads responsible for the presence of Indo-European languages in Chinese Turkestan (that is, the Tocharian languages) would ultimately derive, and the chiefs of the Land of Mitanni in the mid-second millennium would originate from this same complex. (In view of the reported scarcity or non-existence of Indo-European loanwords in the early languages of Mesopotamia, we must assume that until the mid-second millennium BC, these people on the east of the Zagros Mountain range kept themselves to that area). There were of course numerous trading contacts between the Iranian plateau and Mesopotamia—already in the Sumerian period there are attractive, carved, greenstone vessels in Mesopotamia, made of chlorite schist, which must have originated on the plateau—but if we are following the present hypothesis, these contacts would not have had much linguistic impact. Much more work will have to be carried out on the archaeology of Central Asia before this hypothesis can be properly investigated, but it is perfectly conceivable that by the early second millennium, the languages of the Iranian plateau and of the Indus valley, as well as of Turkmenia, were predominantly Indo-European.

The adoption of the horse and the techniques of chariotry may for a while have given some of these people some degree of military advantage over the populations in the Mesopotamia plains, and this may account for the various Indo-European names and words which we find from around 1500 BC onwards. Certainly, the adoption of horse riding transformed the economy of the steppe lands, and the various mounted nomad groups of the first millennium BC—the Saka and the Scythians, the Cimmerians, the Medes and the Tocharoi, all speaking Indo-European languages—developed military technology. The so-called Tocharians of Chinese Turkestan may have reached that area at this time. It is interesting, too, that although most of the military activity reported in the Ṛigveda was conducted from a horse-drawn chariot, as indeed was that of the Hittites and the Hurrian-speakers of Mitanni, there are passages in the Vedic hymns which strongly suggest that by the time of their composition, horses were also being ridden.[12] This suggests a rather later date for the Ṛigveda, and reminds us that at this time there were renewed possibilities for contact between all the lands bordering upon the Iranian plateau.

Much here is hypothetical, but at least a coherent picture can be set out, which explains the observed language distributions (when they enter the light of history) in terms of readily intelligible processes of culture change. It remains to be seen whether so prolonged a separation as this implies between the western Indo-European languages of Europe and the eastern Indo-European languages of Iran and India is a feasible background for the various linguistic resemblances between them. That is a linguistic problem whose outcome will have an important bearing upon the viability of Hypothesis A. It should be remembered that with the increased intensity of interaction from the first millennium BC, when horse riding became widespread, there is the definite possibility of shared language developments of a wave-theory type extending across the steppe lands, between the Slavic languages in the west, the Anatolian languages (and Armenian) and the Iranian and Indic languages. This perspective of a very long time depth for the Indo-Iranian languages should not be lightly dismissed. Certainly the assumption that the Aryas were recent 'immigrants' to India, and their enemies were 'aborigines', has done much to distort our understanding of the archaeology of India and Pakistan.

It may be permissible at this point to draw a very general parallel between the transition in Greece from the Mycenaean to the Classical periods on the one hand, and the passage in north India and Pakistan from the Indus Valley Civilization to the Vedic period, already implied when we compared the Homeric hymns[13] of early Iron Age Greece with the *Hymns of the Ṛigveda*. Neither gives any clear hint of the

[12] For example, Hymn CLXII, 17: 'If one, when seated, with excessive urging, hath with his heel or whip distressed thee ...', Griffith, R.T.H., *The Hymns of the Ṛigveda* (Delhi: Motilal Banarsidass, 1973 [Revised edn, 1st edn, 1889]).

[13] In the Homeric hymns, Evelyn-White, H.G., *Hesiod, the Homeric Hymns and Homerica* (Loeb Classicial Library) (London: Heinemann, 1914), there are very few indications of urban life, although Athena (Hymns XI and XXVIII) bears the epithet 'guardian of the city' (*'erusiptolin*).

urban civilization, which flourished in the relevant area some centuries earlier and then collapsed.

I have recently argued that, in the case of the Greek religion, we see a whole series of transformations from that of the Mycenaean late Bronze Age of around 1500 BC to the religion of the classical Greeks a millennium later. The Mycenaean religion and the Greek religion were very different belief systems, or at least their material manifestations were fundamentally different. But the Greek religion did not replace the Mycenaean as a result of the immigration of 'Greeks'. That is the old view which we can now confidently dismiss. Instead we see a succession of stages when new elements emerged, most but not all of them of local origin.

If we apply the same line of reasoning to the transformation from the Indus Civilization to its non-urban aftermath of a millennium later, we can trace the emergence of a number of elements, few of which need to be of foreign origin. Certainly there are some outside elements; the use of the horse to pull a war chariot is one of these. Precisely the same innovation is seen in Mycenaean Greece, at about the same time, and it is now clear that this happened in Greece without a significant change in population from immigration. Some centuries after the chariot, horse riding in association with new military techniques is seen in both areas. It is not surprising that both innovations had a greater impact in India and Pakistan, where the open terrain offers more scope for the horse (and indeed for the chariot) than does the rocky and mountainous landscape of Greece. There is nothing which forces us to associate these innovations in India with a new population, or with immigrants, any more than in Greece. The adoption of new military techniques will only entail language displacement if they are associated either with significant population change or with new élite dominance.

What we may be seeing at this time is the development of a new ideology, which finds its finest expression in the *Hymns of the Ṛigveda*, and indeed of the *Avesta*, and this may be reflected in the pottery of Cemetery H at Harappa,[14] which has handsome decorated

[14] Sankalia, H.D., 'The "Cemetery H" culture', *Puratattva*, 6, 12–19, 1973, reprinted in G. Possehl (ed.), *Ancient Cities of the Indus* (New Delhi: Vikas Publishing House, 1979), 322–7.

vessels depicting horses, and departs from the geometric tradition of the pottery decoration of the Indus Valley Civilization. (Much the same can, of course, be said of the pictorial pottery of Geometric Greece, where the Homeric heroes are first represented silhouetted in black against the yellow clay.)

We should, in other words, seriously consider the possibility that the new religious and cultural synthesis, represented by the Ṛigveda was essentially a product of the soil of India and Pakistan, and that it was not imported, ready-made, on the back of the steeds of the Indo-Aryans. Of course, it evolved while in contact with the developing cultures of other lands, most notably Iran, so that by a process of peer polity interaction, cultures and ideologies emerged which in many ways resembled each other. It is not necessary to suggest that one was borrowed, as it were, directly from the other.

This hypothesis that early Indo-European languages were spoken in north India with Pakistan and on the Iranian plateau at the sixth millennium BC has the merit of harmonizing symmetrically with the theory for the origin of the Indo-European languages of Europe. It also emphasizes the continuity in the Indus Valley and adjacent areas from the early Neolithic through to the floruit of the Indus Valley Civilization—a point that Jarrige has recently stressed. Moreover the continuity is seen to follow unbroken from that time across the Dark Age succeeding the collapse of the urban centres of the Indus Valley, so that features of that urban civilization persist, across a series of transformations, to form the basis for later Indian civilization. A number of scholars have previously developed these ideas of continuity.

The hypothesis has, however, what may be a damaging weakness. It requires that the first farmers in the area, at sites such as Mehrgarh, should have reached there with their farming economy by the sort of wave of advance process which has been postulated for Neolithic Europe. What works in Europe does not necessarily apply so well for the transmission of farming across or along the western flanks of the Iranian plateau from some nuclear farming area to the north. It remains to be seen whether the wild predecessors of the plants and animals found domesticated at Mehrgarh were already native to the area. If they were not, Hypothesis A may find some support. If they were, it is surely more likely that the process of domestication took place locally, and the theory of an incoming wave of advance is not necessary. In these circumstances we have to look for another explanation.

Hypothesis B: Mounted Nomads of the Steppe

This hypothesis outlines an alternative. Let us admit at the outset that it resembles the old and traditional view in relying on pastoral nomad invaders, but in other ways it is very different. It accepts the likelihood of local farming origins and that the arrival of the Indo-European languages is associated with the arrival of mounted warriors whose original way of life was one of nomad pastoralism; that is to say a process of élite dominance.

The Development of Central Asian Nomad Pastoralism

In order to reach some understanding of the second and first millennia BC in this area, it is essential to look at the origins of nomad pastoralism.[15] This is a difficult theme, since the archaeological traces of pastoral nomads are notoriously less substantial than those of settled farmers.

Development of a primarily pastoral economy

In Central Asia and the European steppes, the principal domestic animals exploited were generally sheep and goats, and horses were herded for their products (milk, meat) as well as their usefulness for traction or as beasts of burden. The essential point is that some arid steppe lands are appropriate for grazing but not for the growing of cereal crops. The pastoral economy is usually symbiotic with the agricultural one as it has been shown that a major component of the diet of these pastoralists was bread. The practice of agriculture is

[15] Anthony, D.W., 'The "Kurgan culture", Indo-European origins and the domestication of the horse: A reconsideration', *Current Anthropology*, 27, 291–314, 1986; Briant, P., *État et pasteurs au Moyen-Orient ancien* (Cambridge: Cambridge University Press, 1982); Khazanov, A.M., *Nomads and the Outside World* (Cambridge: Cambridge University Press, 1984).

thus a pre-condition of a pastoral economy. In general a nomadic way of life may often have developed from the more limited mobility of a transhumant one.

Use of equids as pack animals

There is only limited evidence for this practice of using horses, mules, donkeys, and onagers prior to subsequent stages of development, but the ability to transport a certain amount of equipment by animal, including tents, is a fundamental element in most nomadic economies.

The use of wheeled carts

The use of the four-wheeled cart[16] is archaeologically attested both in Europe and in Asia before that of the two-wheel chariot with spoked wheels. In many cases the draught animals seem to have been equids,[17] but in some areas cattle were also used. This seems to have been the case, for instance, in the Indus Civilization[18] (although the economy there was not of course based on pastoral nomadism). In some cases two-wheeled carts are more common, but in the earlier phases of development, the wheels were solid or composite, not spoked.

Development of the war chariot with two-spoked wheels and drawn by horses

This is not reliably attested anywhere before about 1800/1600 BC. Such war chariots can be seen on Mycenaean[19] gravestones dated

[16] Piggott, S., *The Earliest Wheeled Transport from the Atlantic Coast to the Caspian Sea* (London: Thames & Hudson, 1983); Wiesner, J., *Fahren und Reiten in Alteuropa und im Alten Orient* (Das Alte Orient 38, 2–4) (Leipzig: J.C. Hinrechs, 1939).

[17] Piggott, 1983, *op. cit.*

[18] Allchin and Allchin, *op. cit.*

[19] Littauer, M.A. and J.H. Crouwel, *Wheeled Vehicles and Ridden Animals in the Ancient Near East* (Leiden Brill, 1979); Marinatos, S. and M. Hirmer, *Crete and Mycenae* (London: Thames & Hudson, 1960), pls 146 and 147.

from about 1600 BC, in late Hittite reliefs[20] and in scenes of battles from before the Amarna period in Egypt.[21] The Hurrian called Kikkuli from the Land of Mitanni wrote a treatise in the Hittite language on the training of chariot horses for the Hittite rulers of Hattusas. And the *Hymns of the Ṛigveda* make frequent reference to war chariots.

Fully mobile nomad pastoralism and the military use of mounted horsemen

Surprisingly perhaps we have little evidence that horses were ridden until long after they were used to pull chariots. The earliest representations of horse riding nearly all seem to come after about 1200 BC. That is certainly true in Greece—we have no pictures of Mycenaean horse riding[22]—and it is also true of the Hittites, the reliefs showing mounted warriors all come from the time of the Late Hittite period.[23] The art of the Scythians, and of Mesopotamia, where there are palace reliefs of the Assyrian kings, are the earliest representations we have of horse riding. (There are Egyptian reliefs of an earlier date which do fact show horses being ridden,[24] but these early depictions are not of mounted warriors.)

[20] Hittite war chariots are shown on Egyptian reliefs: e.g. Akurgal, E., *The Art of the Hittites* (London: Thames & Hudson, 1962), pl. 3; Meyer, E. (1914). *Reich und Kultur der Chetster* (Berlin: Verlag Karl Curtis), 13, Fig. 4; and in Hittite reliefs of the late period: e.g. Akurgal (*op. cit.*), pl. 105; Meyer, E., *Reich und Kultur der Chetiter* (Berlin, Verlag Karl Curtius, 1914), pls VI and VIII.

[21] Childe, V.G., 'Wheeled vehicles', Ch. 27, in C. Singer, E.J. Holmyard, and A.R. Hall (eds), *A History of Technology* I (Oxford: Clarendon, 1958), 727, Fig. 527; there are earlier chariot scences from the reign of Amenophis IV, c. 1450 BC.

[22] Portatz, H.A., *Das Pferd in der Frühzeit* (Rostock, 1939); Briant, *op. cit.* The only representation of a horse rider from Mycenaean Greece is a small terracotta figurine from the Late Helladic IIIB period. Hood, M.S.F. (1953). 'A Mycenaean Caralryman', *Annual of the British School of Archaeology at Athens*, 48, 84–93.

[23] e.g. Meyer, *op. cit.* Textual evidence from Mesopotamia suggests that riding was known in the early second millennium BC (Littauer and Crouwel, *op. cit.*).

[24] Wiesner, *op. cit.* See also the wooden model, without good provenance, in the Metropolitan Museum, New York, for which a date as early as c. 1580 BC has been suggested. Zeuner, F.E., *A History of Domesticated Animals* (London, Hutchinson, 1963).

The development of the bit seems to have been an essential innovation for riding, and chariot horses were not initially controlled in this way. Finds of bronze and iron horse-bits offer the most abundant archaeological evidence of horse riding, and they occur by 1500 BC in the Near East, earlier on the steppes, and in Europe and in China after 1000 BC.[25]

Claims have been made that perforated bone objects found very much earlier in central Europe were in fact horse-bits,[26] but they are not numerous, and the innovation (if such it was) did not become widespread nor is it certain that they were used in this way.

The military use of heavy cavalry, using the stirrup

Rather surprisingly, once again, the all-metal stirrup[27] seems to have been a late invention made in China in the fourth century AD and first seen in Europe in the seventh century. It allowed the use of much more formidable weapons, notably the lance, since the horseman could now avoid being unseated during the heavy impact of battle. The barbarian invasions of Europe after the Dark Ages are said to have owed much of their effectiveness to this.

This very schematic outline distinguishes between pastoralism as a new form of adaptation to the steppe lands (allowing them to be exploited for the first time), fully mobile nomad pastoralism based on horse riding, and the warlike, expansionist behaviour which we often associate in our minds with pastoral nomads. This aggressive

[25] Potratz, J.A.H., *Die Pferdetrensen des alten Orient* (Analecta Orientalia 41) (Rome, Pontificium Institutum Biblicum, 1966). Although Littauer and Crouwel (*op. cit.*) indicate the early occurrence of rigid cheekpieces with soft mouthpieces north of the Caucasus.

[26] Piggott (*op. cit.*); Lichardus J., 'Zur Funktion der Geweihspitzen des Typus Ostorf', *Germania*, 58, 1–24, 1980. Even if these were indeed used as bits, they may have been used with chariots rather than for riding; see also. Anthony, D.W. (1986). 'The "Kurgan Culture", Indo-European origin and the domestication of the horse: A reconsideration', *Current Anthology*, 27, 219–314.

[27] Littauer, M.A. 'Early stirrups', *Antiquity*, 55, 99–105, 1981; White, L., 'The origin and diffusion of the stirrup', in L. White, *Mediaeval Technology and Social Change* (Oxford: Clarendon, 1962), 14–28.

behaviour of the mounted warrior only becomes a significant feature in the history of Europe and Asia after about 1000 BC. The suggestion that the Corded Ware/Battle Axe people of central and northern Europe behaved in this way was based largely upon the fundamental misunderstanding of ignoring these distinctions. Likewise the Kurgan peoples of the south Russia steppes need not be regarded as formidable warriors until they were capable of fighting upon horseback. One very relevant factor here may well have been the development of suitable breeds of horse large enough to serve as chargers.[28] The considerable delay between phases (2) and (3) on the one hand and phases (4) and (5) on the other may be due largely to this.

One of the main ideas constituting Hypothesis B is that, with the development of chariotry and then of military horse riding, a new possibility for élite dominance emerged. This would be the basic underlying mechanism for the process of language replacement which took place during the later second millennium BC. But precisely where did these important innovations take place? That question is not an easy one to answer, although it is clear that the development is likely to have occurred amongst people who were already using the horse intensively both as a pack animal and for traction—and this brings us back to the steppes of Eurasia.

It would seem that the horse was not used for traction on the Iranian plateau until rather later than on the steppe lands to the north. Certainly we find cattle, not horses, yoked to the model carts found in the Indus Civilization. In Turkmenia there are comparable models, but with camels[29] pulling the carts, found in what is termed the Namazga IV period, dateable from about 3000 to 2600 BC. In Mesopotamia on the famous standard from Ur[30] just a little later, the animal pulling the cart is sometimes considered to be an onager, and the horse may not yet have been introduced.

[28] Bökönyi, S., 'The earliest wave of domestic horses in East Europe', *Journal of Indo-European Studies*, 6, 1978, 1–16.

[29] Masson and Sarianidi, *op. cit.*; for the camel, see Bulliet, R.W., *The Camel and the Wheel* (Cambridge, Mass.: Harvard University Press, 1975).

[30] Childe, 1958, *op. cit.*; Littauer and Crouwel, 1979, *op. cit.*

Given then that the predominantly pastoral economy of the steppe lands must have developed in the first place from a mixed farming economy on the more fertile steppe margins, can we determine more precisely where this took place? This is one of the most interesting questions of Eurasian prehistory. Consideration of the map suggests that there are really only four possibilities.

1. The south Russian steppe margins, at the west of the great Eurasian steppes, in the Ukraine area. There the point of agricultural origin would be the Neolithic cultures of eastern Europe, termed Cucuteni and Tripolye.
2. The lands north of the Caucasus Mountains, between the Black Sea and the Caspian Sea. The local farming cultures there have been studied by Soviet archaeologists, but are not yet well dated.
3. The farming areas of Turkmenia, along the line of the Kopet Dag, east of the Caspian Sea. The Djeitun culture represented the first farmers in that area. (Most of Central Asia was dominated during the period of the Turkmenian Neolithic by what has been called the Kelteminar culture, which has a characteristic range of pottery and flint types. In many cases the settlements are located on the banks of lakes and small rivers, and it has been suggested that fishing as well as hunting were of considerable economic importance).
4. Any other areas of early farming further east. No other such centres are in fact known at present until one reaches China and the Yangshao culture of Honan province.

It seems likely at present that the fully mobile pastoral economy of the Eurasian steppe land developed either in area (1) or (2). We are thus talking of the range of cultures which go under the name of *yamno*[31] (Pit Grave) or Kurgan (burial mound) cultures. Radiocarbon

[31] Childe, V.G., *The Dawn of European Civilization* (6th edition) (London: Routledge & Kegan Paul, 1957); Gimbutas M., 'Proto-Indo-European culture: The Kurgan culture during the 5th to the 3rd millennia BC', in G. Cardona, H.M. Keonigswald, and A. Senn (eds), *Indo-European and Indo-Europeans* (Philadelphia: University of Pennsylvania Press, 1970), 155–98.

dates do not yet provide unequivocal evidence to decide between them, but it is an integral part of Hypothesis B that the Eurasian steppe lands were colonized by nomadic pastoralists from the west (that is, from the Ukraine). This theory was put forward by Ward Goodenough in 1970 and this somewhat technical archaeological discussion opens up wide vistas.

The development of pastoralism in the steppe lands had consequences in their own way as significant as the introduction of farming to south-east Europe. For here now was a new economic basis which could spread with its own wave of advance. The language of the first nomad-pastoralists could spread, by a process analogous to adaptive radiation, with the same dynamic demographic basis which underlay the rapid spread of farming across Europe. Just as in Europe, the language of the first farmers (of Greece) had an adaptive advantage (its farming basis) which allowed it to spread throughout the area, so on the steppe lands the language of the first effective nomad pastoralists had the opportunity to spread across the region.

I suggest that this is precisely what it did. Sandor Bökönyi,[32] in his study of the prehistory of the horse, has shown that the horse was already known and exploited (presumably for food) in the south Russian steppes at the outset of the period in question. The context there is in the early farming Tripolye and Cucuteni communities of the eastern Balkans. It was the spread, from west to east, of the *yamno* or Kurgan cultures of the first true steppe Neolithic which gave the

[32] Hančar, F., *Das Pferd in prähistorischen und frühe historichen Zeit* (Wien, Herold, 1956); Bökönyi, S., *History of Domestic Mammals in Central and Eastern Europe* (Budapest: Akademiai Kiado, 1974), where a context in the Tripolye B culture is proposed; also Bökönyi (1978, *op. cit.*). A site with notably early finds of domesticated horse bones is Dereivka, of the Srednij Stog culture (Telegin, D.Y., *Dereivka: A Settlement and Cemetery of Copper Age Horse-Keepers on the Middle Dnieper* [B.A.R. International Series 287] [Oxford, British Archaeological Reports, 1986]). As N.J. Merpert, comments on 'The chronology of the Early Kurgan tradition', *Journal of Indo-European Studies*, 5, 1977, 373–8, writes:

'I never believed that it was a migration from the Volga that created the Srednij Stog culture, and I would regard such an assertion as wrong. The basic correlation of the Srednij Stog culture is with the Neolithic of the Dnieper ...'.

See also Anthony, *op. cit.*

steppe lands of Europe and Central Asia their first cultural unity. I suggest that the language of these early steppe pastoralists, who were not yet driving chariots or perhaps riding horses, was already Indo-European. Moreover we can be more specific than that. The language must indeed have been derived from that of those Cucuteni and Tripolye peasants who, with their mixed farming economy, were at the beginning of the transition to nomad pastoralism on the steppe margins. The Slavic language group may represent the much later development within the same area of the language spoken by the descendants of those Tripolye and Cucuteni peasants.

This solution of the problem is rather better substantiated archaeologically at the present time than is its Caucasian alternative. It is also linguistically more convenient, because the contemporary languages of the Caucasus region do not belong to the Indo-European group. The Caucasian languages are numerous and varied, and there is no reason to think of them as a recent importation to the area. They appear on the map, indeed, to form a sort of linguistic barrier between the early farmers of Anatolia and the steppe lands to the north.

Once it is accepted that the first nomad pastoralists of the steppes were already speaking an Indo-European language, derived from south Russia and points west, the rest of the picture is clear enough. The succeeding culture of much of the steppes, which is termed the Andronovo culture, shows considerable unity over a very large area, and it persists to Bronze Age times. There can be no doubt that the horse was being used to pull the carts of the steppe population before this time, and maybe it did begin to have a military significance. At any rate, one may suggest that, at this time, the steppe nomad economy began to have an impact upon Turkmenia and the Iranian plateau. As Masson and Sarianidi write in their consideration of Turkmenia:[33]

> The migration of tribal groups to the south is an almost established fact. The second millennium BC was a period of great migrations and population changes, possibly as a result of the 'population explosion' in the Euro-Asian steppes following adoption of nomadic stock-breeding and primitive

[33] Masson and Sarianidi, *op. cit.*

agriculture which followed the archaic Neolithic economy. At all events, the archaeological material at our disposal leaves no doubt as to the spread of a population with Andronovo and Timber-Grave characteristics. There were two main movements of these steppe tribes into Western Central Asia .... This should, of course, be studied in conjunction with the problem of the diffusion of tribes of the Indo-Iranian linguistic group. I would myself differentiate between the initial population explosion associated with the adoption in the steppes of the nomad pastoral economy and the later movements south, which I imagine as being related more to the élite dominance model. But from this point on, Hypothesis B accords with much of the standard archaeological interpretations for the area.

There can be no doubt that when the peoples of the steppes, then termed, amongst other things, Cimmerians, Sarmatians, and Scythians, first entered the light of history about a thousand years later, they spoke Indo-Europe languages.[34] The same is true of the peoples of the Iranian plateau: the Medes and Persians, and the Saka (that is, the Scythians once again). The Iranian languages are thus naturally to be seen as Indo-European through the dominance of the Iranian plateau by horse-using steppe-nomads from the north. How far east this unity extended is difficult to determine, but the later existence of Indo-European languages in the Turfan depression of Chinese Turkestan suggests that it may have been a long way. Of course by the time it is recorded, in the eighth century AD, Tocharian already formed an Indo-European enclave amongst nomadic pastoralists speaking Ural-Altaic languages.[35]

It is clear that at some point during the first millennium BC there were very significant developments in the eastern part of the Eurasian steppe which resulted in the dominance of populations speaking Ural-Altaic languages over much of the area. Just as initially, in Europe and Central Asia at least, the economy of nomad-pastoralism was associated with Indo-European speakers, so later the nomads were predominantly non-Indo-European in speech, with the exception

[34] Lockwood, W.B., *A Panorama of Indo-European Languages* (London: Hutchinson, 1972); Talbot Rice, T., *The Scythians* (London: Thames & Hudson, 1957).

[35] Sinov, D., *Introduction a l'Étude de l'Asie Centrale* (Wiesbaden: Harrasowitz, 1963).

of just a few pockets, like the speakers of the Ossetian language.[36] The underlying economic or processual reasons for these later changes are not at all clear to me: one is reluctant to blame all of this simply upon the invention of the stirrup. But that problem takes us beyond the time scale of the present inquiry. It is, of course, entirely relevant both for the later language displacements in Anatolia, which led to the adoption of Turkish and the extinction there of Indo-European speech, and for the incursion of the Finno-Ugrian languages into Hungary, and Estonia in the first millennium AD.

Turning once again to the Indus, there is no reason to imagine that our 'nomadic warriors' were responsible for the demise of the Indus Civilization; that was probably a case of system collapse. But these well-organized and mobile tribal groups, with a chiefdom organization, may have profited by the disorder in the Indus to achieve a measure of élite dominance, and hence to bring about an effective language displacement. Thus the early language of eastern Europe, transformed no doubt in its transition to the Eurasian steppes, and transformed again in its adoption to the Iranian plateau and to Afghanistan, would have come to the Indus.

The Choice of Hypotheses: A versus B

At present it is not easy to see how one should choose between these two hypotheses. Both accept the major premise that central and eastern Anatolia was the key area where an early form of Indo-European language was spoken before 6500 BC. From there the distribution of the language and its successors into Europe was associated with the spread of farming.

Hypothesis A suggests that the zone of early farmers speaking Proto-Indo-European extended east to northern Iran and even to Turkmenia at the outset. The spread of Indo-European speech to the south, to the Iranian plateau and to north India and Pakistan, can then be seen as part of an analogous dispersal, related to the demographic changes associated with the adoption of farming.

[36] Lockwood, *op. cit.*, 246.

Hypothesis B does not take this view. It suggests instead that the crucial development for the eastern area was the development in the Eurasian steppes of nomad pastoralism, and that this took place first at the western end of the steppes. In this way, it was argued, the nomad pastoralists of the steppes spoke an Indo-European language at the outset. Their later dominance in Iran and in the Indus is then ascribed to their military effectiveness, based largely upon the use of the horse.

It is of course possible to blend these two hypotheses. Even if we accept Hypothesis A, it is still likely that the first steppe nomads did indeed speak Indo-European languages, and that their adaptation to the steppes first took place in the Ukraine. If we accept Hypothesis B, it is perfectly possible that Indo-European languages were spoken in north Iran and Turkmenia from the time of the first farmers there: the first Indo-European speakers in India would be very much later.

From the linguistic point of view, however, the two hypotheses are very different. The first implies that the Indo-European languages of Iran and India and Pakistan derive from precursors in eastern Anatolia and further east, just as the first Indo-European languages of Europe derived at the same time from precursors in central and western Anatolia. The successors of the western Anatolian languages are the Indo-European languages of Europe; the successor of the central Anatolian languages was Hittite; and the successors of the eastern Anatolian languages were thus the Indo-Iranian languages. We might expect, then, a number of resemblances between Hittite and the Indo-Iranian languages. On the other hand, the languages of eastern Europe would originally have borne little affinity with the Indo-Iranian languages, although convergences could occur as a result of steppe land influences on Iran and India at a later date. The original separation would have taken place by 6500 BC.

On the other hand, Hypothesis B implies that the relationship between the Indo-Iranian languages and those of eastern Europe would be very much closer, with a common origin around 4000 BC. There are some indications which might support such a view, for instance the old classification of the Slavic languages within the eastern or *satem* group, but little emphasis is placed these days upon this simplistic distinction.

Archaeologically speaking, a conclusion is not at present any easier. The decision which has to be made is whether or not the development of the early Neolithic of the Iranian plateau, and especially of Baluchistan was initially, in large measure, the result of a 'spread' of farming there, on a wave of advance model, or instead primarily a local development. A further crucial question is whether or not there is really convincing evidence in the Indus for an episode of élite displacement, with the new élite coming from well to the north, outside the area, somewhere around the middle of the second millennium BC. This has often been suggested. But there are only a few finds which might indicate the arrival of an élite from the north. There are in fact some finds near Mehrgarh[37] in the Indus valley, which closely resemble the culture at the site of Namazga much further to the north in Turkmenia. The famous Cemetery H at Harappa, with its painted pottery, would make an interesting focus of study. Can we regard it as a late development of the Indus Civilization, a transformation from it, in a society which was becoming or had become non-urban? Or do we have to see it as the result of an immigrant group, bringing with it a whole new range of material equipment by which its source can unequivocally be identified? One cannot be sure, but present evidence might suggest the former.

As a tentative conclusion, however, I feel that it is useful in considering the Indo-Iranian languages, to see their distribution as the result of the working out of at least three cultural and economic processes. The first would indeed be the colonization, by early peasant farmers, of tracts of potential farmland in Iran, perhaps as far south as Pakistan (including Mehrgarh) on a variant of the wave of advance model adapted for the environment of the terrains in question. This draws heavily upon the arguments considered for Hypothesis A. The area of origin would be eastern Anatolia, and those areas to the east which one can regard as participating within the original 'nuclear zone' for the initial domestication of plants and animals. At present, however, it seems that the area to the west of the Zagros mountains, including Mesopotamia and most of the Levant, had an early farming population which was not Indo-European speaking.

[37] Jarrige, *op. cit.*

The second process of importance is the development of nomad pastoralism in the steppe lands of Russia, and the wider spread of such nomad pastoralism. The evidence at the moment seems to show that the domestication of the horse took place at the western extremity of the Russian steppes, and that the spread of the nomad pastoral economy took place from west to east. Naturally one should consider whether comparable processes leading to nomad pastoralism were independently under way in other areas. At present, it is possible to consider a nomad pastoralist presence in Central Asia from the third millennium BC as a result of this second process.

The third process is that of élite dominance, where well organized communities of mounted nomad pastoralists, with a ranked social organization, achieved dominance in certain areas by force of arms. We are talking here of events in the first millennium BC, and perhaps back into the second millennium BC, but not earlier, for we have no evidence for mounted warriors at an earlier time.

The situation in each area was no doubt the product of these and other processes. In Central Asia, the second process is likely to have been the most important, at least initially, and in this context the later work of Henning on Tocharian origins is highly significant. He argues for an equation between the Proto-Tocharians and the Guti, who are documented in Babylonia at the end of the third millennium BC. He observes that[38] 'if we regard the Guti as "Proto-Tocharians", their nearest relatives among the Indo-Europeans would be the Hittite nations of Asia Minor', although my arguments would lead to a closer relationship with the early nomad pastoralists of the European steppe lands. There may be other problems, at a detailed level, with some of Henning's proposals, but as he says,[39] 'This is the heart of the theory that I wish to propound. Possibly the archaeologists may welcome a theory that involves considerable movement of people from Persia to the limits of China as early as the close of the third millennium BC.' That is indeed welcome, as an

[38] Henning, W.B., 'The first Indo-Europeans in history', in G.L. Ulmen (ed.), *Society and History, Essays in Honour of Karl August Wittfogel* (The Hague: Mouton, 1978), 215–30.

[39] Henning, *op. cit.*, 219.

observation formulated on linguistic grounds, so long as it can be tied up with the processual realities which we are endeavouring to establish.

In the case of India and Pakistan, the present dilemma remains the decision as to how much emphasis to place on the first of these processes, the farming wave of advance, and how much on the succeeding two. It is at least useful to stress that the situation may not be adequately explained by laying weight upon a single one of these processes. The balance of the evidence, as recently usefully reviewed by Shaffer,[40] is in favour of the presence of an Indo-European speaking population during the Harappan civilization, and not exclusively later. At the same time, the strong continuities between that Harappan civilization and its antecedents, right back to the earlier Neolithic, are becoming more and more evident.

The main difficulty for the Indian evidence arises from the extremely close affinities between Vedic Sanskrit and the Old Iranian language of the *Avesta*. This clearly argues for relatively recent processes at work relating the two areas. One is tempted, then, to suggest that some phenomena of élite dominance were indeed at work during the first millennium BC, or rather earlier, and that the élites of the two areas were closely related. But it is important to observe that this does not militate against the presence of Indo-European speech in north India and Pakistan at a somewhat earlier period. Some sort of 'two wave' hypothesis of this kind may do more justice to the complexity of things for the Indian subcontinent than any simpler explanation.

Above all we need to know very much more about the early archaeology of nomad pastoralism. We need to see whether the sequence of six stages outlined above does really correspond to the reality. These are questions for the future. Meanwhile it is useful to bear both hypotheses in mind. By doing so, and by admitting that at present both have a certain degree of plausibility, we are helpfully reminded how little we at present know. These questions are not in

[40] Shaffer, J.G., 'The Indo-Aryan invasions: Cultural myth and archaeological reality', in J.R. Lukacs (ed.), *The People of South Asia, the Biological Anthropology of India, Pakistan and Nepal* (New York: Plenum Press, 1984), 77–90.

principle unanswerable. When we consider how much we have learnt in recent years about the origins of the Indus Civilization,[41] and when we recall that the important evidence now available from Turkmenia is mainly the result of fairly recent work by Soviet archaeologists, there are certainly grounds for optimism.

[41] Allchin and Allchin, *op. cit.*; Agrawal, *op. cit.*; Possehl, G. (ed). *Harappan Civilisation, a Contemporary Perspective* (Warminster: Aris & Phillips, 1982).

13

The Truant Horse Clears the Hurdles

B.B. Lal

Since horses and chariots are much mentioned in the Veda and later Sanskrit works, if the Vedic Aryans were the builders of the Indus Civilization, there should be remains and representations of horses and chariots among the material remains of the Indus Civlization. B.B. Lal reviews the evidence for the presence of the domesticated horse in Indus sites, finding some evidence of horse remains and representations of the horse. He concludes that, although one would like to have more evidence, on existing evidence the alternative interpretation 'clears the hurdles' in respect of the domestic horse and cannot be dismissed.

[From *India 1947–1997: New Light on the Indus Civilization* (New Delhi: Aryan Books International, 1997), Ch. 15, pp. 109–12.]

Whether or not the horse was one of the animals known to the Harappans has long been a matter of debate. This debate has a rather ideological basis, since one of the arguments to disassociate the Harappans from the Indo-Aryans has been the supposed absence of the horse from the list of animals familiar to the former. And indeed if it were a fact that the Harappans did not know the horse, their claim for any kind of 'Aryanship' must fall to the ground, since right from the Rigvedic times, the horse played an important role in the life of the Indo-Aryans. Anyway, without going into a discussion on the Harappans vis-à-vis the Aryans, here we shall deal only with the association of the horse with the Harappan Civilization.

During the course of his excavations at Mohenjo-daro between 1927 and 1931, Mackay came across, amongst other terracotta models of animals, one example about which he stated:[1] 'Perhaps the most interesting of the model animals is one that I personally take to represent a horse.' Dealing with this topic in 1968, Wheeler wrote:[2] 'One terracotta, from a later level of Mohenjo-daro [evidently referring to the specimen just mentioned], seems to represent a horse, reminding us that the jaw-bone of a horse is also recorded from the site, and that the horse was known at a considerably earlier period in northern Baluchistan.'

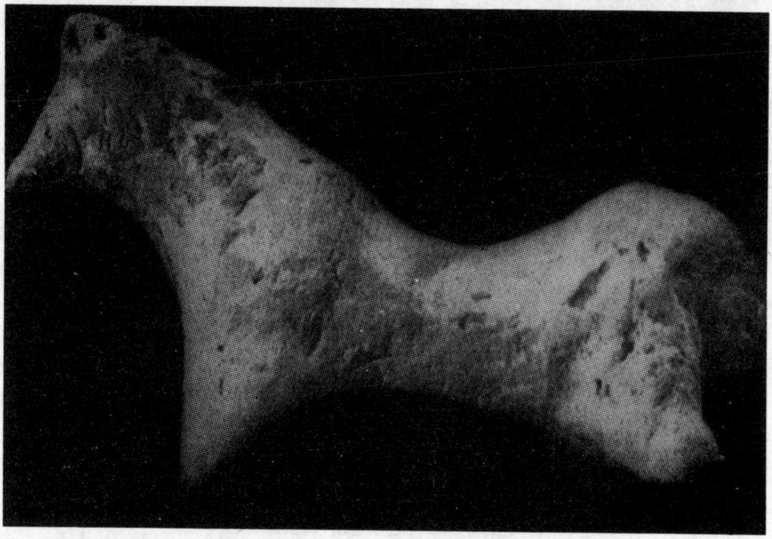

FIG. 13.1 Lothal: Terracotta horse

[1] Mackay, E.J.H., *Further Excavations at Mohenjo-daro*. 2 Vols (Delhi: Government of India, 1938), Vol. I, p. 289; Vol. II, pl LXXVIII, II.

[2] Wheeler, R.E.M., 'Harappa 1946: The Defences and Cemetary R37', *Ancient India*, 3: 58–130, 1947.

However, in spite of these categorical statements, the horse remained a suspect. The reason seems to lie in the fact that whereas other animals like the bull, buffalo, and goat were duly depicted on the seals, the horse was not. But then the same argument would apply to the camel, which is also totally absent from the seals. However, camel's was not the bone of contention since it did not carry with it any ethnic insignia.

Anyway, the Indian excavations have amply proved that the horse was duly known to the Harappans. The evidence comes from Lothal, Surkotada, Kalibangan, etc. and because of the extreme significance of the debate we shall deal with it in some detail.

From Phase III (Period A) of Lothal, which is Mature Harappan, has been recovered a terracotta figurine of the horse (Fig. 13.1). It has an elongated body with thick stumpy tail. A low ridge over the neck marks out the mane. And this terracotta figure is not the only evidence from Lothal. Amongst the faunal remains from the site is a second upper molar. Commenting on it, the experts, namely Bhola Nath, Zoologist, Zoological Survey of India, and G.V. Sreenivasa Rao of the Archaeological Survey of India, state:[3] 'The single tooth of the horse referred to above indicates the presence of the horse at Lothal during the Harappan period. The tooth from Lothal resembles closely with that of the modern horse and has pli-caballian (a minute fold near the base of the spur or protocone) which is well distinguishable character of the cheek teeth of the horse.'

Surkotada in Kachchha has yielded quite a few bones of the horse. These come from all the sub-periods (IA, IB, and IC) of the Harappan occupation.[4] The identification made by Sharma has been fully endorsed by Professor Sandor Bokonyi, Director of the Archaeological Institute, Budapest, Hungary, who is an internationally recognized archaeo-zoologist. In a letter dated 13 December 1993, addressed to the then Director-General of the Archaeological Survey of India, he avers: 'Through a through study of the equid remains of

[3] Rao, S.R., *Lothal—A Harappan Port Town (1955–62)*, Vol. II, p. 641 (New Delhi: Archaeological Survey of India, 1985).

[4] Sharma, A.K., 'The Harappan horse was buried under dune of ...', *Puratattva*, 23: 30–4, 1993; Joshi, J.P., *Excavation at Surkotada 1971–72 and Exploration in Kutch* (New Delhi: Archaeological Survey of India, 1990).

the prehistoric settlement of Surkotada, Kachchha, excavated under the direction of Dr J.P. Joshi, I can state the following: The occurrence of true horse (*Equus caballus* L.) was evidenced by the enamel pattern of the upper and lower cheek and teeth and by the size and form of incisors and phalanges (toe bones). Since no wild horses lived in India in post-Pleistocene times, the domestic nature of the Surkotada horses is undoubtful. This is also supported by an inter-maxilla fragment whose incisor tooth shows clear signs of crib biting, a bad habit only existing among domestic horses which are not extensively used for war.'

Up in the north, Rupnagar (formerly known as Ropar) and Kalibangan have also yielded remains of the horse. Kalibangan material includes an upper molar, a fragment of shaft of distal end of femur and the distal end of left humerus.[5]

From Pakistan too, the evidence, though meagre, is in the positive. We have already referred to the terracotta figurine and jaw-bone of the horse from Mohenjo-daro. Although Vats and the current excavators of Harappa, Meadow and Kenoyer, have not reported any horse bones from the site, an earlier collection from there, sent to the Zoological Survey of India and examined by its specialist, Bhola Nath, did include remains of the horse. Even from a pre-Harappan site in Pakistan, Rana Ghundai, Ross reported a few teeth of the horse, though Zeuner did not agree with the identification. However, the most startling discovery comes from the recent excavation at Nausharo, conducted by Jarrige et al.[6] In the Harappan levels over here have been found clearly identifiable terracotta figurines of this animal.

Though no doubt one would always like to have more and more evidence, even the present evidence is sufficient to dispel any doubt about the association of the horse (*Equus caballus* Linn.) with the Harappan Civilization. The truant horse has indeed crossed the hurdles!

[5] Sharma, *op. cit.*

[6] Jarrige, J.-F. *et al. Excavations at Mehrgarh-Nausharo, 16th to 20th Seasons (1990–94).* Report Submitted to Director-General of Archaeology and Museums, Government of Pakistan.

14

The Horse and the Language of the Indus Civilization

Asko Parpola

Asko Parpola is a Sanskritist and archaeologist who has made important contributions on the connections linking Vedic India, Iran, and Central Asia, and has done major studies of the Indus script. Here he briefly states his views on the horse question and the question of the language of the Indus Civilization. He argues that the patterning of evidence for the horse shows its absence from the Indus Civilization and its sudden appearance a few centuries later, which is consistent with the standard view. But he also argues for an early Aryan presence in India, earlier than the standard view allows for, from as early as the twenty-first century BC, during the last phase of the Indus cities; these, however, are not the Aryans of the Veda, who came later.

[From 'Of Rajaram's "horses", "decipherment" and civilisational issues', *Frontline*, Vol. 17, Issue 23, 11–24 November 2000 (online edition).]

The 'horse argument' is an important criterion in determining the linguistic affinity of the founders of the Indus Civilization, as pointed out in my book *Deciphering the Indus Script* (Cambridge: University Press, 1994), and by Witzel and Farmer in their *Frontline* article.[1] In

[1] Witzel, M. and S. Farmer, 'Horseplay in Harappa', *Frontline*, 17 (20), 30 September–12 October, pp. 4–14.

the Ṛgveda, the horse is an animal of great cultural and religious significance, being mentioned hundreds of times. Yet, so far, not a single representation of the horse has been found on the thousands of seals or the numerous terracotta figurines of the Indus Civilization, although many other animals, real and imaginary, were depicted by the Harappans. Further, Richard H. Meadow, one of the world's best experts on ancient animal bones, assures us that not a single horse bone has been securely identified from the Indus valley or elsewhere in South Asia before the end of the third millennium BC, when the Indus Civilization collapsed. By contrast, horse bones are found, and the horse is depicted, just a few centuries later in the Indus valley, in Gujarat and in Maharashtra, suggesting that by that time speakers of Aryan (or Indo-Iranian) languages had already entered South Asia, bringing with them this animal that was venerated by all early Indo-European-speaking peoples.

On the basis of new archaeological evidence from Afghanistan and Pakistan, I am inclined to think that the infiltration of small numbers of Aryan speakers to the Indus valley and beyond started as early as the last urban phase of the Indus Civilization, from about the twenty-first century BC onwards. (These Aryans were not yet those of the Ṛgveda, who arrived a couple of centuries, later.) The early Aryan-speaking immigrants came through Central Asia from the Eurasiatic steppes, the native habitat of the horse and the region where it appears to have first been domesticated. As demonstrated by H.H. Hock,[2] it is impossible to derive the Aryan or Indo-European languages from South Asia by valid linguistic methods. In other words, it is untenable scientifically to postulate a South Asian origin for these languages.

In my book, I have presented numerous facts suggesting that the Harappans mainly spoke a Dravidian language. The Harappans are estimated to have totalled at least 1 million people, while the primarily pastoralist, Aryan-speaking immigrants could have numbered only a small fraction of this. Eventually, however, the

[2] Hock, H.H. 'Out of India? The linguistic evidence', Bronkhorst, J. and M.M. Deshpande (eds). *Aryan and Non-Aryan in South Asia* (Cambridge, Mass.: 1999).

language of the minority prevailed over the majority. There are numerous parallels to such a development. Almost the whole continent of South America now speaks Spanish or Portuguese, while the Native American ('Indian') languages spoken there before the arrival of the European conquerors are about to vanish. This linguistic change has taken place in 500 years, and was initiated by just 300 well-armed adventurers. In 400 years, the British managed to establish their language and culture very widely in South Asia. To conflate the identity of the Vedic and Harappan cultures and to deny the external origin of Sanskrit and other Indo-Aryan languages is as absurd as to claim, as Dayananda Sarasvati did, that the railway trains and aeroplanes that were introduced in South Asia by the British in the nineteenth and twentieth centuries had already been invented by the Vedic Aryans.

It is sad that in South Asia, as elsewhere in the world, linguistic and religious controversies are the cause of so much injustice and suffering. We should remember that from the very beginning, Aryan and non-Aryan languages and associated cultures, religions, and peoples have intermingled and have become inextricably mixed. Every element of the population has contributed to the creation of the Indian civilization, and every one of them deserves credit for it.

15

Horse Remains from Surkotada

Sándor Bökönyi

The horse question concerns both representations of horses and remains of actual horses. Writers on this question show a great divergence of opinion. For example, the previous two readings disagree over whether the Indus Civilization has produced representations of domestic horses. As to the bones of horses, these and other writers refer to the findings of experts. In addition to the finding of a horse tooth at Lothal, there are the more extensive horse remains at Surkotada in Kacch, reported by A.K. Sharma. The three articles that follow re-examine those remains and assess the evidence for the existence of domestic horses in the Indus Civilization. These articles were published as a set under the title, 'Harappan horses?'. Here again the experts disagree. The respectful and civil manner in which they do so is an example all scholars should follow.

The first of these articles on horse remains is by 'one of the world's leading archaeozoologist' according to the authors of the second article. The technical aspects of identification (much of which I have deleted in this abridgement) are made difficult by the need to distinguish the bones and teeth of true horses, which do not occur in the wild in India, from the wild relative of the horse, the *khur* of Kutch, a half-ass or hemione. The author concludes, there is evidence supporting the possibility of domesticated horses in the mature phase of the Indus Civilization and the end of the third millennium BC (that is, c. 2000 BC). Since wild horses did not exist in India, the author infers that horses were brought in domesticated from inner Asia.

[From 'Horse remains from the prehistoric site of Surkotada, Kutch, late 3rd millennium BC', *South Asian Studies*, 13 (1997), pp. 297–307.]

In India, wild horses (*Equus* sensu stricto) did not exist in post-Pleistocene times, thus horses could not be domesticated there. Horses had therefore to be introduced there in an already domesticated state from the area of distribution of wild horses where early horse domestication centres had developed.

The occurrence of horse bones in a site from around 2000 BC in India always deserves special attention because of the general assumption that there was a close connection between the Aryan invasion and the arrival of horse keeping in India.[1]

Nevertheless, the identification of horse bone remains—particularly if they are heavily fragmented—is rather complicated in Indian prehistoric sites because of the largest subspecies of the half-asses, the *khur* (*Equus hemionus khur*) has been living in the north-western part of the Indian peninsula (Kutch and the Thar desert). This half-ass stands 110–27 cm at its withers which means that only the *kiang,* the Mongolian subspecies (or form?), was larger than this.[2] Strangely enough, Groves puts the African asses, Asiatic half-asses, and also the Hydruntinus-ass into the subgenus (*Asinus*), and at the same time lifts the *kiang* along with half-ass and African ass to species level.[3] Thus he unites asses and half-asses in one higher systematic unit, on the one hand, and breaks up the half-asses into two species, on the other. Eisenmann, however, represents a different view standing much closer to the traditional equid systematics when she 'would be tempted to consider the *kiang* as being a subspecies of *Equus hemionus*' based on a more detailed study on a larger sample.[4]

[1] Parpola, A., 1988, 'The Coming of the Aryans to Iran and, India and the Cultural and Ethnic Identity of the Dasas', *Studio Orientatia*, 64: 195–302.

[2] Groves, C.P., 1974, *Horses, Asses and Zebras in the Wild,* David & Charles, London.

[3] Ibid., p. 187f.

[4] Eisenmann, V., 1986, 'Comparative Osteology of Modern and Fossil Horses, Half-asses, and Asses', pp. 67–116 in R.H. Meadow and H.P. Uerpmann, eds, *Equids in the Ancient World* (Beihefte zum Tübinger Atlas des Vorderen Orient, Reihe A, Nr. 19/1), Ludwig Reichert Verlag, Wiesbaden.

The large size of the bones and teeth of the *khur* certainly makes the distinction of Indian half-ass bones from horse remains particularly difficult, and added to all this the *khur* has the strongest and thickest metapodials among the half-asses.[5] In fact, they are even plumper than those of the true asses and stand very close to those of the horses causing another difficulty for distinguishing *khur* and horse bones.

Horse bones have rarely occurred even in late prehistoric sites in India. Bhola Nath[6] described them in small number from Mohenjo-daro, though from rather recent levels. He also found them in the site of Harappa itself but seemingly from the end phase of the culture. The late Harappan culture of Rupar also yielded some horse remains.[7] Horse bones were also reported from Kalibangan and from the Neolithic-Chalcolithic levels of Hallur (1600 BC). Further, Alur and Sharma could identify a few horse remains from Malvan, Gujarat.[8]

Well-dated, though infrequent, horse bones were described by Thomas[9] from the Early Jorwe (1400–1000 BC) and Later Jorwe (1000–700 BC) periods of Inamgaon, Maharashtra.[10] Unfortunately, Thomas' paper does not contain measurements but a figure contained in it reveals that at least the phalanges come from the horses.

The conclusion drawn by Meadow also reflects the above situation very well. He noted that the domestic horse (along with

[5] Ibid., p. 109.

[6] Nath, B., 1973, 'Prehistoric Fauna Excavated from Various Sites of India with special Reference to Domestication, pp. 213–22 in J. Matolcsi, ed., *Domestikationsforschung und Geschichte der Haustiere*, Akadémiai Kiadó, Budapest.

[7] Ibid., p. 216.

[8] Sharma, A.K., 1990, 'Animal Bone Remains', pp. 372–83 in J.P. Joshi, *Excavation at Surkotada 1971–72 and Exploration in Kutch*, Memoirs of the Archaeological Survey of India 87, Archaeological Survey of India, New Delhi.

[9] Thomas, P.K., 1988, 'Faunal Assemblage', pp. 823–961 in M.K. Dhavalikar, H.D. Sankalia, and Z.D. Ansari, *Excavations at Inamgaon*, Vol. 1, Deccan College Post-Graduate and Research Institute, Pune.

[10] Meadow, R.H., 1981, 'Early Animal Domestication in South Asia: A First Report of the Faunal Remains from Mehrgarh, Pakistan, pp. 143–79 in H. Härtel, ed., *South Asian Archaeology, 1979*, Dietrich Reimer, Berlin.

the donkey) was probably introduced to Mehrgarh comparatively late, possibly in the Harappan period. And he has not found any convincing evidence for the occurrence of horse bones in South Asia before the end of the second millennium BC.

In this respect, Meadow clearly points out the main problem regarding the occurrence of horse bones, and one can only agree with him: most of the prehistoric horse bones of India have been found in multi-layered settlements, sometimes in a poorly determinable archaeological context. One can touch upon similar problems also in Europe where horse bones often surface in Neolithic sites, which are covered by Bronze Age layers.

At any rate, nobody has yet attempted to put the time of the earliest occurrence of the domestic horse in India before 2000 BC simply because they have never been identified in Mature Harappan levels even in a multilayered site. Nevertheless, Sharma[11] has lately claimed to have identified horse bones from all three sub-periods (IA-B-C) of Surkotada in Kutch, north-west India. These bones are well within the span of Harappan chronology, from c. 2300 to 1700 BC.

In Surkotada, the horse bones were not really numerous: they made up 1.2 per cent of the animal remains in Period IA, 2.2 per cent in Period IB, and 1.49 per cent in Period IC.[12] Sharma does not give either the exact number of the horse bones or their description. Nevertheless, spending some time in New Delhi following a workshop on 'Prehistoric contacts between South Asia and Africa' held at Deccan College, Pune, in December 1991, I had the opportunity to carry out a thorough examination of the equid bones found in Surkotada.

The equid remains that had been recovered in the Surkotada excavations and were put at my disposal at the Excavation Branch of the Archaeological Survey of India in Delhi consisted of 34 specimens, mainly teeth. Out of these, the following six can in all probability be considered remnants of true horses [table not printed here].

[11] Sharma, *op. cit.*

[12] Sharma, *op. cit.*

Another upper molar (from Period IA) might also represent a horse, certainly with somewhat less probability.

The distinction of teeth and bones of horse from those of half-ass and of ass has had a long history that probably started with the work of Motohashi,[13] though it originally was aimed only at skulls, and it was extended to loose teeth only by Stehlin in the 1930s.[14] I myself carried out some basic research in this field too in connection with the sporadic and sometimes frequent occurrence of Hydruntinus-ass bones found first in Early, then in Middle Neolithic sites of the Carpathian Basin and the Balkan Peninsula,[15] and also with the huge equid bone assemblage of the early Neolithic site of Umm Dabaghiyah in North Iraq whose identification and study was my task.[16] Since the beginning of large-scale archaeological activity in the Near and Middle East, a number of other authors have also dealt with a few limited aspects of the distinction of equid subgenera, nevertheless, they only touched upon problems which have emerged when they faced the tasks of identification of certain, limited bone samples.

Finally evidence of a somewhat pathological nature seems to suggest the presence of horse remains in Surkotada. In fact, two cases of crib biting, a bad habit that could be exclusively found in domestic horses, were detected among the bones. Crib biting has been observed only among such domestic horses as were being kept alone and were not overloaded with work, thus among horses which were bored. Consequently, bound to a pole or crib in a stall or a yard, they started to bite the wood, resulting in heavy wear on the front of their incisors.

All in all, the evidence enumerated above undoubtedly raises the possibility of the occurrence of domesticated horses in the Mature

[13] Motohashi, F., 1930, Craniometrical studies on skulls of wild asses from West Mongolia. *Memoirs of the Tottori Agricultural College*, 1: 1–62.

[14] Stehlin, H.G. and P. Graziosi, 1935, Richerche sugli Asinidi fossili d'Europa. *Mémoires de la Société Paléontologigue Suisse*, 56 (3): 1–73.

[15] Anthony, D., 1991, 'The archaeology of Indo-European origins'. *Journal of Indo-European Studies*, 19 (3–4): 193–222.

[16] Ibid.

phase of the Harappa culture, at the end of the third millennium BC. It they are not secondary in these layers, which can probably not completely be excluded, they will represent the earliest domestic horses in India according to our most recent knowledge.

It is well-known that wild horses did not exist in India in post-Pleistocene times, in the time of horse domestication. Horse domestication could therefore not be carried out there, and horses reached the Indian subcontinent in an already domesticated form coming from the Inner Asiatic horse domestication centres via the Transcaspian steppes, north-east Iran, south Afghanistan, and north Pakistan. The north-western part of this route is already more or less known; the Afghan and Pakistani part has to be checked in the future.

The horses introduced seemingly had the characteristics of good eastern horses, nevertheless. Due to the hot and humid climate and the small, isolated populations, an essential size decrease occurred in the population. As a result, the majority of the horses consisted of small animals of a withers height around 120 cm, and only a small part made up by individuals of larger size.

Small domestic horses were not uncommon in marginal areas under unfavourable living conditions in prehistoric times—and India has never been ideal horse country.

16

Comment on 'Horse Remains from Surkotada'

Richard H. Meadow
and
Ajita Patel

This reading, by Richard H. Meadow (an archaeologist who has published important work on early animal domestication in South Asia) and Ajita Patel, examines the Bökönyi report and comes to a different conclusion. The authors have serious reservations about the identification of remains at Surkotada as true horses, and in general are sceptical about evidence for domestic horses before the end of the Indus Civilization.

[From 'A comment on "Horse remains from Surkotada by Sándor Bökönyi"', *South Asian Studies*, 13 (1997), pp. 308–15.]

Introduction

We greatly mourn the passing on 25 December 1994 of Sándor Bökönyi, Director of the Archaeological Institute of the Hungarian Academy of Sciences and one of the world's leading archaeozoologists. Dr Bökönyi was a first-rate scholar, a wonderful colleague, and a true gentleman. We feel privileged to have known him and, shortly before his death, to have been able to engage in scholarly debate with him—an exchange, based on differing perceptions of the same body of material, that was never acrimonious, personal, or political.

Dr Bökönyi was not able to complete revision of his manuscript that provides the basis for our comments here, nor was he able to pen a reply before his death. In a long letter dated 19 June 1994, we had written to him detailing our concerns over certain aspects of his article which had been sent to us for review by the editor of the expected forthcoming issue of *Harappan Studies.* On 30 September 1994, however, we did have the opportunity to discuss our comments with him on the occasion of the Seventh International Congress of the International Council on Archaeozoology which was being held in Konstanz, Germany. We went through each point that we had raised and in some cases agreed to disagree. He remained firmly convinced that there are the bones of true horse (*Equus caballus*) in the Surkotada collection, and we remain sceptical. Points of agreement and disagreement, as noted on a copy of the 19 June letter in our possession, are presented as addenda to the comments that follow.

When the article was sent to us for review, we delayed a reply until we had a chance to examine the Surkotada material ourselves. This we did on 25 April 1994 with the assistance and cooperation of the staff of the Excavation Branch of the Archaeological Survey of India at Purana Qila, Delhi. We took that opportunity not only to check the observations made by Dr Bökönyi in 1991, but to take a more comprehensive set of measurements following the protocols developed by Véra Eisenmann.[1] These dimensions are listed at the end of our contribution.

[1] Eisenmann, V., 1986, Comparative osteology of modern and fossil horses, half-asses, and asses, pp. 67–116 in: R.H. Meadow and H.-P. Uerpmann, eds., *Equids in the Ancient World* (Beihefte zum Tubinger Atlas des Vorderen Orients, Reihe A, Nr. 19/1). Ludwig Reichert Verlag, Wiesbaden, 1986; Eisenmann, V. and S. Beckouche, 1986, Identification and discrimination of metapodials from Pleistocene and Modern *Equus*, wild and domestic, pp. 117–163 in: R.H. Meadow and H.-P. Uerpmann, eds., *Equids in the Ancient World* (Beihefte zum Tubinger Atlas des Vorderen Orients, Reihe A, Nr. 19/1). Ludwig Reichert Verlag, Wiesbaden, 1986.

This comment should be taken for what it is—a comment reflecting the scholarly interchange of ideas and opinions about a single collection of faunal material. We do not feel that this is the place to deal extensively with wider issues, such as those addressed by A.K. Sharma,[2] or R.S. Sharma.[3] These we will address in a future publication.

A Comment in Twelve Parts

These comment are abstracted from the letter of 19 June 1994 to Sándor Bökönyi. Significant elaborations on points made in the letter as well as the gist of Dr Bökönyi's verbal replies to us are set off in brackets.

1. Concerning the observations of Groves[4] on the classification of the *khur* and of hemiones of general, by 1986 he had changed his mind about the subgenus for the hemiones, placing them in subgenus *Hemionus*.[5]
2. Bökönyi notes that 'the khur has the shortest and thickest metapodials among the half-asses.'[6] From the measurements listed in Eisenmann and Beckouche (*op. cit.*), however, it seems that the metapodials of the *khur* are not very different in proportion from those of the onager. (In Konstanz, Bökönyi agreed that this more recently published data changed the picture presented by Groves.)
3. Concerning the introduction of horses at Mehrgarḥ, in our view, the issue is the introduction of the domestic horse

[2] Sharma, A.K., 1993, The Harappan Horse was buried under the dunes of ... *Puratattva*, 23: 30–4.

[3] Sharma, R.S., 1995, *Looking for the Aryans.* Orient Longman, Madras.

[4] Groves, C.P., 1974, *Horses, Asses and Zebras in the Wild.* David & Charles, London.

[5] Groves, C.P., 1986, The taxonomy, distribution, and adaptations of recent equids, pp. 11–65 in: R.H. Meadow and H.-P. Uerpmann, eds., *Equids in the Ancient World* (Beihefte zum Tubinger Atlas des Vorderen Orients, Reihe A, Nr. 19/1). Ludwig Reichert Verlag, Wiesbaden.

[6] Groves, 1974, *op. cit.*

(*Equus caballus*) to the Mehrgarh region—better the north Kachi Plain of Balochistan—not to Mehrgarh itself where there is no evidence for the true horse. The original quote from Meadow[7] is as follows:

'The situation with the horse is not so clear. There are, as yet, no convincing reports of horse remains from archaeological sites in South Asia before the end of the second millennium BC. Many claims have been made[8] but few have been documented with sufficient measurements, drawings, and photographs to permit other analysts to judge for themselves. An additional complication is that some specimens come from archaeological deposits which could be considerably younger than the main body of material at the site in question (e.g., at Mohenjo-daro and Harappa). Identifications, no matter how firm, are not particularly useful if the bones on which they are based come from poorly defined contexts.

Here Meadow is speaking of the *bones* of the true horse—their actual remains. We do not doubt that horses came to South Asia at least by the end of the first quarter of the second millennium and *perhaps* even by the end of the third millennium. This is indicated by the figurine evidence at Pirak[9] and also by painted sherds from the Swat valley,[10] all dating to the beginning of the second millennium.

[7] Meadow, R.H., 1987, Faunal exploitation patterns in eastern Iran and Baluchistan: a review of recent investigations, pp. 881–916 in: G. Gnoli and L. Lanciotti, eds., *Orientalia Iosephi Tucci Memoriae Dicata* (Serie Orientale Roma LVI, 2). Istituto Italiano per il Medio ed Estremo Oriente, Rome.

[8] Sewell, R.B.S., 1931, Zoological remains, pp. 469–673 in: J. Marshall, comp., *Mohenjo-daro and the Indus Civilization.* Arthur Probsthain, London; Nath, B., 1962, Remains of horse and Indian elephant from prehistoric site of Harappa, Part 2, 1–14 in: *Proceedings 1st All-India Congress of Zoology.* Calcutta; Sharma, A.K., 1974, Evidence of horse from the Harappan settlement at Surkotada. *Puratattva*, 7: 75–6.

[9] Jarrige, J.-F., M. Santoni and J.-F. Enault. 1979. *Fouilles de Pirak.* Diffusion de Boccard. Paris.

[10] Stacul, G., 1987, *Prehistoric and Protohistoric Swat, Pakistan (c. 3000–1400 B.C.).* Instituto Italiano per il Medio ed Estremo Oriente, Rome.

(Bökönyi took note of these comments and we agreed that only minor changes in his statements would be necessary.)

4. Concerning specimen 2149 that Bökönyi identified as a lower milk P3 or P4, we disagree. With a crown height greater than 75 mm, this specimen is entirely too hypsodont (high-crowned) to be a deciduous (milk) tooth. This we checked with specimens of newly erupted deciduous equid teeth in the collection of the Zooarchaeology Laboratory, Peabody Museum, Harvard University—both modern and archaeological. In addition, tooth 2149 is hardly worn and the distal (toward the back of the mouth) margin of the crown overhangs the 'neck' quite substantially. (The neck is that area of the tooth that lies between the crown and the root.) Such a very high-crowned hardly worn deciduous tooth would be exceptional. The tooth itself is very slender with a greatest breadth (GB) of 14.3 mm, and once it had come into wear, it would measure very much shorter (front to back along the crown) than the documented greatest mesial–distal length of 36 mm. Taking into consideration also the angle of the occlusal (biting) surface in relation to the body of the tooth in side view (a bit angled to the rear of the jaw), it seems clear that this is a lower M1 or M2 and more likely the first. As a permanent molar, the somewhat 'V'-shaped lingual (toward the tongue) valley vaguely visible on the occlusal surface would confirm its identification as an ass (*Equus asinus*) or a hemione (*Equus hemionus*), but not a horse (*Equus caballus*). (Bökönyi agreed that upon consideration our identification seemed possible, and we all agreed upon the problems of identification posed by deciduous teeth and by both deciduous and permanent teeth not fully in wear.)
5. Concerning specimen 23–24, the first phalanx, we think it is rather from the fore limb (anterior) than from the hind limb (posterior) based on the profile of the shaft in dorsal (anterior) view. Identification of the limb, however, is not something that is always very easy especially in a broken specimen like 2304. From the sagittal (dorsal or anterior) length of approximately 74 mm and from careful

examination of the specimen, we were able to estimate a greatest length (GL) of about 82 mm. This is only slightly longer than the longest specimens for hemione published by Dive and Eisenmann (*op. cit.*) and of a size or shorter than the two first phalanges from Shahr-i Sokhta identified as coming from hemiones by Compagnoni.[11] More trouble for hemione identification is the smallest breadth (SD) of 30 mm (30.4 by our measure) which is certainly above any published *modern* hemione breadth. This dimension, however, is nearly matched by the specimens from Shahr-i Sokhta which are reported as having breadths (SD) of 28.2 mm and 31 mm, going with lengths (GL) of 81 mm and 87 mm (!), respectively. Perhaps we should identify the Shahr-i Sokhta material as true horse as well?

In any event, this Surkotada specimen is the best case for a true horse based on size alone, although it is rather too slender for our taste to be a horse. We would rather err on the conservative side in this case and say specimen 2304 is probably from a large hemione, which is what Meadow[12] indicated. An additional observation is that the breadth of the distal articular surface (BFD) of this first phalanx is smaller than the breadths of the proximal articular surfaces (BFp) of the two second phalanges in this same collection which we feel, on the basis of size, are very unlikely to have come from true horses. (In our discussion, Bökönyi continued to maintain an identification of *Equus caballus*, and we agreed to disagree, with Bökönyi saying that he would include further discussion of first phalanges in the revision of his paper. Bökönyi also wondered whether what we said above about the distal first phalanges and the proximal second phalanges might not mean that the second

[11] Compagnoni, B., 1978, The bone remains of Equus hemionus from Shahr-i Sokhta, pp. 105–118 in: R.H. Meadow and M.A. Zeder, eds., *Approaches to Faunal Analysis in the Middle East* (Peabody Museum Bulletin 2). Peabody Museum, Cambridge.

[12] Meadow, 1987, *op. cit.*

phalanges also came from horse.) (Further note: Specimen 2309, a first phalanx, which is illustrated in Sharma [*op. cit.*] was not present in the collection we saw in Delhi.)

...

10. We did not see the evidence for 'crib biting' that Bökönyi observed for specimen 2282—a right premaxillary with upper first and second incisors—and 2288—a first upper incisor. Instead we thought the enamel on the incisors was broken off sometime after death. Examination of the photographs confirms that the enamel on the first incisor of 2282 is broken off; the enamel on the labial margin of the second incisor near the occulusal surface seems worn and polished, but whether this reflects crib-biting is unclear. (Bökönyi remained convinced of his identification of the pathological condition. We need to examine the teeth again, probably under a microscope.)
11. (Bökönyi notes that 'All in all, the evidence enumerated above undoubtedly raises the possibility of the occurrence of domesticated horses in the Mature phase of the Harappa culture, at the end of the third millennium BC. If they are not secondary in these layers, which can probably not completely be excluded, they will represent the earliest domestic horses in India according to our most recent knowledge.') As mentioned above, we believe that we should expect to find the true horse in the subcontinent by the very end of the third or the beginning of the second millennium BC, although so far the firm bone evidence still is not there, in our opinion, in spite of Bökönyi's careful and methodical attempt to document it in his paper. In this regard, it is important to note that Surkotada had dates that go into the second millennium, and the date of the 'Harappan' layers themselves is not all that clear.[13]

[13] Joshi, J.P., 1974, Surkotada: a chronological assessment. *Puratattva*, 7: 34–8; Possehl, G.L., 1994, *Radiometric Dates for South Asian Archaeology*. The University Museum, Philadelphia.

12. (At the end his paper, Bökönyi compares the situation in South Asia with that in the French Bronze Age. The way he phrased it, it could be taken as a direct comparison of the two areas, which is the way we took it at first. In fact, as he made clear to us in Konstanz, it was the general phenomenon of smaller horses in marginal areas and not the specifics that he was comparing. We still think that the two cases really are not comparable, as there was probably an ancestral wild horse population in western Europe. Our comments on the lower 'premolar' [which we believe is a molar] are presented above.)

Conclusions

In sum, based on what we observed in Delhi and have outlined above, we cannot accept without serious reservations Bökönyi's identifications of any of the Surkotada material as true horse, but in the end that may be a matter of emphasis and opinion. In any event, we applaud the very careful way Bökönyi expressed himself in his article and can only hope that the above comments are helpful in showing the non-specialist how technical and far from straightforward are some of the issues involved.

One final point needs to be made. Even if one or even a few bones should turn out to be undoubtedly from true horse, that does not mean that every equid bone, by association, is from horse. Each specimen has to be evaluated on its own merits, and for some—perhaps even most—one can only identify the genus (*Equus*) but not the species (*E. hemionus, E. asinus, E. caballus,* or hybrids) from which they came.

17

The Domestication of the Horse in Asia

David Anthony

The third piece of this trio of articles on horses is by David Anthony who has written on the archaeological evidence of Indo-European origins. He lays out briefly the current state of knowledge about the domestication of the horse, from about 4000 BC in the Ukraine, 'centuries before wheeled vehicles'. Horses and spoke-wheeled chariots are found in the steppes of Russia and Kazakhstan dating to 2100–1800 BC, which is towards the end of the mature phase of the Indus Civilization. This tends to support the standard view.

[From 'Current thoughts on the domestication of the horse in Asia', *South Asian Studies* 13 (1997), pp. 315–18.]

The time and place of the domestication of the horse and its earliest use as a transport animal are topics that remain clouded by uncertainties. The subject has been complicated by the politicized history of the study of the Aryans and their migrations. The earliest direct evidence for cultural control of horses consists of bit wear on the premolars of a stallion excavated at the Copper Age site of Dereivka on the Dnieper River in Ukraine; the occupation level is dated by seven radiocarbon determinations to 4200–3800 BC, calibrated.[1,2,3] The stallion skull and mandible were excavated from an apparently undisturbed context in the Copper Age settlement, but yielded an anomalous radiocarbon date of ca. 3000 BC,[4] possibly because of the thick coat of glue and lacquer that covered it in the museum for 25 years before it was tested. Experiments by Anthony and Brown suggest that this horse was bitted with a hard bit, minimally bone, for at least 300 hours.[5] Bitting implies either driving or riding. If the Dereivka stallion dates to ca. 4000 BC, centuries before the earliest evidence for wheeled vehicles, driving is unlikely; it is therefore thought by Anthony and Brown to have been ridden. Bit wear has also been detected[6] on five horse premolars from the Copper Age site of Botai in northern Kazakhstan, a settlement of more than 150 pit-houses where horses constitute more than 99 per cent of the 330,000-specimen faunal sample. Botai is dated by five radiocarbon determinations to about 3300–2900 BC.[7] Botai-culture sites have yielded no domesticated animals except dogs and, apparently, horses, although Sandra Olsen has recognized a few camel bones of unknown status among the Botai fauna. The earliest archaeological

[1] Anthony, D. and D. Brown. 'Looking a gift horse in the mouth: Identification of the earliest bitted equids and the microscopic analysis of bit wear', pp. 98–116, in: P. Crabtree, D. Campana, and K. Ryan, eds, *Early Animal Domestication and its Cultural Context*, (MASCA) Research Papers in Science and Archaeology, Supplement to Volume 6 (The University Museum, Philadelphia, 1989).

[2] Anthony, D. and D. Brown. 'The origins of horseback riding'. *Antiquity*, 65 (246): 22–38, 1991.

[3] About the absolute age of the settlement and cemetery of Dereivka on the Middle Dneiper. Paper presented at the conference, *Early Horsekeepers of the Eurasian Steepes, 4500–1500 BC*, 19–29 June, Petropavlovsk, Kazakhstan. Paper presented at the conference *Early Horsekeepers of the Eurasian Steppes, 4500–1500 B.C.*, 19–24 June, Petropavlovsk, Kazakhstan.

[4] Telegin, *op. cit.*

[5] Brown, D. and D. Anthony. 'Bit wear and horseback riding'. Paper presented at the conference *Early Horsekeepers of the Eurasian Steppes, 4500–1500 B.C.*, 19–24 June, 1995, Petropavlovsk, Kazakhstan.

[6] Brown and Anthony, 1995, *op. cit.*

[7] Zaibert, V, *Eneolit Uralo-Irtyshskogo Mezhdurech'ya.* Petropavlovsk Nauka, 1993.

traces of a steppe culture that might be described as proto-Aryan occur with the Sintashta and Petrovka cultures of the upper Tobol-Ishim river drainages in the northern steppe zone of Russia and Kazakhstan. These sites are dated to about 2100–1800 BC, contained burials with spoke-wheeled chariots and horses, and represent the earliest stage in the development of the Andronovo horizon, which was in contact with Bactria and Margiana.[8, 9, 10]

8 Anthony, D. and N. Vinogradov. The birth of the chariot. *Archaeology*, 48(21): 36–41, 1995.

9 Parpola A. 'Formation of the Aryan branch of Indo-Aryan'. Paper presented at the conference. *Early Horsekeepers of the Eurasian Steppes, 4500–1500 B.C.*, June 19–24 1995, Petropavlovsk, Kazakhstan.

10 Kuzmina, E. *Otkuda Prishli Indoarii?* (Moskva: Rossiiskii Institut Kul' turologii, 1994).

18

Decipherments of the Indus Script

Kamil V. Zvelebil

It is not possible to provide samples of the hundred or so proposed decipherments of the Indus script. This article by Kamil Zvelebil, the eminent authority on Dravidian linguistics is a very good critical survey of many of the decipherment attempts. The author concludes that some progress has been made. The direction of writing had been firmly established (by B.B. Lal, among others) to be from right to left. The Indus script has some 400 signs, of which about 200 are used frequently. It is mainly logographic (having signs for ideas rather than for sounds) and certainly not alphabetic since it has too many signs. But none of the proposed decipherments are successful. Zvelebil further concludes that the Indus script is not related to the later Indian scripts (Brahmi, Kharoshti) and that the Harappan language is probably not Indo-European.

[From 'Dravidian and "Harappan"', in *Dravidian Linguistics: An Introduction* (Pondicherry: Pondicherry Institute of Linguistics and Culture, 1990), pp. 84–98.]

In 1875, Sir Alexander Cunningham reported the discovery of a 'most curious object' which was found at Harappa by Major-General Clark, then Commissioner of Avadh. It was a seal made of 'dark brown Jasper' and engraved on it was a humpless bull, looking to the right, with two 'stars' under its neck. Above the bull was an inscription engraved in six characters. Though the inscription was unintelligible to Cunningham, he nevertheless concluded that the characters of the script were not Indian and therefore the seal was 'foreign to India'. This seems to have been the first reported discovery of a steatite seal with Harappan script.[1]

In 1886, more seals were brought to light; but their origin, significance, and age remained obscure to scholars for quite some time to come. Larger amounts of texts became available only after the first regular excavations at Harappa were started by Rai Bahadur Daya Ram Sahni in 1920–1, and their prehistoric nature was established only by Sir John Marshall and his colleagues, Mackay, Gadd, and Smith in about 1924, after the discovery of Mohenjodaro by R.D. Banerji.

As Wheeler pointed out long ago, Harappan civilization is the most spatially extensive of all the early civilizations we know. The Mature Harappan phase seems to have extended from about 2000 to 1700 BC, but most Harappan sites seem to have been occupied for no more than 200 years (with the exception of the few large cities). The final appearance of the Harappan cultural style was probably in Gujarat–Maharashtra around 1300 BC. There are about 1000 Harappan sites spread over an enormous area. Recently, the French discovered a settlement close to the Oxus River, deep in Central Asia, and the Russians some apparently proto-Indian seals at Altyn Tepe. This raises, on the one hand, the possibility of Altaic connections and, on the other hand, of Indo-Aryan loanwords in Harappan vocabularies.

The seals are generally made of steatite alias soapstone, a singularly soft stone which tends to disintegrate when it becomes too moist. Seal cutting must have been a master craft of the Indus people. According to Walter A. Fairservis Jr., the Harappan seal cutter was a highly accomplished master-craftsman. Among a large population, though, seal-bearers were a relatively small group. Nonetheless, even small Harappan settlements had their quota of seal bearers and users. On analogy with the Sumerian seals which

[1] The seal itself was found sometime in or before 1872–3, and is now preserved in the British Museum, London.

can be read and understood, the Harappan seals may also be roughly divided into two major groups: a larger class of owners' seals used in administration and trade, with the name of the seal of owner with or without further determinatives (occupations, clans, ranks, titles, etc.) added; and a smaller class of dedicative seals where the recipients of the gifts are gods or their representatives (temples, priests, rulers?).

Ever since the first specimens of the Indus script were published, they presented a standing challenge to scholars, resisting, so far, all attempts at decipherment. The problem consists of the fact that we have to do with an *unknown script* in an *unknown language*, with no bilingual inscription found so far. To make the matter worse, there are only eight texts longer than fifteen signs in the whole corpus; the longest inscription has twenty-six signs written on three sides of a triangular prism. The longest continuous text has seventeen signs in three consecutive lines. The average length of an inscription is almost exactly five signs. Sometimes texts are confined to one or two signs. This script, invented around 2500 BC, consists of some 419 signs occurring in seal texts and graffiti 13.376 times in 2,290 known texts. Of the 419 signs, 113 occur only once, forty-seven occur twice, fifty-nine occur fewer than five times. Thus approximately 200 signs are in general use. About thirty-five signs can possibly be compared with proto-Elamite. These findings demonstrate that the Harappan script is in principle of the same type as the other known writing systems of the third millennium BC, representing probably the first phase of phonetization in which pictures of concrete objects are used both for the names of those objects and for other, homophonous words with entirely different meaning. In terms of historical analogies: Proto-Sumerian is dated ca 2900 BC, Proto-Elamite 2800 BC, and Harappan ca 2300 BC. It terms of the number of signs, the 419 Harappan symbols are considerably fewer than Sumerian (ca 600), Egyptian (ca 700) and Chinese (ca 3500). The problem of the seal-cutter/scribe was often to provide maximum information in minimum space, and hence, maybe, the technique of combining as many as four different signs. As stressed above, in actual fact, the total number of signs in regular use is less than 200. These findings (the number of signs and the occurrence of some signs as isolate single signs making up an entire inscription) demonstrate that the script was definitely not alphabetic nor purely logographic, but most probably logosyllabic or something of that order, that is, some signs represent words (lexemes), others may serve purely for their syllabic values, representing probably grammatical markers; in fact, in principle, a script like the modern Sino-Japanese, only much less complex.

The Indus script does not bear a close resemblance to any other known script so that it could be proved genetically related to any. The idea of writing may have come from Elam, but the script was probably invented independently. Already Hunter (1934) and Gelb (1963) among others noted the possibility of a common source of some signs in the corpus of Proto-Sumerian, Proto-Elamite, and Proto-Indic. Both Proto-Sumerian and Proto-Elamite appear to have a distinct chronological priority over Harappan. However, none of the speculations in any of these directions has so far helped in the actual decipherment.

To sum sup the enormous difficulties of the Harappan problem: (a) an unknown language in an unknown script; (b) the absence of any bilingual text; (c) the 'unfortunate' nature of the texts—they are simply too short and very probably too limited in character; (d) the absence of any real clue (like place-names or personal names); and (e) Harappan civilization is geographically remote from other civilizations of its time, and also historically remote from later cultural developments on the Indian subcontinent.

The decipherment of any unknown script and/or language presupposes the availability of some clue or reference. Where a clue or reference is absent, the decipherer can only exercise his own imagination, and the acceptance of any decipherment is an act of faith. In the absence of a bilingual clue, of geographical and other proper names, and of lengthy inscriptions, the prospects of ever understanding the Indus script and language have generally been considered very meager. And, indeed, until approximately 1965, the attempts at the decipherment of the Indus Valley script and language must all be characterized as totally invalid, in spite of such tremendously honest work as that of G.R. Hunter (1939) or such highly imaginative approaches like those of Bedrich Hrozny (1943–8) or Father H. Heras (1953). There was the usual crop of amateurish nonsense or attempts typical of lack of chronological accuracy, linguistic naivety, untenable aprioristic assumptions and assertions—in short, the would-be decipherers largely ignored the criteria of rigorous approach and underestimated one or more, or all, of the difficulties mentioned above.

Tangible results have been achieved only since the introduction of computer techniques by Soviet and Finnish scholars in the early sixties. With the Soviet team's first announcement in 1965, important qualitative changes ushered in a new era of serious and partially successful treatment of the Harappan problem. Among all the pre-1965 attempts, only two will be briefly mentioned: the work of Hunter and the labours of Heras. In contrast, a more detailed critical information will be given on the following ventures: those of Knorozov and his team, the Finnish group, I. Mahadevan, W. Fairservis, Kinnier-Wilson, and S.R. Rao.

Sign lists and concordances to the Indus inscriptions were published quite early, in the 1930s: S. Langdon (1931), C.J. Gadd and S. Smith (1931), M.S. Vats (1940); but especially one must in this context mention with great admiration the excellent work performed without the aid of computer technology by G.R. Hunter in his book *The Script of Harappa and Mohenjo Daro and Its Connection with Other Scripts*, London, 1934. Hunter's was the most precise, most honest, and most rigorous work on Harappan script before the contemporary stage began in the early 1960s. As for Heras, one should remember his attempt because it was de facto the first systematic and consistent attempt to decipher the script and read the language. Of course, he has failed; but he reached the conclusion that the Harappan language was a kind of ancient Tamil, and many of his intuitions were adopted twenty years later by the Russian and Finnish teams. It is only fair to say that even the very recent attempts to decipher the script do not go very much beyond of what Heras had achieved intuitively. It is quite apparent that these contemporary attempts have drawn much inspiration from Heras, both as to the method of segmentation of signs, as well as to the interpretation of their function and meaning; the whole idea of homophones, of the rebus principle is, as a matter of fact, already contained in his work.

The computer was first used by the Russians under the inspiring leadership of Yurij V. Knorozov. What the computer enabled was, primarily, to compile concordances of texts for statistical and positional analyses of the signs. However, one must admit that the widely advertised possibilities and reliability of the computer-decipherment was largely exaggerated. As of today, no programmes exist on the basis of which electronic computers could cope with the actual reading of the signs, let alone a translation of the texts. Hence, scholars proceed to work without the aid of computers, too (for example, W.A. Fairservis). And, as will be shown, although the computers have achieved a lot, they have not substantially and essentially brought us nearer the actual interpretation and decipherment of the inscriptions.

We must distinguish between attempts at phonetic decipherment, that is, attempts ultimately resulting in the 'reading' of the texts in their underlying actual language, and formal, structural-systemic analysis and description of the Indus texts based on positional statistics. These two steps represent two very distinct procedures, and this distinction one must always bear in mind while discussing what has and what has not been achieved. Scholars have progressed quite far with the second step—that is, with the formal/structural analysis. In contrast, they were unable to move significantly ahead with the actual decipherment and reading of the inscriptions.

In this type of script, the signs can be read either semantically (ideographically) or phonetically. In the former case, a given pictogram stands for the object it depicts, and it can be understood without reference to the underlying language. All decipherments which will be discussed have this in common while the ideographic reading is frequently (not always though) fairly acceptable, and often identical in the various attempts, the phonetic readings differ widely and are, from the point of view of linguistics, mostly unacceptable because they cannot be verified so far by any objective, independent, rigorous procedure. It has become apparent that the assignment of concrete linguistic values or meanings, and of grammatical functions even to the most frequently and regularly occurring signs is virtually impossible.

It is not necessary to use a computer to see that certain signs occur more frequently than others. Next question is: In what order do the signs occur? Do they fall into regular positions obedient to some convention, ether of the Harappan seal writing, or some morphemic structure, or some fixed order in certain phrases? Clearly relative position offers us a clue as to sign behaviour (together with the statistical frequencies) and, in addition, some control is necessary if we are to properly analyse the role of the individual signs relative to one another. Hence the need for a *grid* system. Different decipherers have coped with these problems in their own ways: the Soviets breaking the inscriptions into what they call 'blocks' and coming up finally with what they consider root morphemes and a few suffixes. In very similar ways, the Finns. A grid consisting of fourteen columns was constructed by Fairservis. Mahàdevan came with his method of parallelisms. All of these scholars accepted the principle of *homophony* (the so-called rebus principle) as actively employed by the Harappan scribes. And yet, in spite of the fact that all of them, too, accepted as a basic axiom that the underlying language was some form of Dravidian, their results widely disagree.

The Soviet teams and groups headed by Y.V. Knorozov boast of the distinction to have introduced the computer into the problem of the decipherment. They indeed were the first. According to Professor Olderogge, they began working in the middle of 1964, and since then they have published an important series of papers in Russian and English entitled *Proto-Indica* (1965, 1968, 1970, 1973, and 1979) announcing their results of the computer-aided investigation. The computer programmes were prepared very carefully by M.A. Probst, and most of the analysis and interpretation was done by Knorozov, Volchok, Alekseev, Kondratov, and Gurov. The Soviet and the Finnish attempts can be treated together since the methodology adopted by both teams is broadly identical: first, preparing careful computer programmes; next, to determine functional characteristics of each sign by statistical-positional analysis; third, to ascertain the probable phonetic value by the technique of homophony applied after linguistic reconstruction. Hence, both teams have also agreed broadly on the three basic conclusions though, as we shall see, in detail they disagree: (a) the inscriptions generally read from right to left; (b) the signs are mostly logographic and the rebus principle is widely employed; and (c) the underlying language is Dravidian.

However, the careful and often thought-provoking positional-statistical analysis of the texts, and the faultless programming notwithstanding, their further procedure is entirely intuitive-speculative, the conclusions possible but completely hypothetical, and, above all, absolutely unverifiable.

The Soviet and the Finnish scholars have overreacted to their own results. Their initial enthusiasm has taken them too far into vague and complex speculations, and, in addition, they had a tendency to believe that they were looking at something 'mysterious', almost 'mystical', rooted in the Harappan world view which could well be ancestral to the intricacies of later Hindu civilization. This is particularly true of the work of Asko Parpola. I believe on the contrary with W. Fairservis that the Harappans were thoroughly pragmatic, unlikely to have constructed other than a functional world view rooted in the control of a ranked society based on village agriculture which in turn was based on the availability of water resources. As Fairservis says, 'village India written large'. We shall not go into the details of the Soviet teams' decipherments.[2] Their work has of course its great merits, particularly in its pioneering nature, its primacy of employing the computer, its formal analysis of the texts and, last but not least, in the excellent mathematical preparation of the computer programming. However, they have not convincingly deciphered even one single short Harappan inscription, and they have not been able to offer a verifiable reading of any Harappan text.

Almost simultaneously with the Soviet teams' activities, a Finnish group based at Copenhagen and Helsinki used the computer programmes prepared by Seppo Koskenniemi. Asko and Simo Parpola were chief investigators. More recently, Kimo Koskenniemi has developed computer programmes to generate a corpus of texts, analysis of duplicate texts, and a revised concordance based on single-sign occurrences (1982). The main role of the Soviet teams consisted in the pioneering use of computers; then they based their interpretations mainly on the insights of the Spanish Jesuit Father Heras, and thus bolstered up substantially the Dravidian hypothesis.

[2] The Soviet methods and early results were subject to a very detailed criticism by A.R.K. Zide and myself in a monograph which we translated from Russian into English with a critical commentary, cf. Zide, Arlene R.K., and Kamil V. Zvelebil (eds), *The Soviet Decipherment of the Indus Valley Script: Translation and Critique*, The Hague-Paris, 1976.

The greatest merit of the labours of the Finnish scholars represents the preparation of the corpus (1979) and two concordances (1973, 1982), and the daring, often provocative but always stimulating interpretations of Asko Parpola. While working out the list of signs, all teams, particularly the Finns, encountered two main problems: How to distinguish between different graphemes? And in what sequences should the graphemes be ordered? It is very true what the Finns say in their 1979 (p. 13) publication: A false identification of two distinct graphemes is equally detrimental as a false separation of two allographs. The problem would not arise if all the signs were drastically individual. But in the Indus script, many signs have been inscribed in 'more or less' similar but 'not quite identical' form. What, however, does this 'more or less' similar mean? What is the value of 'quite' in 'not quite identical'? It must be admitted that the Finnish scholars do very carefully try to set up criteria for identifying two or more graphic forms as variants of a single grapheme—and yet, none of these can be taken as really conclusive. In the course of this process, they offer some sharp but deserved criticism of Mahadevan's sign list. Thus, e.g., it is really almost incredible that Mahadevan lists as separate signs (his) nos. 110 and 112, the symbols for 'seven', appearing once as ||| |||| and next time as ||||/|||. On the other hand, the Finns (and Fairservis) take Ψ and ⊢ШШ as identical. These signs may be identical, but it is by no means certain that they are. The difference could of course be explained either as a difference in 'regional' style or in gradual development, but it could also indicate some minor variation of a basically identical emic unit (that is, phonetic or even semantic variation); and, one should not hesitate to say, Ψ and ⊢ШШ could even be two completely different signs, (for example, one indicating ('meaning') 'wheat', another 'barley'.

In their most recent publications (especially the 1982 concordance), the Finns' view is that the Indus script is 'a relatively crude morphemographic writing system' in which the graphemes usually stand for the lexical morphemes. This view is almost identical with the present position of Mahadevan.

Once contradiction in the Finnish approach should be mentioned. On the one hand, the principle of economy is repeatedly stressed by Parpola as very important in the Harappan script. How to reconcile this principle with the many graphic variants—or rather what is considered to be only 'insignificant' graphic variants of one sign, for example,  =  = ? If a script is so strictly economical, it should not display such wealth of merely graphic variations; in other words, every variant should be meaningful.

As for the function of the seals, the Finns, too, distinguish roughly between the owners' seals with owners' proper names ending in , and dedicative seals, less frequent, ending in . This gave them one of their basic clues;  is a genitive-possessive suffix,  is a dative marker. I shall return to these two signs later.

A.R.K. Zide and myself, and later I alone, have repeatedly criticized in detail the Finnish initial attempts and, in particular, their enormous enthusiasm due to which they definitely overestimated the value of their own decipherment, taking for absolutely granted the Dravidian hypothesis, and building upon it an entire system of a Proto-Dravidian Harappan astral religion and similar constructs. Easy conclusions were made and discarded on scantly material and on unverifiable data, and etymologies played with rather ruthlessly. One must of course admit that if Asko Parpola would not have let his imagination soar high from time to time, it would also not bring him the positive results it definitely did. And, we should stress, these are secondary phenomena. The greatest merit of the Finnish work is the excellent concordances they prepared—and this work will always remain one of the cornerstones of the entire process of decipherment.[4]

[3] Thus e.g. in June 1974, Parpola wrote that 'Statues of naked dancing girls have been found in the Indus, and they point to the existence of the devadasi institution. These sacred prostitutes probably formed groups according to the number of the various asterisms.' Almost every word of that pronouncement is a wild misstatement.

[4] Zide, A.R.K. and K. Zvelebil, *Review of Works on Indus Valley Script* (by Knorozov ed. and Parpola et al.), *Language* 46 (1970) 4.952–68; Zide, A.R.K. and K. Zvelebil, *Review of Parpola et al.*, Decipherment ... and Progress ..., *Indo-Iranian Journal* XII (1970) 2.126–34; Zvelebil, Kamil, 'The so-called "Dravidian" of the Indus inscriptions', *Proceedings of the 3rd International Conference-Seminar of Tamil Studies*, Pondicherry, 1973, 32–41.

J.V. Kinnier-Wilson offered in 1974 the beginning of a decipherment which he called 'a new approach to the problems of the Indus script'. He began from a relatively safe basis: the numerals. His conclusions were tentative, cautious, and modest. He operated mostly within one consistent framework—that of economics (weights, measures, etc.). He constantly supported his identifications with Sumerian parallels. He was in favour of regarding the language of at least some strata of the Indus people as a type of Sumerian since he suggested that the two scripts, Indus and Sumerian, branched out from a single stem at some early period and that original features are preserved in both. But Dravidian, too, would be a likely candidate. The function of the Indus seals he saw almost exclusively as economic, and thus he searched not only for units of weight, etc., but also, for example, for a grain-sign which he found in . On the whole, Kinnier-Wilson's attempt should be regarded with sympathy for its subdued tone, and its common-sense approach. Nevertheless, it cannot be accepted as a real wide opening of a road to actual decipherment either.

An American archaeologist, Walter A. Fairservis Jr., was inspired to attempt a decipherment by the excavations which he had been performing frequently on the Harappan site of Allahdino, about twenty-five miles north-east of Karachi. In 1976 he began pondering the meaning of the script in the context of rich archaeological evidence, and first proposed a model of decipherment proceeding on the assumption that the normal direction of the script was from left to right (1976, 1977). This came as a surprise in view of the near-unanimous and well-established concensus of a long line of scholars who all agreed that the direction was from right to left. Fairservis (1977) has advanced several arguments in support of his view but they were successfully refuted by Mahadevan in an excellent paper published in *Purātattva*, No. 9, 1980. the wrong choice of direction has rendered the initial attempts of Fairservis invalid; in fact, we may agree with Mahadevan when he says that 'no attempted decipherment ... based on a left to right direction can be taken seriously'. On the other hand, it must be admitted that no other scholar had dedicated so much careful attention to the techniques of Harappan writing as Fairservis had done. Also, the advantage of his approach is undoubtedly his outstanding archaeological erudition and his intimate knowledge of Harappan material culture. As was to be expected, his point of departure was to establish certainties demonstrable in archaeological evidence (like for example, the dependence of the civilization on cultivation of wheat and barley), and to proceed from those material certainties to their relationships to a pertinent body of sign and symbol—without doubt a healthy, commonsense procedure. From the beginning, his conclusions were that the seal inscriptions are basically iconographic and are the fruition of an ancient system of rank and title. After rather careful considerations, repeatedly commented upon critically by many colleagues, Fairservis came around 1980 with the hypothesis that the Harappan language is a form of Dravidian which in its basic root morphemes is closest to Tamil-Kannaḍa, with a logographic script containing about 400 graphemes that should be read generally from right to left. In March 1982, he modestly admitted that 'what follows is meant to be a model only, it is not to be taken as a claim that the Harappan script is deciphered.' He again repeated his basic—and to my mind sound—axiom that no decipherment of the script can occur without reference to existing knowledge, which is very considerable, of the Harappan civilization. Why did he point to early Tamil-Kannaḍa as the most likely candidate to have retained the vocabulary of Harappan civilization? Because, he says, the North Dravidian group was essentially older than the Harappan and was concerned culturally with other problems than city life and the expansion of village farming. Perhaps this is not a bad idea worth testing. Also, Fairservis pleads for a reconstruction by the Dravidianists of the obvious artifact vocabulary familiar to the archaeologist which would include words for characteristically Harappan objects (he offers such word-list)—another idea worth attention. In support of the Dravidian hypothesis, he unfolds very impressive archaeological-anthropological evidence into which we simply cannot go here. He then bases the actual attempt at decipherment on the following premises: (1) The seals are concerned with the identification of the bearer as an individual—in other words: search for proper names, ranks, titles, occupation, pace of residence. (2) The script is logo-syllabic, like modern Sino-Japanese. (3) The homophonic or rebus principle was in use. (4) Dravidian—presumably early Kannaḍa-Tamil—is the most likely candidate since it has a word for grain which also means 'moon/month' (**nel-a*), and since its original system of numerals was to the base 'eight', as in the Harappan script.

Obviously the greatest drawback of Fairservis is his incompetence as Dravidian linguist. He is undoubtedly an outstanding archaeologist, has ingenuity, patience, perseverance, honesty, and originality of ideas. But his linguistic knowledge of Dravidian is replete with striking errors, and his linguistic thinking is naive. This can be manifestly seen in this contribution to the *Scientific American* (March 1983). His so-called readings published there make no sense from a Dravidianist's point of view. In August 1976, the optimism of Fairservis reached its peak; he was convinced that he had found a definite clue to the actual decipherment. Since then, he has come a long way. He has stressed lately the fact that the Harappan civilization was a *literate* civilization but that those who have the philological and linguistic skills necessary to tackle the problems of script and language do not have the command of archaeological knowledge. Vice versa, the archaeologists have fatal lack of philological and linguistic skills. The Harappan script is the product of the Harappan civilization, and hence it must reflect its function as a written media for the Harappans whoever they may have been. It follows that the best test of the validity of a decipherment lies in just how much the results reflect of what is archaeologically and anthropologically known, verifiable and validated. This takes us finally to the possibility of some kind of solution which must begin with broad and intensive cooperation among archaeologists, anthropologists, cryptographers, philologues and linguists.

In India, computer analysis of the Indus script is being carried out from 1971 on. After some early work at Madras, Iravatham Mahadevan secured the aid of the best Indian computer experts in Bombay, and in 1977 appeared a magnificently produced book on the Indus script. Mahadevan's concordance based on the analysis of 11,303 legible sign-occurrences (which made the sample the largest ever analysed since Hunter's 1934 figure was ca 3750, the Soviet team's ca 6300, and the Finnish team's 9147). The list of signs contains 417 distinct signs. The Mahadevan-Finnish concordances taken together may undoubtedly serve excellently as complementary.

In his decipherment, Mahadevan started from the basic groundwork provided by the Soviet and Finnish teams but applied an entirely different technique—the technique of parallelisms developed for Hittite by Emil Forrer. The observation of parallel phenomena is its basis. Encouraged by his overall correct interpretation of the Tamil-Brāhmī inscriptions Mahadevan made the method of parallelisms the basic tool of his attempt taking his comparisons mainly, but not only, from the Tamil-Brāhmī cave inscriptions. After he had published his own concordance, he set up some basic features of Harappan grammar which he described as 'intelligible to the eye if not to the ear'. This means that it is basically a formal structural analysis and description independent of any identification with a concrete language. Lately, in his method of bilingual parallels, he introduced two important changes: (a) Instead of looking for homophones (rebus principle) he would search for ideographic parallels from later bilingual Indian traditions (available both in Indo-Aryan and Dravidian languages) (b) The frequent terminal signs are no more considered formative or inflectional suffixes but they are rather indicative of the class of persons to whose names they were suffixed—that is, they are ideograms. He would now identify the sign ↑ with spear or weapon and hence with the meaning 'soldier'. The yoke-carrier sign refers to an official 'bearing the yoke of responsibility'. Hence, the combination of spear plus yoke carrier is 'read' by Mahadevan as 'official with military duties'. This is attractive and 'phantasievoll', but of course completely arbitrary, and hence rather uncertain—a kind of game. However, Mahadevan has disciplined himself to the honest admittance that the script has not been deciphered, and that even the language underlying the script has not been recognized. Therefore, he performs his formal structural analysis, rather than attempting concrete readings, and in that field, as his latest papers demonstrate, he had achieved considerable progress.

We shall now try to show what indeed has been achieved, what has not been achieved, and what could and should be done to achieve more—although there are grave doubts as to the ultimate success of any complete and verifiable decipherment of the Harappan script and language. When critically judging what has and what has not been achieved we must make a distinction between *evidence* and *proof*. None of the proposed models of actual decipherment has so far won general acceptance because none of the potential decipherers can prove their conclusions to be correct. In contrast, honest, albeit partial, evidence, although it cannot prove anything, can suggest greater or lesser possibilities and probabilities.

What, then, has been achieved?

Apart from the publication of the concordances, which is in itself a great achievement, the two relatively secure results obtained so far are: (a) the determination of the direction of writing; and (b) the segmentation of texts into probable 'words' and phrases' through simple word-division techniques based on formal positional analysis and statistical counts.

(a) The Indus script runs normally form right to left, and this is probably the best established fact about the script. For detailed arguments, one should consult Marshall (1931), Gadd and Smith (1931), G.R. Hunter (1934), A.S.C. Ross (1939), G.V. Alekseev (1965), B.B. Lal (1966, 1968), and I Mahadevan (1970, 1980).

(b) The Indus script consists almost certainly mainly of logograms. Almost all investigators have proposed that the script is most probably a logosyllabic system comprising word-signs and phonetic syllables, typologically similar to the modern Sino-Japanese script. However, no one has as yet been able to establish by objective and independent analytical procedures the existence of purely phonetic syllabic signs in the Indus script. Asko Parpola has recently proposed that the script is morphemographic, using signs with inherent semantic and phonetic values, applicable in either function. Mahadevan wishes to work with the hypothesis that the script consists essentially of word-signs and not phonetic units with alphabetic/syllabic values. Some of the world-signs stand for lexemes as free forms, but some signs may indeed stand for grammatical markers.

(c) If so, then we may reach a third conclusion: the word-signs of the Indus script are formed as (1) ideograms (that is, picture-signs standing for concrete objects and concepts suggested by such objects), (2) phonograms (derived by the rebus principle from homonyms of the words represented pictorially), (3) conventional signs which are not pictures but arbitrary symbols or marks (for example, strokes other than the numerals). Let me hasten to add that (a) phonograms formed by the rebus principle can be recognized only if the underlying language is known, and (b) it is impossible to ascertain the meanings or phonetic values of the conventional signs directly in the absence of bilingual records.

This is, roughly speaking, all that has been truly achieved. Everything that goes beyond that is sheer speculation. In other words, it is significant that what has been achieved are mostly negative results.

1. The Indus script is certainly not alphabetic or quasi-alphabetic judging form the number of signs and their functional/distributional characteristics. The precise nature of the script, however, has not yet been fully established.
2. The Indus script is not closely related to any of the contemporaneous pictographic scripts of the third–second millennia BC, although traces of diffusion and some similarities can be found, in particular with proto-Elamite.
3. The Indus script is not related to any later Indian script—either Brāhmī or Kharoṣṭhī.
4. Not one of the suggested grids has been proved powerful enough to 'do the job' of decipherment.
5. The Harappan language is most probably not related to the Indo-European family as there is no evidence for prefixing or inflexional endings in the Indus script. It is almost rules out that it would be an archaic form of Sanskrit (as proposed by S.R. Rao).
6. The Harappan language is most probably not related to any West Asian language since they place the attribute after the substantive-head of the attributive phrase. However, there may be some distant, as yet very vaguely understood, connection with Elamite.
7. The most common supposition that the several most frequent terminal signs of the Indus script (=U=, ↑, ...)

represent grammatical suffixes like case endings or derivational morphemes has apparently not been confirmed by the concordances.

8. A major negative conclusion which must be unfortunately stressed most vigorously is that none of the published claims of decipherment of the Indus script (and language) is valid.

We may legitimately ask: Can the Indus script be at all deciphered? Are all further attempts bound to be futile and a waste of time and resources?

One is very much tempted to answer in the positive—unless, of course, a bilingual inscription is discovered, or unless a large text containing definite and verifiable clues is brought to light; if not, one must unfortunately admit, all further attempts may prove hopeless. And yet, to give up is impossible. No code, no cipher can ultimately resist decipherment. So far, none has.

What, then, should be the strategy employed? What could and should be done?

Because the chances of finding a bilingual or a large text are rather remote, scholars already engaged in the formal structural analysis should go ahead with their analytical work, refining it further along the lines indicated by Mahadevan in his paper of 1983. I regard the approach of Mahadevan via the structural-analytic procedures—based, naturally, on the achievement already gained by the application of computer analysis by the Russians and the Finns—as by far the most promising, and its possibilities not yet at all exhausted.

Second: The structural-analytical procedures should be accompanied by the approach as indicated by Fairservis, that is, to attack the problem via the evidence of habitational archaeology within the framework of our rich knowledge of the material culture of the Harappans.

Third: Although it is a priori possible that the Harappan language belonged to an unknown family which had disappeared without leaving any trace, the most probable candidate is and remains some form of Dravidian. Hence, Dravidianists should cooperate positively and sympathetically but with extreme caution and merciless rigour with the would-be decipherers, and also try to reconstruct possible

Dravidian world-lists of items typical for Harappan civilization provided by archaeologists.

Four: The search for a bilingual text should go on with utmost intensity irrespective of our meager expectations, and that not only in the whole vast area of the Indus civilization but also in other adjacent regions like Mesopotamia and Iran. Particular attention as far as the seal texts are concerned should also be paid to Sumerian parallels because their cultural context is largely similar to that of the Indus seals, and because we know for certain about direct (commercial? diplomatic?) contacts between Harappans and Sumerians. Another area to be exploited are the early proto-Elamite levels in Iran: in that area, perhaps, we may hope for a discovery of longer texts or even bilinguals.

Five: Attempts at phonetic reading of the Indus texts should not be undertaken prematurely just to satisfy the ambition of the decipherer. All linguistic speculation, even when based on structural-formal analysis should be taken with a very large pinch of salt.

While all this goes on, we should never forget the words of J. Chadwick who wrote: 'To preserve an open mind is incredibly difficult, because we are either mesmerized into swallowing camels, or so prejudiced we cannot manage the odd gnat.'

Bibliography

Dravidian and Harappan

(A particularly drastic selection was necessary in this section)

Burrow, T., 'Dravidian and the decipherment of the Indus script', *Antiquity* XLII, 172 (Dec. 1969), 274–8.

Clauson, Gerard and John Chadwick, 'The Indus script deciphered?', *Antiquity* XLIII, 171 (Sept. 1969), 220–7.

Cunningham, A., *Archaeological Survey of India. Report for the Year 1872–73*, Vol. 5, p. 108, pl. xxxiii, figs. 1 and 2.

Emeneau, M.B., Review of proto-Indica 1968, first announcement, progress, etc., *JAOS* 91 (1971) 4.541–2.

Fairservis, Walter A., Jr., The origin, character, and decline of an early civilization, *American Museum Novitates* No. 2302, 1967.

——, *The Roots of Ancient India.* New York, 1971. 2nd ed. 1975.

——, 'The script of the Indus valley civilization', *Scientific American*, March 1983, 44–52.

Kinnier Wilson, J.V., *Indo-Sumerian: A New Approach of the Problems of the Indus Script.* Oxford, 1974.

Knorozov, Y.V., N.V. Gurov, and B.Y. Volchok, *Proto-Indica 1968: Brief Report on the Investigation of the Proto-Indian Texts.* Moscow: Academy of Sciences Institute of Ethnography, 1968.

Knorozov, Y.V., M.G. Albedil, and B.Y. Volchok, *Proto-Indica 1979: Report on the Investigation of the Proto-Indian Texts,* Moscow: Nauka, 1981.

Koskenniemi, Kimmo and Asko Parpola, *Corpus of Texts in the Indus Script.* University of Helsinki Research Reports, No. 1, Helsinki, 1979.

____, *A Concordance to the Texts in the Indus Script.* Helsinki, 1982.

Koskenniemi, Seppo, Asko Parpola, and Simo Parpola, *Materials for the Study of the Indus Script, I: A Concordance to the Indus Inscriptions.* Helsinki, 1973.

Lal, B.B., 'The direction of writing in the Harappan script', *Internal Conference of Asian Archaeologists,* New Delhi, 1961, *Summary of papers,* p. 37.

____, 'From the megalithic to the Harappan: Tracing back the graffiti on pottery', *Ancient India* 16 (1960), p. 4ff. 1962.

____, 'The direction of writing in the Harappan script', *Antiquity* XL, No. 157 (1966), 52–5.

____, 'Indus script: Inconsistencies in claims of decipherment', *The Hindustan Times Weekly Review* (Delhi), 6 April 1969, p. 14.

Mahadevan, Iravatham, 'Dravidian parallels in proto-Indian script', *JTS* II. 1 (May 1970), 157–276.

____, 'Method of parallelism in the interpretation of proto-Indian script', *Proc. Of the 3rd International Conference-Seminar of Tamil Studies,* Paris, 1970 (eds X.S. Thani Nayagam and F. Gros), Pondicherry, 1973, 44ff.

____, *The Indus Script: Texts, Concordance and Tables.* Memoirs of the Archaeological Survey of India No. 77. New Delhi, 1977 [A magnificent corpus of the Harappan inscriptions].

____, *Decipherment of the Indus Script: Progress and Prospects: Heras Memorial Lectures, 1980.* Bombay: The Heras Institute.

____, 'Dravidian models of decipherment of the Indus script: A case study'. *10th Annual Conference of Dravidian Linguistic Association,* New Delhi, 1980.

____, 'Towards a grammar of the Indus texts: Intelligible to the eye, if not to the ears', *Tamil University, Thanjavur: Seminar on the Indus Script,* 10–14 April 1983.

——, 'What do we know about the Indus script? Neti neti ("Not this nor that")', Presidential Address, Section V, *Indian History Congress*, Dharwar 2–4 November 1988, Dinamani Press, Madras, p. 29 [The best recent assessment of the 'state of the art'; honest and witty].

Pande, H. Ch., *Soviet Studies on Harappan Script.* Ed. By Henry Field and E.M. Laird. Field Research Projects, Florida, 1969.

——, *Review of Finnish Decipherment of Proto-Dravidian Inscriptions.* Ed. Henry Field, Field Research Projects, Florida, 1970.

Parpola, Asko, *The Indus Script Decipherment: The Situation at the End of 1969*, The Scandinavian Institute of Asian Studies, Joint Reprint Series Number Three, Madras, 1970 (also in *JTS*, II, 1, April 1970, 89–109).

Parpola, Asko, 'The Indus script: A challenging puzzle', *World Archaeology* 17, 3 (Feb. 1986, 399–419 [A sober and honest assessment of the 'state of the art']).

Parpola, Asko, Seppo Koshenniemi, Simo Parpola, Pentti Aalto, *Decipherment of the Proto-Dravidian Inscriptions of the Indus Civilization: A First Announcement.* Coperhagen, 1969.

——, *Progress in the Decipherment of the Proto-Dravidian Indus Script.* Copenhagen, 1969.

Parpola, Asko, Seppo Koskenniemi, Simo Parpola, and Pentti Aalto, *Further Progress in the Indus Script Decipherment.* Copenhagen, 1970.

Southworth, Franklin C., 'Lexical evidence for early contacts between Indo-Aryan and Dravidian', in: *Aryan and Non-Aryan in India, Michigan Papers on South and South-east Asia*, No. 14 (1978), p. 1, Ann Arbor, 1979.

Thapar, Romila, 'Indus script; Romila Thapar's View', *Hindustan Times Weekly Review*, New Delhi, 30 March 1969, i–ii.

——, 'A possible identification of Meluhha, Dilmun and Makan', *Journal of the Economic and Social History of the Orient*, XVIII (1975), Part 1, 1–42.

Vacek, Jaroslav, 'The problem of the Indus script', *Archiv Orientalnt***, 38 (1970), 198–212.

Zide, A.R.K., and K. Zvelebil, 'Review of Parpola et al., "Decipherment ... and Progress ..."', *IIJ* XII.2 (1970), 126–34.

——, *Review of Works on Indus Valley Script* (by Knorozov ed., and Parpola et. al.), *Lg.* 46 (1970) 952–68.

——, *The Soviet Decipherment of the Indus Valley Script: Translation and Critique.* Janua Linguarum Series Practica 156, The Hague-Paris, 1976.

Index